THE GREAT

EXCHANGE

Justification by faith alone
in the light of recent thought

Philip H. Eveson

Published in association with FIEC by DayOne

Copyright © Day One Publications 1996
First printed 1996

Most scripture quotations are from The New International Version © 1973, 1978,
1984, International Bible Society. Published by Hodder and Stoughton.

ISBN 0 902548 73 5

Published by Day One Publications
6 Sherman Road, Bromley, Kent BR1 3JH

All rights reserved

No part of this publication may be reproduced, or stored in a retrieval system, or
transmitted, in any form or by any means, mechanical, electronic, photocopying,
recording or otherwise, without the prior permission of **Day One Publications.**

Designed by Steve Devane and printed by Clifford Frost Ltd, Wimbledon SW19 2SE

Dedication
In Memory of my parents
Mary Blodwen Eveson
1911–1956
George Wellesley Eveson
1909–1983

THE GREAT
EXCHANGE

FACING THE ISSUE is a series of books designed to help Christians to think biblically on a variety of pressing issues that confront evangelicals at the present time. The themes are primarily theological but, as the Bible never teaches doctrine in isolation, all have a keen practical edge to them.

The series began its life in the cut and thrust of discussion in the Theological Committee of the Fellowship of Independent Evangelical Churches whose brief is to monitor and respond to challenges and changes in the world of evangelical theology. The committee, whose members currently are Brian Edwards (chair), Andrew Anderson, Paul Brown, Andrew Bryant, David Field, Stanley Jebb, Hywel Jones and Jonathan Stephen, commissions the writers, discusses their approach with them, and is available for consultation. Though united in our understanding of the gospel, we do not always come to exactly the same conclusions on every detail. So the views put forward by the authors do not necessarily reflect in every respect those of the committee or, for that matter, those of the FIEC or the Publisher.

The series is written with the general reader in mind and the books do not assume a background training in theology. They are, however, written by people of proven ability in grappling with important theological trends. We hope that each book will stimulate thought and action, both controlled by the Bible.

Andrew Anderson
Series Editor

1996 is the year we remember the 450th anniversary of Luther's death. The gospel of God's justifying grace enabled him to die well. He needed no priest to give him the last rites or any requiem masses. As death approached, Luther kept repeating the words of John 3:16, 'For God so loved the world that he gave his one and only Son, that whoever believes in him shall not perish but have eternal life.' Finally Dr. Jonas asked him. 'Do you want to die standing firm on Christ and the doctrine you have taught?' Luther mustered up enough strength to shout out, 'Yes!' A few minutes later he passed into the presence of his Lord.

I did not set out to write a book on justification. Lecturing to students at the London Theological Seminary on Paul's Letter to the Galatians meant a critical evaluation of articles and books which considered justification from different perspectives, some of them radically different from my own Nonconformist protestant background. Opportunities then came to speak on these modern views at ministers' fraternals, the Westminster Fellowship and the Evangelical Movement of Wales Theological Training Course at Bryntirion, South Wales. An article subsequently appeared in the British Evangelical Council Journal 'Foundations' and, more recently, I gave a paper at the Westminster Conference on 'The Council of Trent and Modern Views of Justification'. In the meantime, an invitation came to address the members of the Theological Committee of the Fellowship of Independent Evangelical Churches (FIEC) on Tom Wright's views. I was most surprised when they then asked me to write a book on the subject. At first I thought they wanted a little booklet giving a critical assessment of recent thinking on justification but it soon became evident that they were looking for a more substantial book on the topic.

Having now completed the work, I must first of all thank the members of the FIEC Theological Committee for encouraging me to write and for their valuable comments and criticisms of an initial draft. I am grateful to the Revd. Brian Edwards the chairman of the Committee for challenging some of my conclusions and to the Revd. Andrew Anderson, the general editor of the series, for making the text more readable. My colleagues at the London Theological Seminary have been very supportive, especially the Revd. Dr. Hywel Jones and Revd. Graham Harrison who have made many helpful suggestions. I would particularly like to record my thanks to the Revd. Dr. Don Carson who encouraged me in my task and, in the middle of his busy workload, was kind enough to read through the entire manuscript. His incisive remarks have been much appreciated. The officers and members of Kensit Evangelical Church, Finchley, where I minister, have been very understanding and I thank God for their prayerful support. Finally, I would like to pay special tribute to my wife - a most 'suitable helper' to me. She has read many drafts more than once and has helped prepare the indices.

The book is dedicated to the memory of my father and mother. It was my father who first taught me the importance of justification by faith alone and encouraged me to memorize those passages of scripture that teach the very heart of the gospel. The reality of God's justifying grace was brought home to me most forcefully when, at the age of thirteen, I watched my mother die of cancer. As she lay in our sitting-room, I shall never forget her final words in which she peacefully and confidently committed her life to the Saviour whom she trusted and loved.

It is a great privilege and an awesome responsibility to write on such an important subject, especially at a time 'when the foundations are being destroyed'. How can one possibly do justice to it! It is my earnest prayer that what is written in the following pages will be of some help in making clear the very essence of the gospel and in establishing Christians in their most holy faith. To God alone be the glory!

Philip H. Eveson
November 1996

I n many Christian circles today the term justification is often avoided. It is thought to be too difficult or old-fashioned. Yet the word is frequently used in everyday speech. We may ask, for instance, 'What justification do you have for saying that?' Then, again, in the world of word processors justification is a familiar expression in reference to aligning texts. The end result is that people are computer literate but ignorant of its Christian usage and significance in the context of the gospel's saving message.

A Neglected Doctrine

The rallying cry of the Protestant Reformation – 'justification by faith alone' – means nothing to the present generation. What was of great importance to many from the sixteenth to the nineteenth centuries at all levels of society is now of mere academic interest. To make matters worse, preaching and teaching on this basic theme has noticeably diminished and even become non-existent in many churches. As long ago as 1952 Alan Stibbs, who was then Vice-Principal of Oak Hill Theological College, declared that the doctrine of justification by faith needed to be reinstated 'because it is neglected, and does not hold the place that it should, either in our praise to God or in our preaching to men. A proper sense of its full glory and wonder is weak, if not lacking, among many Christians.'[1] In 1986, before he became Archbishop of Canterbury, George Carey remarked that justification by faith 'is hardly a common expression these days, even in the Church'.[2]

Away from the grass-roots level, the subject has been discussed at some length by theologians of various schools of thought in the interests of church unity. This has led to agreed statements being published. Yet the issues and arguments seem far removed from the experiences and situations of the people in the pew, let alone the teeming masses outside the church.

In recent decades, since Vatican II, greater freedom has existed for Roman Catholics to mix with Protestants. It is not unusual for Roman Catholics to meet with evangelicals in college Christian Union Bible study and prayer groups, in evangelistic campaigns or charismatic gatherings, and in local inter-church functions. They are often involved with evangelicals over ethical issues such as abortion and euthanasia. There are Roman Catholics who will call themselves evangelical and can be clearly distinguished from others by their moral integrity and deeply spiritual life.

To the ordinary church-goer or occasional visitor it is not so easy these days to distinguish a Protestant liturgical service from a Roman. The latter now uses English or some other vernacular language instead of Latin and includes more informal elements such as popular choruses and spiritual songs, while the former has gone back to using unreformed items of dress and furniture, and liturgies that include prayers for the dead.

In many minds, then, the old divisions have already been broken down so that there is a decided lack of interest in focusing on doctrinal differences that seem unimportant. To support this line of reasoning, reference is often made to the Scripture verse about the spirit not the letter of the law being the essential thing. As long as there is a love for the Lord Jesus Christ, a concern to make Christ known to others, and a desire to meet together in fellowship, what is the value of drawing attention to bygone wars of religion, to arguments over doctrine, many of which seem to have been caused through a misunderstanding about words?

It has been suggested that evangelicals and Roman Catholics should bury the hatchet and work together for the common good in the face of secularism, paganism and militant Islam. Both groups are apparently in agreement in affirming their acceptance of justification by faith. But is it really the case that Roman Catholics agree with Protestants, especially those of evangelical persuasion, on this item of faith which has for centuries kept them apart?

New Thinking
While there are those who claim not to understand the biblical and theological reasons for the great divide over this question of justification, or who may not consider it to be sufficiently significant to continue a policy of no cooperation, it is a subject being hotly debated at the present time in scholarly circles. Many articles and books on this

theme have been published in recent years. It is now fashionable to denounce the Lutheran interpretation of Paul and of the Judaism of his day and to present what many feel to be a refreshingly new and simple approach to the understanding of justification.

In addition, bold attempts are being made to bring justification back into the everyday thinking and preaching of the church. Concern is expressed that the church is not presenting the truth of justification. In a sincere desire to make the matter relevant to today's needs, the term is, unfortunately, being given meanings that are at best secondary, so that the essence of the truth is lost and it ceases to be the gospel's cutting-edge. These are the matters which are addressed in the following pages.

The book is divided into four parts. Part one uncovers what the Bible teaches on the subject of justification including a chapter on the vocabulary associated with it. In part two attention is drawn to the traditional opposing positions on justification and the attempts that have been made recently to cross the divide. Part three discusses recent scholarly work on the subject. In the final part the crucial importance of getting it right is emphasised both for the future of the church and the eternal well-being of its individual members. An attempt is also made to show the relevance of the subject in today's world.

Notes

1. A. M. Stibbs, 'Justification by Faith: The Reinstatement of the Doctrine Today', Evangelical Quarterly, Vol. 24, No.3, 1952, p.156.
2. G. Carey, I Believe, SPCK, 1991, p. 32.

Part 1

The Biblical Evidence

2 Justification in Paul's Letters

We are dependent on God's Word, the Scriptures of the Old and New Testaments, for all that we know, believe and preach concerning the gospel of God's saving power in Jesus Christ. As Paul reminds Timothy, 'from infancy you have known the holy scriptures, which are able to make you wise for salvation through faith in Christ Jesus' (2 Timothy 3:15). 'Salvation' is a comprehensive term concerning every aspect of God's gracious action toward sinful humanity, culminating in the wholesomeness of life in the new heavens and new earth. One crucially important element in that salvation concerns the justification of sinners.

Justification is not a human idea which the church or an individual has invented in order to express something of God's saving activity. It is a truth revealed to us by God himself in the Bible. It is part of God's saving plan which has been disclosed in the gospel and which is to be proclaimed from the housetops. What is more, as with every other aspect of God's revealed truth, God's action in justifying sinners leads us back into the mystery of God and his unfathomable ways. We are left amazed, stunned and humbled, and to all eternity we shall be 'lost in wonder, love and praise'. In his letter to the Romans, Paul cannot but worship and adore as he comes to the close of his presentation of the gospel: 'Oh, the depth of the riches of the wisdom and knowledge of God! How unsearchable his judgments, and his paths beyond tracing out! Who has known the mind of the Lord?...For from him and through him and to him are all things. To him be the glory for ever! Amen' (Romans 11:33-36).

In dealing with the subject of justification, the Bible does not leave us with an unexplained concept or statement of fact. There is definite teaching on this important issue concerning a person's right standing or status before God. It also draws in other vital elements of the gospel including such concepts as substitution, propitiation and imputation, elements which are either missing or undervalued in some modern treatments of the subject. In other words, there is, very definitely, a biblical doctrine of justification, not merely a biblical concept of justification.[1] The Bible not only presents us with the fact that sinners are justified by God's grace and the results and implications of that legal position, it also tells us how sinners are able to be in this happy situation of being declared righteous by God. Romans chapter five begins with the fact of justification ('Therefore since we have been justified...') and then proceeds immediately to consider the resulting blessings ('we have peace with God...'). But this statement of fact is introduced with the word 'therefore,' which is a reminder that it is connected to the previous chapter. There, Paul is at pains to show that we are not justified by our works, but by faith alone. He also explains in chapter three how the righteous God can still remain righteous and at the same time pronounce unrighteous people righteous.

As we survey the biblical evidence for belief in justification by faith alone, the natural place to begin is with the letters of the apostle Paul. We begin with Paul because the special vocabulary associated with justification, which we shall consider in chapter five, is concentrated in his writings and he presents the most complete treatment of the subject. From there we shall proceed in chapter three to look at what the other New Testament authors have to say about this vital doctrine. This will also involve examining the Gospel evidence to see whether the Lord Jesus Christ dealt with justification during his earthly ministry. In chapter four we turn back to the Old Testament and inquire into its teaching on the topic.

In brief, Paul defines justification as God's declaration that sinners who believe in Christ are fully pardoned, acquitted of all guilt and are in a right legal standing before him, on the basis of what God has done in Jesus Christ. It is in his letter to the Romans that Paul gives a detailed presentation of the theme. Paul also considers the subject in his letter to the Galatians. With great passion he warns his converts of the danger of accepting another gospel, a gospel of justification that includes works as well as grace, which is not the gospel. He also alerts the Philippian believers lest they be lead astray on this vital issue (3:2-11). In his correspondence with the Corinthian church, Paul introduces justification as of central importance to the gospel and insists that all boasting should be 'in the Lord' (1 Corinthians 1:30-31; 6:11; 2 Corinthians 3:9; 5:19-21; 10:12-18). Finally, when writing to Titus, in one of his great summary statements of the gospel, Paul clearly emphasises justification by faith alone (3:4-8).

Paul presents the truth of justification by faith alone as the crucial and initial element in the sinner's redemptive relationship with God through Jesus Christ. It is not to be confused with reconciliation, restoration, liberation or transformation. Justification is not another word for reconciliation.[2] Rather, it is to be seen as providing 'the logical foundation for reconciliation.'[3] Liberation or redemption is part of God's gracious provision through which he justifies sinners but it is not to be identified with justification. Again, the regeneration, transformation and sanctification of the individual take place in association with justification but these terms are not synonymous with justification.

The essence of Paul's teaching on the subject is presented in Romans 3:21-26. Leon Morris considers these verses to be 'possibly the most important single paragraph ever written'.[4] All the key theological terms relating to justification are clustered together here, many of them having already been introduced in 1:17ff.

The Open Secret

'But now' (3:21) points to the dawn of a new era. Something wonderful has happened. While the phrase could have logical force, referring to the next stage in the argument, it is more likely to be a reference to time. The situation has been drastically altered by the coming of Jesus Christ and by his death on the cross. Paul is picking up the point he started with in 1:16-17 that the gospel reveals the righteousness of God. While the wrath of God has been very evident in giving people over to their sinful passions, there is this thrilling disclosure, for all the world to know, that God has decisively intervened to bring people of all nationalities into a right position with himself through Jesus Christ.

Continuity and Discontinuity

'**Apart from law**' (v21) highlights the break with the past. The period before the 'now' was the era of the Mosiac covenant, characterised by law. It was a temporary administration made with one nation, Israel, and having laws which kept them apart from others, which highlighted sin but had no power to change the human predicament (cf. Romans 4:13-15). When thinking of the working out of God's plan of salvation in history, the two great epochs are categorised by Paul in terms of law and faith. The period prior to the coming of Christ is described as a state of confinement under the law ('held prisoner under law') and 'under the supervision of the law' (Galatians 3:15-4:7). The decisive moment in the history of salvation occurred when 'faith came' which means when Christ came who is the object of faith. By using this term 'faith' - four times in Galatians 3:23-25 - to describe the coming of the new dispensation, Paul highlights in a startling manner the fact that the people of God are no longer characterised by law but by faith in Christ. In 2 Corinthians 3:4-11 Paul describes the old era as an administration of condemnation and death. It can now be described as the 'old' covenant (3:14) because of the one who has established the 'new covenant' through the blood of his cross (1 Corinthians 11:25).

'**To which the Law and the Prophets testify**' (3:21) stresses the continuity. The whole Old Testament, Paul is saying, anticipates and points to this new era. In fact, justification through Jesus Christ is not a novel idea, it is what has been in God's mind from the beginning (cf. Ephesians 1:4-5). Indeed, such men as Abraham and David were justified in this way, as Paul indicates in Romans 4. This shows that when Paul speaks of the 'coming of faith' he does not mean that no one had exercised saving faith prior to the coming of Christ. As we saw in the previous paragraph, 'faith' in that context describes the new era in God's saving purposes. The gospel of God's justifying grace is the fulfilment of what is hinted at in the Mosaic religious system, the history of Israel and the prophetic messages. Now it has come to light and has been made plain ('it has been made known') through God's intervention in Christ.

The righteousness of God

The phrase 'the righteousness of God' in Romans 3:21 and 22 recalls 1:17 and 3:5 (NIV's 'righteousness from God' is an unnecessary interpretive rendering that confines the meaning).[5] In verses 25 and 26 'his righteousness' is found twice in reference to God. The phrase occurs twice more in Romans 10:3. Nowhere else does Paul use the expression except in 2 Corinthians 5:21. Outside the Pauline literature it occurs in Matthew 6:33, James 1:20 and 2 Peter 1:1 with a meaning different from that of Paul.

What does 'righteousness of God' mean in Paul's letters? A modern influential view sees it as a technical term used in Jewish apocalyptic writings for God's salvation-creating power: God's righteousness is his power which creates salvation.[6] It is assumed that this understanding would have been familiar to the readers in Rome. This is highly debatable. Judging by the way the term is used elsewhere in the New Testament, it does not appear to be a special term for God's power, and Paul certainly does not describe righteousness in these terms. It is the gospel, not righteousness, which is the power of God to salvation.[7]

Another recent way of understanding the phrase is to see it against the Old Testament background as a reference to 'God's faithfulness in keeping his promise to Abraham'.[8] While there is much to be said for this view, its one serious disadvantage lies in the fact that it does not take into account 2 Corinthians 5:21, 'so that in him we might become the righteousness of God' and the very similar statement in Philippians 3:9, 'the righteousness that comes from God and is by faith'. It is surely better to treat each occurrence of the phrase in the light of its immediate context, and not discount the possibility that more than one meaning may be attached to it.

Here in Romans 3:21-26 'the righteousness of God' is identified with justification. Verse 26 includes the verb 'to justify' as well as the adjective 'righteous'. God has intervened 'now' in Jesus Christ to provide for the justification of sinners. In 3:21-22, as in 1:17 and 10:3, the expression has a fulness of meaning that includes God's righteous character as seen in his faithfulness to his promises, God's saving activity intervening to justify his people, and God's gift of a right legal position before him. In Romans 3:5 and 3:25-26 the context demands that God's righteous character is in view. The former reference is to God's righteousness expressed in judgment, while the latter refers to the vindication of God's righteous character. 2 Corinthians 5:21, on the other hand, can only mean God's gift of a right legal status before God through Jesus Christ and it is this which lies at the heart of Paul's teaching on justification.[9]

Paul expounds justification in chapters four and five of Romans where righteousness is spoken of as God's gift (5:17) and is reckoned to the believer (4:3-11). Imputation or 'interchange', what Luther called 'the wonderful exchange', is at the heart of God's justifying grace. Sin is not reckoned to believers but to Christ and he bears it; the obedience or righteousness of Christ is reckoned to believers so that they are constituted righteous (2 Corinthians 5:21). In 1 Corinthians 1:30 Christ is described as our righteousness from God. Again Philippians 3:9, 'not having a righteousness of my own that comes from the law, but...the righteousness that comes from God and is by faith', parallels Paul's statement in Romans 10:3 'not knowing the righteousness of God and seeking to establish their own righteousness, they did not submit to the righteousness of God' (a literal translation). The Philippians passage clearly shows that righteousness is a gift from God ('the righteousness from God') and that must be taken into account in any discussion of the term 'the righteousness of God'. Philippians 3:9 also associates this righteousness with faith in Christ. Incidentally, faith is stressed in Romans 1:17 and that adds weight to the view that the gift element cannot be ignored when interpreting 'the righteousness of God' there. These examples would suggest that those who make a big point of distinguishing between 'righteousness of God' and 'righteousness' in Romans are going beyond the evidence.[10]

Faith

This 'righteousness of God' is received **'through faith of Jesus Christ'** (lit. v22). Paul has already emphasised the place of faith in 1:17 and quotes Habakkuk 2:4, 'the righteous will live by faith'. 'Faith and nothing but faith' is the probable meaning of the literal expression 'from faith to faith'. The NIV renders it as 'faith from first to last'. 'Faith' is again mentioned in this paragraph in chapter three verses 25 and 26 as well as towards the end of the chapter in verses 28 and 30. The whole of chapter four is given over to the subject of faith as opposed to works. 'Faith' characterises the justified person, not 'works of the law'. This 'faith' does not mean 'faithfulness' nor does the context encourage the view that 'faith of Jesus Christ' should be taken to mean Christ's faith or faithfulness. Jesus Christ is the object of faith.[11]

There is no value in faith as such, it is simply the means whereby sinners embrace the one who saves them. Faith is stressed in Ephesians 2:8-9 'through faith...not by works, so that no-one can boast. For we are God's workmanship...'. In Galatians 2:15-5:6 so strongly does Paul insist on justification by faith alone that he states, 'The only thing that counts is faith' (5:6); and that with the coming of Christ the gospel era can be described as the era of faith: 'Now that faith has come' (3:25). It is not works, or Christian graces like love that justify, but Christ who is received by faith. Nevertheless, the apostle is quick to add that the faith which justifies is living, 'expressing itself in love' (5:6).

The righteousness of God is universally available

The phrase **'for everyone who believes'** is not a redundant expression and is to be understood in the light of the sentence that follows, 'For there is no difference.' To whom is this 'righteousness of God' available? On the one hand it is *only* available to those who have faith in Jesus Christ. On the other hand, it is available to *anyone* who has faith in Christ. Jew and Gentile alike have need of it if they are to be justified, because all are in the same sinful position. It is open to any Jew or Gentile.

The universal condition of humanity

What Paul has been arguing in Romans 1:18-3:20 is summarised here in 3:23, **'There is no difference, for all have sinned and fall short of the glory of God'.** It makes no difference whether a nation has the Bible or not, or whether people try to carry out the religious and moral requirements of the law of God or not. All nations and every single person within those nations are in exactly the same position by nature. The verbal form Paul uses, 'sinned', suggests that he has in mind what he will later develop in 5:12-21. All sinned 'in Adam'. Adam is the federal head of humanity. He is man's representative and when he sinned, all humanity sinned in him and all died in him. It is also true that in this state all, whether Jew or Gentile, are actual rebels and are not in a right legal position before God. 'There is no one righteous no, not one' (3:10). That is the position of every single person, for all are by nature 'in Adam'. Moreover, all humanity is continually coming short of the glory of God. It is unable to see and participate in the splendour and stunning grandeur of God.

God's free grace

Human beings are **'justified freely by his grace'** (v24). It is amazing to think that the God spoken of here is the one against whom people have rebelled. This is what makes the statement all the more remarkable. 'Freely' emphasises the fact that it is a gift. But justification is not merely a free gift. It is a free gift to those who do not deserve it. 'Grace' means that it is totally unmerited. God's undeserved favour is displayed in justifying sinners who actually deserve condemnation. Paul draws attention to the grace of God in salvation many times in his letters. In Ephesians he praises God's 'glorious grace' and 'the riches of God's grace' which have been lavished on believers (1:6-8). He leaves them in no doubt that 'it is by grace you have been saved' (2:5, 8). Paul reminds Titus that the 'grace of God that brings salvation has appeared to all men' and that they have been 'justified by his grace' (2:11; 3:7).

Redemption

The costly nature of God's justifying grace is now introduced with the words **'through the redemption that came by Christ Jesus'** (v24). Justification is not equated with redemption. What is taught here about redemption has to do with the way by which our justification is made possible. Galatians 3:10-14 also mentions redemption in the context of justification. Redemption means liberation on payment of a price. It implies a situation of imprisonment or slavery. Romans 3:9 states that 'Jews and Gentiles alike are all under sin'. It is a theme which Paul develops in chapter 6 of Romans, when he speaks of 'the reign of sin'. Not only are all guilty on account of sin but all are enslaved by sin. Human beings are in the realm of sin and under the power of sin. Then, again, in Galatians Paul speaks of being 'under the law', 'under the curse', 'in slavery under the basic principles of the world' and 'slaves to those who by nature are not gods' (3:10; 3:23; 4:3,8). Redemption is from all these forms of slavery and is 'in Christ Jesus'. Christ 'gave himself a ransom for all' (1 Timothy 2:6).

Romans 3:25 indicates the costly nature of the ransom that purchased deliverance by the use of the phrase **'in his blood'**. Ephesians 1:7 even more closely identifies redemption with the blood of Christ. 'Blood' refers to the sacrificial death of Christ. He is the Passover lamb (I Corinthians 5:7). Twice Paul tells the Corinthians that they 'were bought at a price' and now belong to the Lord (1 Corinthians 6:20; 7:23).

Wrath removed

The redemption by Christ involves more than liberation from sin and evil powers. We are liberated from 'death-row'. Galatians 3:13 speaks of 'Christ redeeming us from the curse of the law by becoming a curse for us'. The curse is nothing other than the wrath of God directed against human sin which the law spotlights. Instead of 'curse' Paul uses the word **'propitiation'** or 'the turning away of wrath' in Romans 3:25 (NIV inadequately translates: 'a sacrifice of atonement'). It is a reminder of his earlier references to the wrath of God and the day of God's wrath (1:18; 2:5,8).[12] Warning people of 'the coming wrath' was an integral part of Paul's preaching (1 Thessalonians 1:10). This wrath concerns God's vengeance, his just retribution on sinners. It is a punishment which involves being 'shut out from the presence of the Lord' on that day and experiencing everlasting destruction (2 Thessalonians 1:5-9). The staggering truth is now taught that God himself planned and publicly displayed Christ as the means for removing his own wrath. The unmixed wrath of God that will be seen on the day of judgment fell on Jesus Christ. On the cross the curse or punishment which sin deserves was taken by Christ.[13] 2 Corinthians

5:21 expresses the same truth: 'God made him who had no sin to be sin for us'. This substitutionary sacrifice, this vicarious punishment is for all who have faith ('**through faith**'). Such is the message of the cross (1 Corinthians 1:18). No wonder Paul glories 'in the cross of our Lord Jesus Christ' (Galatians 6:14)!

The tolerance of God

In verse 25 reference is made to God's forbearance or tolerance: '**in his forebearance he had left the sins committed beforehand unpunished**'. The tolerance of God is yet another item that has been mentioned earlier in 2:4. In the context of chapter three it means more than God's patience which holds back the day of judgment and wrath so that the final punishment does not fall immediately on sinners (cf. Acts 17:30f). It refers to God's attitude toward believers of the old era, whose sins were not held against them. They were forgiven and accounted righteous in God's sight even though their sins were not actually dealt with at that time. In 2 Samuel 12:13, for instance, after David's great sin is exposed by Nathan the prophet, David in repentance confesses, 'I have sinned against the Lord'. To this Nathan replies, 'The Lord has taken away your sin. You are not going to die'. The sacrificial system of the old covenant could not in reality atone for sin. God left the sins of his people unpunished until the present time (cf. Hebrews 9:15,26). What the Old Testament sacrifices symbolised, Christ has finally and completely fulfilled in his death.

The vindication of God

'**He did it to demonstrate his justice** (righteousness) **at the present time, so as to be just** (righteous) **and the one who justifies those who have faith in Jesus**'. Everything about the cross of Jesus vindicates the righteousness of God. God is seen to be righteous in passing over the sins of the righteous in Old Testament times as well as in justifying the ungodly who now believe in Jesus. At the same time God is seen to be true to his promises made with the people of old. Divine justice is satisfied by the death of Christ. Christ has paid the punishment by receiving the wrath of God which sin deserves, in order that guilty sinners, past, present and future, whether Jew or Gentile, who look to God's promised Messiah, Jesus Christ, might be forgiven, acquitted and pronounced righteous. With a message like this we can appreciate Paul's eagerness in wanting to share it with Jews and Gentiles alike, right at the heart of the Roman empire.

Faith not works

From Romans 3:27 to 4:25 Paul expounds the truth of justification by faith alone. Before this can be considered there is a preliminary matter that needs to be settled. It is this: does Paul teach justification by works in Romans 2:5-16? It must be said immediately, that if this were the case, he would be contradicting his main teaching from chapter 3:20 to 5:1. But Paul is not dealing with salvation or the subject of justification at this point. It is the grim, dark picture of the day of wrath and condemnation, when God will judge every single person by his Son Jesus Christ, that is in view. He is not talking of justification but of judgment. It will be a righteous judgment based on works alone. The same is taught by Jesus in Matthew's Gospel (12:37; 25:31-46) and by John in the book of Revelation (20:11-15). The righteous, who have been justified by faith, will be seen to be righteous by their works and the unrighteous will be seen to be unrighteous by their works. For the righteous it will mean eternal life, for the unrighteous there will be nothing but the full horror of the wrath of God. On that day of judgment justice will be scrupulously fair for both Jew and Gentile. The mere possession of the law of God by the Jew will not put them in an advantageous position, 'it is those who obey the law who will be declared righteous' (Romans 2:13). That is the only reason for mentioning justification. He is not making any further point from the reference.

It may well be possible in theory for a person to achieve justification by doing God's revealed will. In our Lord's case, theory turned to actuality for he was justified on account of his righteous life (1 Timothy 3:16). But as far as the whole human race 'in Adam' is concerned, it is impossible. Paul's further point is that God judges according to standards of which, whether Jew or Gentile, we are all aware. The standard will either be the revealed law of God or the consciousness of right and wrong felt by humanity generally. By those standards all are condemned. No one has ever lived up to their own standards, let alone the perfect standard of God himself revealed in his law and in the life of Jesus. Jew and Gentile are therefore in the same position. All are condemned, all are under the wrath of God and all are in need of salvation. We are all sinners by nature and by practice.

It follows from this that keeping the law of God will not put a human being right before God (Romans 3:27-4:25). Even to belong to the nation specially chosen by God, to be a member of God's covenant people, carrying out the duties and requirements of the law, does not mean one is necessarily righteous in God's sight. Seeking to obey the law and, in the case of sinful lapses, religiously observing the provisions of the law to obtain ritual purification and atonement, is not good enough. Doing all these works of the law to the best of one's ability does not put a person right with God. No one was ever justified by that means.[14] There were people who were right with God in the period prior to Christ's coming, such as Abraham and David, but they were justified not on the basis of belonging to the covenant community or on the basis that they carried out all the covenant obligations. The only way anyone was justified in Old Testament times was by faith in God's promise. The promise concerns the Messiah, Jesus Christ, who is a descendant of Abraham and David 'according to the flesh' (Romans 1:3; 9:5). It is only by faith in Jesus Christ that Jew and Gentile are acquitted and stand in a right legal position before God. This is what Paul is at pains to show, particularly in Romans and Galatians.

The Spirit is also included in the promise to Abraham (Galatians 3:14). This is because the Spirit is closely associated with Jesus. He is the Spirit of Christ. Those who are justified have the Spirit and Paul speaks of the righteousness of the law being fulfilled in them through the Spirit. The indwelling Spirit is a notable feature of Paul's teaching in Romans 8 and Galatians 5. The faith that believes is the result of the Spirit's work and leads a person to do from the heart what is pleasing to God.

Notes

1. Cf. A. McGrath, *Iustitia Dei: a History of the Christian Doctrine of Justification*, Vol.1, Cambridge, 1986, p. 2 and his more popular book *Justification by Faith: What it means for us today?* pp. 143-144. He is right to make a distinction between the biblical concept and later church doctrine, but he needs to stress that there is a biblical *doctrine* not merely a biblical *concept*. N.T. Wright in his lectures on justification is adamant that the biblical doctrine does not include *how* a person comes to be accepted by God but rather it is the declaration by God of covenant membership. Cf. chapter 6 below.

2. Dunn, *Romans 1-8*, Word Biblical Commentary 38A, Word, 1988, p. 259. Commenting on Romans 5:10 he writes: 'The temptation to press for a clear distinction between "justification" and "reconciliation" should be avoided...the close parallel between v 9 and v 10b shows that Paul regards the one as equivalent to the other'. Cf. also C. K. Barrett, *The Epistle to the Romans*, Harper and Row, 1957, p. 108.

3. R. Y. K. Fung, 'Justification by Faith in 1 & 2 Corinthians', in *Pauline Studies, Essays Presented to F. F. Bruce*, eds. D. A. Hagner & M. J. Harris, Paternoster, 1980, p. 255. Cf. also M. E. Thrall, 'Salvation proclaimed: V. 2 Corinthians 5:18-21', *Expository Times*, Vol. 93, 1981-1982, p. 230: 'Justification is the necessary presupposition of reconciliation'.

4. Leon Morris, *The Epistle to the Romans*, Eerdmans/IVP, 1988, p. 173.

5. For a discussion of whether 'righteousness of God' is a subjective or objective genitive cf. C. E. B. Cranfield, *Romans* Vol.1, T. & T. Clark, 1975, pp. 96-99; D. J. Moo, *Romans 1-8*, Moody, 1991, pp. 65-70.

6. Cf. E. Käsemann, 'The Righteousness of God in Paul', in *New Testament Questions of Today*, SCM, 1969, pp. 168-182; *Commentary on Romans*, Eerdmans, 1980, pp. 23-30.

7. Cf. S. K. Williams, 'The "Righteousness of God" in Romans', *Journal of Biblical Literature 99*, 1980, p. 258.

8. Cf. S. K. Williams, 'The "Righteousness of God" in Romans', p. 265.

9. Protestant scholars of the past and present have seen 2 Corinthians 5:21 as an unambiguous reference to a status of righteousness which is credited to the believer. For the view that even here 'the righteousness of God' means God's 'covenant faithfulness' cf. N. T. Wright, 'On becoming the righteousness of God: 2 Corinthians 5:21', in *Pauline Theology Volume II*, ed. D. M. Hay, Fortress Press, 1993, pp. 200-208. He takes it to mean that, as Christ's ambassador and minister of the new covenant, Paul himself has actually become a visible expression of the covenant faithfulness of God.

10. Cf. S. K. Williams 'The "Righteousness of God" in Romans', p. 265 and P. T. O'Brien, 'Justification in Paul and Some Crucial Issues of the Last Two Decades', in *Right with God,* ed. D. A. Carson, Baker/Paternoster, 1992, pp. 77-78.

11. For a thorough refutation of the view that 'the faith of Christ' means 'the faithfulness of Christ' cf. J. Murray, *The Epistle to the Romans,* Part One, Eerdmans, 1960, Appendix B, pp. 363-374. See also D. J. Moo, *Romans 1-8,* pp. 224-225 and the discussion of the phrase by R. B. Hays (who supports 'the faith/faithfulness of Christ') and J. D. G. Dunn (who supports 'faith in Christ') in *Society of Biblical Literature: 1991 Seminar Papers,* Scholars Press, 1991, pp. 714-729, 730-744.

12. For the meaning 'propitiation' rather than 'expiation' or 'mercy seat' cf. Cranfield, *Romans,* pp. 214-218; Moo, *Romans,* pp. 232-242; J. R. W. Stott, *The Message of Romans,* IVP, 1994, pp. 113-116.

13. Cf. Cranfield, *Romans,* p. 110: 'the reality of the wrath of God is only truly known when it is seen in its revelation in Gethsemane and on Golgotha.'

14. Cf. R. Haldane, *Exposition of the Epistle to the Romans,* Banner of Truth, 1958, pp. 79-94. He shows that those who have the law must produce exact and perfect obedience to it if they are to be declared righteous on the judgment day. In answer to the argument recently revived by E. P. Sanders that the law itself provided for sinful lapses through the sacrificial system Haldane replies, 'The legal expiations had no virtue in themselves; but inasmuch as they were figures of the expiation made by Jesus Christ, they directed men to His sacrifice. But as they belonged to the temporal or carnal covenant, they neither expiated nor could expiate any but typical sins, that is to say, uncleanness of the flesh...which were not real sins, but only external pollutions. Thus...all real sins remained on the conscience...for from these the law did not in the smallest degree discharge' (p. 89). In other words, there is no salvation in the law itself. The means of atonement in the law only typified the true atonement presented in the Gospel.

3 Justification in other New Testament books

The Ministry of John the Baptist and Jesus

The Gospel accounts begin with the activity of John the Baptist. The time of fulfilment begins with John who is the end-time messenger sent to prepare the way of the Lord (Malachi 3:1; 4:5-6; Mark 1:2; Luke 1:17,76; 3:4). His preaching and baptism were startlingly revolutionary. He was calling his own people to repent and be baptised. John's challenge came to those who prided themselves on being God's people, having the law and being in a right relationship with God. They were the clean people over against the unclean Gentile sinners who did not even possess the law, never mind keep it. Calling such people to repent and be baptised emphasised the point that Paul was to make later, that Jews as well as Gentiles were unclean sinners who were unfit for God's presence and to be members of God's kingdom. Whereas the kingdom or rule of God was once associated with national Israel in the land of promise, it is now to be re-established and associated with the coming of the Messiah. In this way John 'preached the good news to them' and prepared for Jesus the Christ (Luke 3:18).

Jesus proclaimed the gospel of the kingdom and associated himself with it. He also saw himself as the 'Servant' of Isaiah's prophecy, who had come to seek and to save the lost, to give his life a ransom for many, by being 'numbered with the transgressors' (Mark 10:45; Luke 22:37; Isaiah 53:12). Like John, Jesus clashed with those who thought themselves to be in a right position before God through birth and law-keeping, and he very pointedly declared that he had not come to call the righteous but sinners to repentance (Mark 2:17). Like the prophets before them, both John and Jesus preached to their own people of sin and the need for a heart religion. The privileged status of the Jews as the people of God, appointed to bring light to the nations, could not be appealed to as the ground for acceptance by God and membership of the re-established kingdom. To be right with God and members of this kingdom they must repent and believe the gospel. This is nothing other than a revolution, involving a new spiritual birth (John 3:1-8).

The Pharisees and scribes, who were the upholders of the law, had to be shown that even they were sinners and that no amount of law-keeping could put them in a right legal position before God. Neither was the appeal to their natural birth, which automatically made them children of Abraham and members of the old covenant community, acceptable for entrance into the kingdom (Luke 3:8; John 8:33-47). Entry into God's kingdom and a right legal position before him meant that scribes and Pharisees, as well as tax collectors and 'sinners', must see their need and sinfulness. The law was there to emphasise human sinfulness and to direct people to put their trust in the promise contained in the law. This is why Jesus was so hard on the teachers of the law and those who prided themselves on keeping the law. He sought to root out all hypocrisy and self-righteousness. Even the best of people are sinners by nature and by practice. Jesus said to the Pharisees, 'you are the ones who justify yourselves in the eyes of men, but God knows your hearts' (Luke 16:15). A true recognition of the sinfulness of the human heart and a looking to God's promised Messiah, the offspring of Abraham and David, is the only way to be justified. The new covenant, hinted at by Moses in Deuteronomy 30:6 and prophesied by Jeremiah 31:31-34 emphasises a heart religion, where all know the Lord and the forgiveness of sins.

Luke

In the story of the Rich Man and Lazarus, the rich man represents the religiously self-sufficient who have not appreciated the thrust of what Moses and the Prophets were saying. Lazarus represents the humble poor, like Mary and Joseph and the shepherds, who believe and belong to the true children of Abraham (Luke 16:19-31; cf. John 5:45-46). Again, Jesus told the parable of the Pharisee and the Tax Collector in direct reply to those 'who were confident of their own righteousness and looked down on everybody else' (Luke 18:9). The tax collector may well have been as materially rich as the Pharisee, but unlike the Pharisee who boasted of his religious observances, he recognised his own sin and need and looked to the Lord for mercy. This is the one who 'went home justified before God' (v 14).

In the above example Luke has recorded a statement of Jesus which actually uses the word 'justified'. What is implicit in much of Jesus' teaching is here made explicit. God justifies, not the so-called righteous who have no awareness of sin and need, but the ungodly, the sinners, who look only to the grace of God. It is Luke, in his second volume, who also includes a reference to justification by faith alone, when he presents an early example of Paul's preaching. As he comes to the climax of his message Paul proclaims the superiority of the gospel to the law. 'Through him (Jesus) everyone who believes is justified from everything you could not be justified from by the law of Moses' (Acts 13:39). While the Mosaic law could never justify from anything, a perfect justification is provided by Jesus Christ to all who believe in him.[1] Peter also insists, at the special church assembly in Jerusalem, that 'faith accomplishes what the law cannot do'. He closes by showing that Jew and Gentile are in need of the same grace of God, 'We believe it is through the grace of our Lord Jesus that we are saved, just as they are' (Acts 15:7-11).

Matthew
While the ethical element, in the sense of doing what is right according to God's will, is often present in Matthew's use of 'righteousness' and 'righteous', this is not the whole story.[2] 'Righteousness' can be described as a gospel righteousness. It is a righteousness associated with entering and submitting to God's rule and for which one will be persecuted. It includes 'not merely ethics, narrowly conceived, but believing Jesus and welcoming him as Messiah'.[3] This righteousness focuses on Jesus who said to those in bondage to legalism, 'Come to me, all you who are weary and burdened, and I will give you rest' (Matt. 11:25-30). He came not only to set an example but 'to inaugurate the fulfilment of God's saving purposes'[4] (3:15 'to fulfil all righteousness'), 'to give his life as a ransom for many' (20:28) and to inaugurate the new covenant in his blood (26:28).

The fallen state of humanity in sin is assumed when Jesus says 'if you then though you are evil know how to give good gifts...'. The call, therefore, is to seek first the kingdom of God and his righteousness (Matthew 6:33; 7:11). Later, Jesus speaks of John the Baptist as coming 'in the way of righteousness' or as the NIV interprets it, 'to show you the way of righteousness' (21:32). Tax collectors and prostitutes are entering the realm of God's saving power whereas the religious leaders, such as the chief priests and Pharisees, remain unrepentant and unbelieving.

The first of the Beatitudes demonstrates that the kingdom belongs to those who are 'poor in spirit' (5:3). Those in this 'blessed' or privileged position have come to the end of themselves. They are not necessarily financially poor but they are like David, 'poor and needy', and are looking to the Lord alone to save them (cf. Ps. 34:6; 40:17). 'There is no more perfect statement of the doctrine of justification by faith only than this Beatitude' writes Lloyd-Jones in his *Studies in the Sermon on the Mount.*[5]

The righteousness of the scribes and Pharisees, on the other hand, is not radical enough (Matthew 5:20). They do 'acts of righteousness' (6:1; lit. 'righteousnesses') to be seen by men. They have a self-centred piety in which there is deliberate self-conscious hypocrisy. Jesus castigates them with these damning words: 'on the outside you appear to people as righteous but on the inside you are full of hypocrisy and wickedness' (23:28).

Those who have received God's righteousness and entered God's kingdom 'hunger and thirst for righteousness' (5:6). In other words, they yearn not only for personal righteousness of life, but that God's kingdom of righteousness might come, and that his will might be done on earth. This is a theme picked up in 2 Peter 3:13 as the apostle looks forward to a new heaven and earth 'the home of righteousness'. The 'sons of the kingdom' in contrast to 'the sons of the evil one' will 'shine like the sun in the kingdom of their Father' (Matthew 13:38,43; cf. Daniel 12:3). No hypocrisy will be seen in these righteous ones on that day when God separates the sheep from the goats. It will not be a case of looking to their good works to save them. The question which the righteous ones ask makes it clear that they did not do good works in order to be accepted. They showed from their hearts their love for Christ by loving his people (25:37-40). Righteousness is therefore a gift from God of a right legal standing before him, associated with Jesus and God's will.

John's Gospel

After Jesus emphasises the need of new birth in John 3:1-10 (cf. 1:13), our attention is immediately drawn to the love of God in Christ (3:11-18). Eternal life comes through looking to the heavenly Man crucified in the place of sinners. John comments that only those who believe in God's Son have life. To believe on the Son means no condemnation. On the other hand, not to believe means that one is already condemned. 'Whoever believes is not condemned, but whoever does not believe stands condemned already because he has not believed in the name of God's one and only Son' (John 3:18). This is the verdict, and the condemnation includes the wrath of God remaining upon that person (John 3:36). The same truth is reiterated in John 5 where we are told that the one who receives God's word through Jesus has eternal life 'and will not be condemned; he has crossed over from death to life' (vv 22-24). This means that they are in a right legal position before God here and now through faith in Christ. The future judgment is not ignored as the following verses in John 5 indicate. It will ratify what is already a reality (vv 25-30).

All this reminds us of Paul's statement that 'there is now no condemnation for those who are in Christ Jesus' (Romans 8:1). Justification is a verdict in the present that a person is not guilty and will not receive punishment. While Luke presents the positive side in Jesus' teaching on justification ('he went home justified'), John records discourses which focus on the negative side of the same truth ('not condemned' and 'will not be condemned').

John 16:7-11 use terminology that is important to the subject of justification, namely, 'sin, righteousness and judgment'. All three terms, it will be noted, are to be understood in relation to Jesus Christ: 'because men do not believe in me'; 'because I am going to the Father'; 'the prince of this world now stands condemned' as a result of the cross (cf. 12:31-33). It is, of course, a notoriously difficult passage to interpret and it is not impossible that more than one meaning is intended. The Holy Spirit, the Paraclete, is given as a result of Jesus' departure and he will convict the world of sinful human beings, seduced by the devil, of its guilt which is spelt out in terms of its sin, its righteousness and its judgment. It is because the world does not believe in Jesus, who calls people to repent of their sin and believe, that the Spirit convicts the world of its sin and need.

Again, the Spirit convicts the world of its false and hopelessly inadequate righteousness. It was in the name of righteousness that Jesus was crucified. Because Jesus was going to the Father via the cross, thus marking him out as 'the Righteous One', the Spirit convicts even the religious, moral world of its unacceptable and useless righteousness. The righteousness that counts is that of our Advocate who is now with the Father, Jesus Christ and his atoning death (cf. I John 2:1-2). The Spirit also convicts the world of its false judgment. The world in its devilish blindness condemned Jesus. Because the ruler of the world, the devil, stands condemned as a result of the triumph of the cross, the Spirit convicts the world of its unrighteous judgment and that, in following the devil, it also stands condemned.[6]

John's Letters

Although John does not deal directly with justification in his letters, there are some verses which are important to the subject. In his first letter he deals extensively with the subject of sin. First of all he stresses the sinfulness of all, even of Christians (1 John 1:8-10; 2:1). We are all sinners by nature and practice. Christians can be commanded not to sin (2:1) because they are born of God, have God's nature and are no longer in the same sinful state (3:4-9; cf. Romans 6:2). Nevertheless, because they are still sinners the atoning death of Christ ('the blood of Jesus') carries on its purifying effect in those who are truly living in fellowship with God (1:5-7). Specific sins need to be individually confessed and again, God is 'faithful and just and will forgive us our sins and purify us from all unrighteousness' (1:9; cf. Psalm 143:1-2).

Is the word 'just' or 'righteous' merely another term for 'faithful' in 1 John 1:9? While some have argued this, there is no good reason for treating it as a synonym.[7] The phrase is reminiscent of Deuteronomy 32:4, 'A faithful God who does no wrong, upright and just is he.' We must allow each word to have its individual meaning. 'Righteous' forms a contrast with 'unrighteousness' at the end of the sentence.

Others understand 'righteous' as a reference to God's saving action in forgiving.[8] But this does not take account of the fact that God also punishes sinners. Here 'righteous' or 'just' emphasises the moral nature of God's forgiveness. 'Faithful' reminds us that God is true to the promises of the new covenant in forgiving sins. 'Righteous', on the other hand, refers to the fact that God's forgiveness is not at the expense of his justice in punishing sin. God has said that he will by no means clear the guilty: 'he does not leave the guilty unpunished' (Exodus 34:7). How then can God forgive and not punish sinners?

Forgiveness, in the Bible, cannot be divorced from its teaching on justification. It cannot be glibly said that it is in God's nature to forgive. It is also in God's nature to punish sin. Sin must be punished for God to be true to his righteous nature revealed in his law. Yet God has gone on record to forgive sin and purify the unrighteous (Micah 7:18-20). How can God deal with sin and yet forgive and make it possible for the sinner to be righteous? The only moral ground on which God could ever do such a thing is 'the blood of Jesus'. The love of God provides for the covering of the wrath of God in addition to the purification of our sins. 'This is love: not that we loved God, but that he loved us and sent his Son to be the propitiation for our sins' (1 John 4:10). Paul expresses the same truth in Romans 3:25-26. This is the way God can be both just and the justifier of guilty sinners who look to Jesus Christ, the righteous one, who paid the penalty due.

This subject is considered again in 1 John 2:1-2 where law-court language is in the background. Jesus Christ is 'the Righteous One', who 'speaks to the Father in our defence'. John is fond of calling attention to Jesus as the righteous one (cf. 2:29; 3:7). In Jesus there is no sin (3:5); that is why he is righteous. The Son of God who lived in this world 'in the flesh' is in a right legal position before God on the basis of a life lived in conformity to God's will. This is one qualification for Jesus acting as our Advocate. The other is his action in turning away God's wrath with respect to our sins through his sacrificial death (v2). On the basis of his own righteous life culminating in the righteous action associated with his death he is able to plead the cause of those he represents in the heavenly court-room (cf. Job 16:19). 'Jesus is supremely able to ask for that righteousness to be extended to all God's children who are in fellowship with him.'⁹ The grounds of acquittal, forgiveness and of a right legal standing before God for all who belong to Jesus are, in other words, Jesus' blood and righteousness. As a result of God's love in Christ, God is no longer their judge but their Father (3:1-2). Adoption into God's family and membership of the covenant community are results of justification.

Hebrews

The epistle to the Hebrews warns of the reality of the divine punishment and its justness (2:2; *endikos* means 'based on what is right, just, deserved'; cf. Romans 3:8). The retribution is deserved. Those who despise the gospel are heading for eternal judgment and the curse of God (6:2, 4-8). They have no part in that kingdom which is unshakeable (12:25-29). The wrath of God is something to fear (10:26-31). Yet God is also revealed as gracious (2:9) in that his Son became the man Jesus in order that he might die to make propitiation for the sins of the people (2:17).¹⁰ This was the culmination of a life of obedience in which he delighted to do the will of God (5:8-9; 10:5-10). His love of righteousness and hatred of wickedness (1:9) 'was the essential preliminary to his atoning death on the cross'.¹¹

Melchizedek is portrayed as the type of the messianic priest-king, the king of righteousness and peace (7:2; cf. Psalm 72:2-7). To these two aspects of Christ's character the prophets bear witness. Messiah is 'the prince of peace' (Isaiah 9:6) and 'the righteous Branch' whose name is 'the Lord our Righteousness' (Jeremiah 23:5-6; 33:15-16). All this is fundamental to the gospel, which the writer to the Hebrews describes as the message or teaching about righteousness (lit. 'the word of right-eousness 5:13). Christ our righteousness is set over against the dead works from which we need to repent (6:1) and to be cleansed by the blood of Jesus (9:14).

Another crucial ingredient of the Gospel is 'faith in God' (6:1). This positive disposition of faith toward God balances the negative renunciation of dead works. It is only through the blood of Jesus, the new and living way, that we are able to draw near to God (10:19-22). Those who have a right legal standing before God live by faith (10:37-39) and many examples from the Old Testament are given for encouragement (11:1-12:2) including Abel, who was a righteous man, and Noah who 'became heir of the righteousness that comes by faith' (11:4, 7). Clearly this righteousness is not the result of human works but is given by God to those who believe. This message about righteousness is nothing other than Paul's teaching on justification by faith alone, or to put it in the words of a 20th century French commentator on Hebrews: 'the first Christian instruction involves initiation into justification by faith'.[12] It is on this firm basis that the letter goes on to encourage Christians to 'spur one another on towards love and good deeds' (10:24).

Peter

I Peter 3:18 says something similar to what we found in 1 John and Hebrews: 'For Christ died for sins once for all, the righteous for the unrighteous, to bring you to God'. Peter has Isaiah 53:11 very much in mind, where the righteousness of the Servant is contrasted with the sinfulness of those for whom he suffered. Reconciliation is, of course, the main point of the verse, 'to bring you to God'. However, justification is the necessary foundation of reconciliation. The reference to 'unrighteous' is a reminder to the reconciled of their previous position before God. They are now among the righteous (cf. 3:12 and 4:18). In order for them to be in this new legal position before God and hence to be no longer alienated from God, Christ, the righteous one, suffered on behalf of the unrighteous. Earlier in 1:2 and 1:19, the blood of Christ is mentioned, while in 2:22, Peter refers to Christ's spotless life, using Isaiah 53:9, before moving on in verse 24 to speak of his bearing 'our sins in his body on the tree'. Christ is both their righteous representative and substitute. It is in this way, on account of his righteous life and atoning death, that these formerly unrighteous people now have a right status before God and are reconciled to him. They go on to live for righteousness (2:24).

Revelation

In the book of Revelation John describes justification by using two very different pictorial forms. First, justification is symbolized by several references to white garments or robes (3:4-5; 4:4; 6:11; 7:9, 13-14). In the Old Testament, Isaiah likens the righteous deeds of Israel to dirty rags (Isaiah 64:6) and yet at the beginning of his book there is the promise that 'though your sins are like scarlet, they shall be as white as snow' (1:18). In Zechariah's prophecy, Joshua the high priest is given clean rich robes instead of his filthy ones (3:3-5). His filthy clothes represent the guilt of himself and the people which God removes (cf. vv1, 4, 9). This typifies what God will do through his servant, the Branch (v8; cf. Isaiah 52:13-53:12; Jeremiah 23:5; 33:15). In chapter 13:1 Zechariah also promises that in that day 'a fountain will be opened to the house of David and the inhabitants of Jerusalem, to cleanse them from sin and impurity'. All this provides the background to this theme of the white robes in Revelation. The Laodiceans were spiritually naked and needed to purchase white robes to cover their shame (Rev. 3:18). On the other hand, the redeemed stand before God arrayed in robes that have been washed and whitened in the blood of the Lamb (7:13-15). What a powerful image, crimson blood producing white clothes! They are clothed in the righteousness of Christ which is associated with his sacrificial death.

The other picture of justification that John gives in Revelation is in chapter 12. Actually a number of Old Testament associations are brought together in this chapter that bear upon the subject. The reference to Satan the accuser of the brothers reminds us of the book of Job, particularly the heavenly court scene in the first two chapters. In Zechariah 3:1-10, besides the exchange of filthy for clean robes, there is the scene of the heavenly court where Satan acts to accuse Joshua the representative of God's people. The picture we have in Revelation 12:7-12 is of the adversary, Satan, as a kind of public prosecutor. The war in heaven is 'not military but moral and legal'.[13] Satan represents justice and there is a moral conflict in heaven. Military might cannot remove him, for as long as there are sinners to be accused he has a legitimate case. Michael is 'the defending barrister', but he is not the one who gains the legal victory. The victory belongs to Christ through his death at Calvary. Sinners are justified on the grounds of Christ's work alone.

This survey of the New Testament evidence has already included references from Genesis to Malachi but it is now necessary to consider in more detail the general thrust and important verses of the Old Testament relating to justification.

Notes

1. F. F. Bruce, *The Book of Acts*, Eerdmans, 1988, p. 262f.

2. Cf. B. Przybylski, *Righteousness in Matthew and His World of Thought*, Cambridge, 1980: righteousness is 'proper conduct before God' p. 99.

3. D. A. Carson, *Matthew*, The Expositor's Bible Commentary, vol. 8, Zondervan, 1984, p. 450.

4. D. A. Hagner, *Matthew 1-13*, Word Biblical Commentary 33A, Word, 1993, p. 56.

5. D. M. Lloyd-Jones, *Studies in the Sermon on the Mount*, IVP, 1959, p. 42.

6. Cf. D. A. Carson, *The Gospel According to John*, IVP/Eerdmans, 1991, p. 537-539; W. Hendriksen, *A Commentary on the Gospel of John*, Banner of Truth, 1961, pp. 324-326.

7. A. E. Brooke, *A Critical and Exegetical Commentary on the Johannine Epistles*, T. & T. Clark, 1912, p. 19.

8. C. H. Dodd, *The Johannine Epistles*, The Moffatt New Testament Commentary, Hodder & Stoughton, 1946, pp. 22f.

9. S. S. Smalley, *1,2,3 John*, Word Biblical Commentary, vol. 51, 1984, Word, p. 37f.

10. Cf. P. E. Hughes, *A Commentary on the Epistle to the Hebrews*, Eerdmans, 1977, pp. 120-123 for the translation 'propitiation'. At 9:5 the term means 'mercy seat'. For a full discussion of the word *hilastérion* cf. L. Morris, *The Apostolic Preaching of the Cross*, Tyndale Press, 1965, pp. 144-213.

11. Hughes, *Hebrews*, p. 65.

12. C. Spicq quoted by Hughes, *Hebrews*, p. 191f.

13. John Sweet, *Revelation*, SCM/Trinity Press International, 1990, p. 199.

4 Justification in the Old Testament

The apostle Paul tells us that the law and the prophets bear witness to God's justifying righteousness. In making this statement he is not only saying that particular passages point to this great subject but that the entire Old Testament does so. Before coming to specific verses that directly bear upon the theme there are some general observations to be made.

The Initial Family Bond

The biblical doctrine of justification presupposes the living and true God, the Creator and Ruler of the whole universe, and the recognition that human beings are created by God and are responsible to God. 'God said, "Let us make man in our image, in our likeness...". So God created man in his own image...male and female he created them' (Genesis 1:26-27). God created man in his image so that a personal relationship of mutual love might exist and that man might act as God's viceroy over the newly created earth. That original bond between God and man is described in covenantal terms. A general blessing is pronounced: 'God blessed them and said, "Be fruitful and increase in number; fill the earth and subdue it. Rule over..."' (Genesis 1:28). A curse is also threatened for disobedience: 'you must not eat from the tree of the knowledge of good and evil, for when you eat of it you will surely die' (2:17). In that initial family bond, where man is described as God's son (5:1-2; Luke 3:38), righteousness involved loyalty to that covenant relationship. On the divine side it meant the obligation to punish disobedience as well as to bless. It should be noted, however, that God is the sovereign. He makes the rules and he is not accountable to man: on the contrary, man is accountable to God.

Human Sin and Divine Grace

Justification also implies human sin and divine grace. There would be no need for justification if human beings had remained faithful to the initial covenant bond. Such terms as 'judge', 'judgment' and 'justification' arise in the context of human sinfulness. Again, there would be no possibility of justification were it not for the grace of God. These twin themes of man's sin and God's grace are present in chapter three of Genesis. The account is given of how sin entered the world through the rebellion of our first parents. God is now shown to be the divine judge who pronounces sentence. At the same time, God's grace is revealed in the promise of victory through the offspring of the woman (Genesis 3:15). In addition, the provision of proper clothing for the couple is both a reminder of their sinfulness and an act of grace (3:21). Prior to Adam and Eve's disobedience nakedness was neither a problem to them nor to God (2:25). After their disobedience they sought to hide from each other and from God. Their awareness of being naked was an indication of their guilt and shame. For that guilt and shame to be removed they must be properly clad. Thus their clothing was a continual reminder that they were now sinners.[1] They could not approach God unclothed.

That it was God who provided the suitable clothing was, nevertheless, an indication of his grace.[2] The paltry efforts of the human couple were totally inadequate. To be adequately and decently covered God must clothe them. Their sin and guilt could not be properly covered through their own desperate efforts. For human beings to approach God it was necessary to have clothes provided and approved by him. In place of the skimpy belt of fig leaves God chose tunics or shirts of skin. There could be no greater contrast. It shows how easy-going and utterly inadequate were the human efforts to deal with guilt and shame, and how thorough-going and costly was God's way. It involved the taking of life. As E. J. Young suggests it would appear that 'this act of God in the taking of animal life laid the foundation for animal sacrifice'[3] Here, then, we have in this chapter all the basic ingredients concerning the biblical doctrine of justification, which will be opened up and developed with the accumulation of divine revelation through the Old Testament period, until the climax is reached in the New Testament. Promise and type give way to fulfilment and reality in the coming of Messiah, God's Son. We can only briefly draw attention to these themes of sin and judgment, of grace and promise and of the provision of proper covering with which to approach God.

Solomon, in his great prayer at the dedication of the temple, is conscious of the sin of Israel (1 Kings 8:33, 35, 46-47, 50) and confesses that 'there is no-one who does not sin' (v46). The Psalmist declares that as God looks down on humanity he sees that 'there is no-one who does good, not even one' (Psalm 14:3). Jeremiah teaches that 'the heart is deceitful above all things and beyond cure. Who can understand it?' (17:9) God reveals through Ezekiel that 'the soul who sins is the one who will die' (18:4). The Preacher insists that 'there is not a righteous man on earth who does what is right and never sins' (Ecclesiastes 7:20). Indeed, Ecclesiastes can be thought of as a sermon or commentary on the early chapters of Genesis, with its emphasis on the transitory nature of life in this fallen world and the power of death. All feel the curse. Isaiah sums up the situation in these words:

'The earth is defiled by its people; they have disobeyed the laws, violated the statutes and broken the everlasting covenant. Therefore a curse consumes the earth; its people must bear their guilt (24:5-6).

'But Noah found favour in the eyes of the Lord' (Genesis 6:8). This is the first actual reference to grace in the Bible and it is set against the dark background of human wickedness and God's anger. With an eye to God's promise made in Eden Noah's father was expecting a deliverer to be born (5:29). Noah was not the promised offspring but God saved Noah with a view to fulfilling his promise. A new section of Genesis opens in 6:9 with the statement that 'Noah was a righteous man, blameless among the people of his time, and he walked with God'. Despite belonging to a race of sinners, by God's grace Noah was righteous. This meant he was in a right legal position before God and did what was pleasing to God. He stood out as free from blemish among his contemporaries and had a close personal relationship with God like Enoch before him. These themes of grace, hope, promise, and a right legal status before God are all present against the background of God's wrath and judgment.

God's Saving Plan

The emphasis on a promised offspring becomes even more prominent from the time of Abraham, when we are told that 'through your offspring all nations on earth will be blessed' (Genesis 22:18). In fact, the book of Genesis, through its special headings to each section ('this is the account of' or better 'this is the family history of': 2:4, 5:1, 6:9, 10:1, 11:10, 11:27, etc.), focuses the mind on the promises of God. They act like signposts which encourage the reader to look forward to the fulfilment of God's saving purposes for all peoples on earth. At the close of Genesis blessing comes to Egypt, a representative of the nations, as a result of the offspring of Abraham. Through the sufferings of righteous Joseph at the hands of his own people life comes to many in accordance with God's plan. 'You intended to harm me, but God intended it for good to accomplish what is now being done, the saving of many lives' (50:20). But this is not the real fulfilment, it is only a token and type of greater things to come. Jacob and Joseph are seen as men of faith who put their trust in the promise of God and look forward to the day when the promise will be fully realised (49:29-32; 50:24-25).

From this point on, the history is dominated by the covenant which God made with the twelve tribes of Jacob under the leadership of Moses at Sinai. This covenant is another milestone in the divine plan to teach the people of God important lessons and to encourage them to continue to look for the fulfilment of God's promise. They are redeemed from Egyptian slavery and formed into a nation in which the kingdom of God is to be seen on earth as they live together in the land of Canaan. They are given God's law and in every department of life they are to be seen as God's holy people. The law not only presents Israel with the moral standard which God requires and with detailed rules based on that standard, it provides, through its sacrifices and cleansing rituals, visual aid teaching on sin and its consequences, the way of acceptance with God and the forgiveness of sins. Blessing is promised for obedience and a curse is pronounced for disobedience and apostasy.

Deuteronomy also emphasises the promises to the patriarchs and the need of a heart religion which only God can give. It also teaches that God's choice of Israel to bring blessing to the world is due to the grace of God and not their own righteousness. The true prophets of the Lord who come later, both in historical writing and prophetic word, seek to draw attention to the demands of the covenant, to the curses that will inevitably fall on the people for their disobedience and lack of trust in God, and to the great fulfilment of God's promises to the patriarchs in a new covenant, and to a ruler of Davidic stock who will bring lasting deliverance and universal peace. This new administration will not merely replace the former but will bring about the great reality to which the old Sinai covenant at best could only point. The hymns and wisdom literature of the Old Testament in their own way also call attention to these themes of grace, faith, a religion of the heart, a right legal position before God and future blessing associated with the Davidic king.

Our attention now shifts to those specific texts in the Old Testament that directly bear upon the subject of justification.

1. Genesis 15:6, 'Abram believed the Lord, and he credited it to him as righteousness'.

This verse is quoted in Romans 4:3, 20-24; Galatians 3:6 and in James 2:23. Abraham is the father of the Jewish nation and therefore what is said of him is very important. We are first of all informed that his faith was credited as righteousness. This is the only place in the Old Testament where faith is counted as righteousness.[4] It is also significant that this is the first occurrence of the word 'believe' in Scripture.

God graciously called Abraham from an idolatrous background and made a covenant with him. All nations would find blessing through him and his offspring. It is interesting to discover the subject of justification in this setting. While it was common in Jewish circles to think of Abraham's faith as a meritorious work, both Paul and James view the text in context. Genesis 15 does not speak of faith as a work done by Abraham. Faith is reliance on God's promise. It was not Abraham's act of believing that was credited to him for righteousness. There is no thought of God treating faith as though it were righteousness. The act of believing is not a substitute for good works. Righteousness is a gift given by God to those who rely on the promised offspring. Abraham believed the promise concerning the offspring and this led God to account to him a righteousness which he did not merit or inherently possess. Righteousness is what acquits a person in a human court and likewise before the heavenly Judge. 'Normally righteousness is defined in terms of moral conduct...and might well be paraphrased as God-like, or at least God-pleasing, action'.[5] Abraham, however, does not do righteousness but has righteousness credited to him. Thus Abraham was justified by faith alone in that he was judged by God to be in a right legal position before him and acquitted through faith in God's promised offspring. This is the doctrine of justification by faith alone.

Abraham's faith was later severely tested in his submission to God's call to sacrifice his own unique son but, as James indicates, that act of obedience showed the genuineness of his faith. Through the various visual aids in the covenant ceremony (cf. Genesis 15:17) and all the experiences connected with his son Isaac, including the miraculous birth and the circumstances surrounding the offering of his son, God taught Abraham about the coming offspring. It is left to Paul to spell out the connection between the offspring, who is Jesus Christ the Son of God, and the gift of righteousness. There are a number of passages in the New Testament which stress that Abraham and the other patriarchs looked to the promise which finds its fulfilment in Jesus Christ. Our Lord himself said, 'Abraham rejoiced at the thought of seeing my day; he saw it and was glad' (John 8:56). Paul declared that all the promises of God find their 'Yes' in Christ (2 Corinthians 1:20). Hebrews comments that though the patriarchs died before the things promised arrived yet they 'saw them and welcomed them from a distance' (Hebrews 11:13).

2. Psalm 32:1-2, 'Blessed is he whose transgressions are forgiven, whose sins are covered. Blessed is the man whose sin the Lord does not count against him...'

These verses express the privileged and happy state of the forgiven sinner. The weight of his rebellion against God, and its consequences, has been lifted. His sin has been properly covered and the Lord 'no longer considers the person a sinner' (cf. 2 Samuel 19:19).[6]

It is the phrase 'whose sin the Lord does not count against him' which Paul seizes in his use of this verse in Romans 4:7-8. Paul quotes the text not so much to show that forgiveness is involved in justification, which it obviously is, but because it includes the verb 'to impute' or 'to reckon'. It emphasises again that justification is an act of God's free grace which is not based on a person's works. It involves the non-accrediting of sins. Again, the forensic or judicial element is present. The divine Judge is acquitting and treating the person as righteous. Whereas Genesis 15:6 presents the positive side, in which righteousness is reckoned to the person, here the negative is highlighted. Sin is not reckoned to the person.

3. Habakkuk 2:4b, 'the righteous will live by his faith'.

These words are quoted by Paul in Romans 1:17 and Galatians 3:11, and by the writer of Hebrews in 10:38. It is generally recognised that the personal pronoun 'his' refers to 'the righteous' and not to God.[7] There is more uncertainty over the meaning of the word 'faith'. While, generally in the Old Testament, the word means 'faithfulness', its use in Habakkuk favours the meaning 'trust'. The prophet is called to wait in faith for God to act. He is to rest in God's word, come what may. 'Though it linger, wait for it' (v3). Chapter three then expresses in poetry trustful reliance on God. This is what 'faith' means. A contrast is drawn between the one who is arrogant and not upright and against whom woes are pronounced, and the righteous one who lives by his trust in God. The reference to 'living' is a reminder of the life associated with obedience to the covenant obligations: 'Now choose life, so that you and your children may live and that you may love the Lord your God' (Deuteronomy 30:19-20; cf. Leviticus 18:5). The opposite is death and destruction for all who are disobedient and turn away from God's way. It is an echo of the tree of life in the garden of Eden and the death that came through disobedience.

Paul is quite in order to use this passage from Habakkuk as a key text in support of his argument that it is by faith alone and not by the works of the law that we are justified (Galatians 3:11). It is also significant that he should take this one passage from the Old Testament where the noun 'faith' has the meaning of 'trust' rather than faithfulness, and that it is connected to 'the righteous' and the verb 'live'. There is much discussion as to whether Paul links faith with 'righteous' or with 'live'. In the final analysis it really does not matter. The quotation is important for stressing that the gospel of God's justifying grace means 'faith from start to finish' (Romans 1:17). They are righteous by faith and live daily by faith. The unrighteous are the ones who do not believe the promise of God, and however many works they do, they are under the wrath of God and their end is death.

4. Isaiah 53:11b, 'by his knowlege my righteous servant will justify many, and he will bear their iniquities'.

Instead of the Levitical offerings for sin presented by the priests, the Servant of the Lord offers himself as *the* sacrifice for sin. Those offerings not only pointed to the expiation or covering of sins through the shedding of blood, but to the appeasing of God's wrath, indicated in the symbolism of the smoke of the burnt offering rising as a pleasing sacrifice acceptable to God. That the blood of bulls and goats cannot in themselves take away sins and remove the divine wrath is evident in the plea of Moses, the servant of the Lord, to be accursed instead of his people (Exodus 32:32). That plea was turned down by God but it certainly prepared for this prophecy of Isaiah where *the* Servant of the Lord actually comes under the curse of God on account of his people's sins.

In addition, the Servant is described as the righteous one who justifies many. E. J. Young speaks of the glorious interchange which determines the connotation of the verb 'to justify'. The Servant bears the iniquity of sinners and they in turn receive his righteousness.[8] He provides righteousness for the many. It can only mean, as Motyer comments: 'that there are those ('the many') whom he clothes in his righteousness, sharing with them his own perfect acceptability before God.'[9] The righteousness that Abraham received through faith in the promise, Isaiah depicts as being provided by the Servant.

The work of the Servant calls to mind the prophecy of Daniel. He speaks of Messiah being 'cut off' and putting an end to sacrifice and offering. In that same context we are told of God's purpose 'to finish transgression, to put an end to sin, to atone for wickedness, to bring in everlasting righteousness' (Daniel 9:24-27).

Phinehas, Aaron's grandson, points us towards Isaiah's righteous

Servant. As an expression of his faith in God, Phinehas' zealous action stopped the plague which had already claimed thousands of lives (Numbers 25:6-13) His intervention removed the divine wrath and God confirmed the lasting nature of his priesthood, a priesthood which finds its fulfilment in Christ (Hebrews 7:11-28) and prophesied by Isaiah. This is not all, Psalm 106:30-31 draws on this incident and states that the action of Phinehas 'was credited to him as righteousness for endless generations to come'. There is an interesting parallel here between an endless priesthood and the endless benefit of the accredited righteousness. In Motyer's words, Phinehas foreshadows the Lord Jesus 'in the divine status of *righteousness* accorded to him as mediator, anticipating the One whom Isaiah calls "that righteous One, my Servant" (53:11; Heb. 7:26).'[10] This is the one who justifies the many.

5. Psalm 143:1b-2, 'in your faithfulness and righteousness come to my relief. Do not bring your servant into judgment, for no-one living is righteous before you.'

'Faithfulness' and 'righteousness' are covenant words and the psalmist prays the Lord will answer him on the basis of God's righteous character. God can be trusted to do what is right according to the covenant promises and threats (cf. verses 11-12). Yet, the psalmist is aware that the righteousness of God also means that if God were to judge him according to the righteous standard of his own nature, revealed in the law, he would have no right legal standing. His sinfulness would be all too obvious. There is, in fact, no-one on earth who is righteous. This is the same truth that is presented in Psalm 130:3, 'If you, O Lord, kept a record of sins, O Lord, who could stand?' (cf. Psalm 14:2-3). Job expresses the same dilemma in these terms: 'But how can a mortal be righteous before God?' (Job 9:2; cf. 7:17; 15:14; 25:4-5). It is made quite clear that to justify the wicked is an atrocious thing; 'Acquitting the guilty and condemning the innocent - the Lord detests them both' (Proverbs 17:15). Nevertheless, the psalmist cries for mercy on the basis of God's righteousness. His plea is not based on any achievements or merits of his own. His entire trust is in God's righteousness.

These verses call to mind two passages from the New Testament.

After appealing to a number of Old Testament verses to prove that Jew and Gentile alike are all sinners, Paul writes in Romans 3:20: 'Therefore no-one will be declared righteous in his sight by observing the law.' But then he immediately follows this up by that glorious statement which has been considered in chapter two concerning God's righteousness made known in the gospel. The other New Testament text is 1 John 1:9, 'If we confess our sins, he is faithful and just to forgive us our sins and purify us from all unrighteousness'. God's faithfulness and righteousness, as revealed in the promised Saviour, are the basis on which to plead.

Conclusion

We are reminded in the last book of the Bible of that fundamental promise found in the first book of the Bible, that the offspring of the woman would bruise the serpent's head and that that promise has been wonderfully fulfilled with the coming of Jesus Christ, his atoning death, resurrection and ascension to the throne of God (Genesis 3:15; cf. Revelation 12:1-12; 13:3). A moral victory has been won; justice has been done; the ancient serpent has received a mortal wound; and the sinner who belongs to Jesus is freed and can no longer be accused. 'Who will bring any charge against those whom God has chosen? It is God who justifies. Who is he that condemns? Christ Jesus, who died - more than that, who was raised to life - is at the right hand of God and is also interceding for us' (Romans 8:33-34). It also means that a proper garment to cover nakedness and shame, typified in the covering God gave to Adam and Eve, has been provided by God, again through our union with Jesus Christ. Jesus alluded to this robe in the parable where the man is refused entry into the wedding feast for not possessing the proper wedding clothes (Matthew 22:1-14). This is the righteousness which Paul describes as a divine gift which the believer receives by faith (Romans 5:17).

'How can a mortal be righteous before God?' Job asks. (Job 9:2) That is the basic problem. We cannot come and go as we please before the Almighty. He is of purer eyes than to look upon our depraved lives. We are all sinners and God is right to be angry with us. He is now our judge and is fully justified in condemning us to the punishment that fits the crime, eternal death. That is what the Old Testament continually impresses upon us and the New constantly underlines it. 'The wages of sin is death' says Paul in Romans 6:23. 'The lake of fire is the second death. If anyone's name was not found written in the book of life, he was thrown into the lake of fire' (Revelation 20:14-15). At the same time the kindness and love of God is displayed in God's Son, Jesus Christ, the Messiah and Servant of the Lord promised in the Old Testament, who came to seek and to save those who lie in the shadow of death. As a result of Christ's righteous life, his atoning death, his bodily resurrection and his ascension to the Father's throne in glory, those who are united to Christ through faith alone, are no longer condemned. They no longer face God's wrath and eternal ruin, but are already able to stand upright in God's presence, unashamed, clothed in the righteousness of Christ and washed in his precious blood. If they were to die, at that very moment, like the repentant thief on the cross, they would be presented 'holy in his sight, without blemish and free from accusation' (Colossians 1:22; cf. Ephesians 1:4; 5:27; Jude 24).

Faith believes the promise of God in the gospel concerning Jesus Christ. The faith by which we embrace Christ is a faith given through the work of the Holy Spirit. It is, therefore, a living faith which perseveres to the end (Colossians 1:23) and which is active in doing the good works which God has given us to do (Ephesians 2:8-10). Those who die in the Lord rest from their labours 'for their deeds will follow them' (Revelation 14:13). On the day of judgment they will be judged as those who are righteous in Christ and their deeds will indicate that they are righteous.[11]

Notes

1. *Calvin's Commentaries* vol. 1, *Genesis,* Baker reprint, 1979, p. 182.

2. *contra.* G. J. Wenham, *Genesis 1-15,* Word Bible Commentary, Vol. 1, Word, 1987, p. 85.

3. E. J. Young, *Genesis 3*, Banner of Truth, 1966, p. 149.

4. Cf. Psalm 106:30. Phinehas' intervention 'was credited to him as righteousness'. Moo is of the opinion that even in this case 'God's reckoning Phinehas as righteous (see

Numbers 25) is a declarative act, not an equivalent compensation or reward for merit' (*Romans,* p. 265).

5. Wenham, *Genesis,* p. 330.

6. A. A. Anderson, *Psalms* Vol. 1, New Century Bible, Marshall, Morgan & Scott, 1972, p. 256.

7. Cf. D. W. Baker, *Nahum, Habakkuk and Zephaniah,* Tyndale Old Testament Commentaries, IVP, 1988, pp. 60f.

8. E. J. Young, *The Book of Isaiah,* Vol. 3, Eerdmans, 1972, p. 357.

9. J. A. Motyer, *The Prophecy of Isaiah,* IVP, 1993, p. 442.

10. J. A. Motyer on 'The Psalms' in *New Bible Commentary 21st century edition,* eds. D. A. Carson, R. T. France, J. A. Motyer, G. J. Wenham, IVP, 1994, p. 556.

11. For another biblical overview cf. E. P. Clowney, 'The Biblical Doctrine of Justification by Faith', in *Right with God: Justification in the Bible and the World,* ed. D. A. Carson, Paternoster, 1992, pp. 17-50.

5 The 'Right' Words

G. C. Berkouwer wrote: 'The confession of divine justification touches man's life at its heart, at the point of its relationship to God'.[1] In particular, as we have seen from the previous chapters, it is about humans being in a right legal position before God. Having considered the biblical evidence we must now give some attention to the biblical terminology. A word of warning, however, needs to be issued. There is the danger of thinking that a detailed examination of words is all that is required in presenting the scriptural understanding of justification. Such reasoning fails to appreciate that the Bible can teach and give further light on a subject without necessarily using the precise terminology. To concentrate purely on a study of words, even in their original contexts, can lead to an unbalanced view of the subject. Nevertheless, it is important to be clear concerning the language used. We shall therefore survey the words associated with justification, discuss their meaning in different contexts and make a number of observations.[2]

Justification and Righteousness

From the biblical perspective these two words are linked. In Greek, both terms belong to the same word-group, the *dik-* family. English is forced at times to use two different word-groups, the 'just-' and 'right-' families. For instance, the noun *dikaiosynē* and the adjective *dikaios* are usually translated 'righteousness' and 'righteous' respectively. When it comes to translating the verb *dikaioō* there is no modern English equivalent within the 'right-' family. No such verb as 'to rightify' exists although there is an old English verb 'to rightwise'. Instead, it has been the common practice from the sixteenth century to express the verbal idea by employing the 'just' word-group, and so we have the word 'justify'. Sometimes 'justice' is used by translators as a synonym for 'righteousness' and 'just' as a synonym for 'righteous'. Why not be consistent then, and take advantage of all the words of the 'just-' family to translate the *dik-* word-group? One reason is that such terms as 'justice' and 'just' suggest a narrower range of meaning associated with fairness in implementing the law. It is better, therefore, to speak of a 'righteous' person and of the 'righteousness' of God on the one hand, and of God 'justifying' the ungodly on the other. Incidentally, Hebrew also uses one main word-group, the ṣ-d-q family. These three root letters are familiar to us in the name 'Melkizedek' ('zedek' in its transliterated form is ṣedeq). The Greek translation of the Old Testament, the Septuagint (LXX), generally uses the dik- word-group to translate words belonging to the Hebrew ṣ-d-q word-group.

Justification
Unlike some theological terms such as 'Trinity', 'justification' is a biblical word. Our English word 'justification' sometimes renders different words from the dik- group. One of these, dikaiōsis, commonly means, in classical Greek, 'condemnation' or 'punishment' although it occasionally has the sense of 'vindication'. It is found twice in the New Testament in Paul's letter to the Romans in the sense of 'vindication' and 'acquittal'. At the end of chapter four, in reference to Jesus Christ, we are told that he 'was delivered up because of our offences, and was raised because of our justification.' (v25 New King James) In the next chapter it appears again at verse eighteen, 'Consequently, just as the result of one trespass was condemnation for all men, so also the result of one act of righteousness was justification that brings life for all men.' Another word from the same word-group, dikaiōma, which normally means 'regulation' or 'right action' in the New Testament, is used in verse sixteen to express the same idea of acquittal: 'The judgment followed one sin and brought condemnation, but the gift followed many trespasses and brought justification'.

In all three passages 'justification' is the best translation.[3] Certainly, 'righteousness' would not be an appropriate alternative. It is also clear from the context how we should understand the term. Justification is to be taken as the opposite of condemnation. The word 'condemnation' occurs again at 8:1, where Paul provides a summary statement and a reminder of what he has argued in 5:12-21: 'Therefore, there is now no condemnation for those who are in Christ Jesus.' Condemnation refers to the pronouncement of a guilty sentence and the punishment due. Justification, in this context, must mean the declaration of a verdict of not guilty, of acquittal and of a right status before God. 'Righteousness' (*dikaiosynē*) can also have this meaning as will be noted below.

Righteousness

This is a comprehensive term with a wide range of meanings in the Scriptures. In the history of its interpretation a number of definitions have been attempted. Older scholars understood the basic meaning to be action that conforms to a particular norm.[4] More recently the trend has been to define 'righteousness' in terms of relationships: it is taken to mean loyalty to the demands of a relationship.[5] Given these definitions, there are those who would emphasise the ethical implications of righteousness, namely, right behaviour, ethically right actions that conform to the norm or that meet the obligations of the relationship. The Greeks understood righteousness in this way as an ethical virtue.[6] On the other hand, others stress that righteousness is primarily a legal concept and that this is the way the Hebrews understood it. It is the right standing of a person in relation to a court's decision.[7]

These various definitions and stresses need not be mutually exclusive. They can all be linked under the concept of the covenant.[8] The covenant idea is of fundamental importance in biblical theology. In the context of the covenant, 'righteousness' means a right legal status before God and conduct that is consistent with God's demands as revealed in the covenant stipulations. As in a marriage bond, a covenant involves commitment by both parties. In God's gracious covenant with Israel, righteousness means God and his people being loyal to that covenant. God is committed to doing what is right. Therefore, God's righteousness is his faithfulness to his word of promise or threat, as indicated in the covenant. Those brought into this special covenant relationship are called to do what is right by keeping God's commandments. Their righteousness is their faithfulness to the covenant commands. The demands of the covenant are rooted in the being and character of God so that righteousness can be more broadly defined as conformity to God's standard. Within this covenant framework, then, righteousness can mean a legal standing and an ethical virtue.

There are two Hebrew words for righteousness, ṣeḏeq and ṣᵊḏāqā. It is difficult to discern any difference in meaning, except that in usage only ṣeḏeq is found in such phrases as 'honest scales' (lit. 'scales of righteousness') in Leviticus 19:36 and Deuteronomy 25:15. (Cf. also Psalm 4:5 'sacrifices of righteousness', Psalm 23:3 'paths of righteousness'.) The Greek Old Testament generally uses dikaiosynē to translate both ṣeḏeq and ṣᵊḏāqā.

In surveying the use made of these Old Testament words for righteousness, the above phrases provide interesting examples with which to begin. The phrase 'scales of righteousness' does not mean morally superior scales but accurate or correct ones. Such examples suggest that righteousness has this fundamental meaning of 'conformity to a norm'. In the context of God's relationship with Israel in the covenant, that norm is the law of God.

When used of human beings, 'righteousness' can be defined in terms of personal morality, social justice and fairness in law-suits (e.g. Ezekiel 18:24; Leviticus 19:15; Isaiah 5:7). It is human activity which conforms to God's revealed will but it arises out of God's special relationship with his creatures. Righteousness is God-pleasing or even God-like behaviour.[9] On the other hand, it is possible to have a righteousness that is thoroughly unclean and unacceptable to God. The confession of Isaiah 64:6 states that 'all our righteous acts (lit. 'righteousnesses) are like filthy rags' (Cf. also Isaiah 48:1). It is expected, however, that those who are in a right legal standing before God will do what is right (Cf. Isaiah 56:1; lit. 'doing righteousness').

This behavioural righteousness is set against the background of legal or forensic righteousness or what can be termed 'justification'. Righteousness in this sense refers to the standing of a person in relation to the judge's favourable decision. It means 'acquittal' or 'vindication' in a court of law. In Israel, the law is God's law and the judges must judge according to it, in the light of their covenant obligations. The supreme judge is God himself and what matters in the final analysis is to be in a right legal position before God, to be acquitted by him. This understanding of righteousness as a legal standing is clear in the passage where Isaiah denounces the leaders of the people who 'deny justice to the innocent' (Isaiah 5:23). The more literal translation of the AV reads: 'take away the righteousness of the righteous from him'. It is clear that 'righteousness' cannot mean right behaviour because no one can take away a person's moral character and attainments. What these leaders are doing is taking away the right status before the law of those who have a just claim to it. In this connection, it is instructive to note Genesis 15:6, that unique passage in the Old Testament where again the righteousness of the individual is not spoken of as a human activity. Instead of Abram doing righteousness, righteousness is credited to him. As we have already indicated in chapter four this is one of the most important verses in the Old Testament concerning justification by faith alone.

Turning now to its use in relation to God, there are very many verses in the Old Testament which speak of the righteousness of God, particularly in the Psalms and Isaiah. God's righteousness refers, in the first place, to his moral character. Biblical theology this century has been embarrassed to speak of God's being or nature, lest it give the impression of speculative Greek thought and so it has emphasised God's activity.[10] Sadly, it must also be said that it has not taken seriously the Bible's claim that God revealed to Israel truth about his being and character. We read in Isaiah 5:16 'the holy God will show himself holy by his righteousness'. Compared with the gods of the surrounding nations, what makes God truly God is his essential righteousness which he has displayed in this world. In addressing God the Psalmist declares, 'your righteousness is an everlasting righteousness, and your law is truth' (Psalm 119:142 New King James). It is a revealed attribute which is experienced by human beings. Because it is in his nature to do what is right, God can be depended on to act in an upright, fair and consistent manner. Righteousness is one of those attributes fundamental to his sovereign rule. Psalm 89:14 reads, 'Righteousness and justice are the foundation of your throne...'.

Within the context of his covenant with Israel, righteousness is often understood as God's activity in doing what is right in accordance with what he has promised or threatened. God's righteousness is therefore his justice in vindicating his oppressed people, in condemning the wicked within Israel and judging the other nations

(Psalms 9:4,8; 50:6,16ff). God's righteousness means his victory in war. After such a victory over the enemy, Deborah sings of the 'righteous acts (lit. 'righteousnesses') of the LORD' (Judges 5:11). God's righteousness is often associated with his saving intervention on behalf of his people. The book of Psalms and the prophecy of Isaiah often draw attention to this. As the following texts show, God's righteousness is another way of referring to God's salvation: 'I am bringing my righteousness near, it is not far away; and my salvation will not be delayed' (Isaiah 46:13); 'My righteousness draws near speedily, my salvation is on the way...But my salvation will last for ever, my righteousness will never fail' (Isaiah 51:5-6; also verse 8); 'My mouth will tell of your righteousness, of your salvation all day long' (Psalm 71:15); 'The LORD has made his salvation known and revealed his righteousness to the nations' (Psalm 98:2).

In some passages, God's righteousness is not so much God's saving activity as the basis for his saving activity. The psalmist knows that 'nothing less than the divine nature ensures that God will do what is *right.*'[11] By virtue of his covenant promises God has committed himself to intervening on behalf of his people. In Psalm 31:1, for example, the psalmist cries out to the LORD 'deliver me in your righteousness'. He prays, in other words, on the basis of God's righteous character, which means God will do what he has covenanted to do. Righteousness is associated with faithfulness in Psalm 143:1 'in your faithfulness and righteousness come to my relief'. Later, in the same psalm, a similar cry goes up to God, 'in your righteousness, bring me out of trouble'. This strong covenantal association is the reason why the Greek Old Testament used the word 'righteousness' (*dikaiosynē*) to translate the Hebrew word ḥeseḏ ('mercy' or 'covenant love') on nine occasions (e.g. Exodus 34:7, Proverbs 20:28 and Isaiah 63:7).

God's righteousness, then, is first and foremost his nature as a moral being. He is the standard by which to assess what is right. God's righteousness also means God acting in accordance with his own righteous character to fulfil the promises and threats he has made. His promises include deliverance from sin and its consequences, while his threats mean punishment for those who remain opposed to God. There is an eschatological or end-time dimension to this righteousness in Malachi 4:2 where we read that in connection with the coming 'day' for those who fear God's name, 'the sun of righteousness will rise with healing in its wings'. The prophets have this expectation of God acting in righteousness to bring about everlasting righteousness (Isaiah 51:5-8). It is associated with the day of the LORD, the coming of Messiah and the work of the Servant of the Lord (Isaiah 32:1, 61:1-3; Jeremiah 33:15-16; Daniel 9:24).

In the New Testament the term 'righteousness' (*dikaiosynē*) is coloured by these Old Testament associations. In reference to human beings it has both an ethical and legal dimension. In Matthew's Gospel, for instance, the ethical or behavioural meaning predominates, whereas, in Paul, it is the legal aspect that surfaces. Nevertheless, righteousness, in the sense of Christian behaviour, is always set against the background of a right legal position before God. After Paul has presented legal righteousness or justification in chapters three to five of Romans, he speaks of righteousness in chapter six as acts of obedience on the part of believers. John regards 'doing righteousness' as an indication of the new birth (I John 2:29). Like the Old Testament, the New Testament distinguishes between the godly who do the right ('those who fear him and work righteousness' Acts 10:35; cf. Psalm 106:3) and the totally unacceptable righteousness so widely witnessed within the old covenant community and expressed in the religion of the Pharisees (Philippians 3:6-9; cf. Isaiah 64:6). The false and futile righteousness of the religious and moral world is denounced (Matthew 5:20; John 16:8-10; Romans 10:3) and in contrast the righteousness of Christ is presented as not only an example to follow (I Peter 2:21-24) but the gift, by God's grace, of a right legal status given to all believers (Romans 5:17-18; I Corinthians 1:30).

We have already considered 'the righteousness of God' as used by the apostle Paul in chapter two. It will now be clear from our examination of the Old Testament evidence that the phrase has a fulness of meaning that should make us wary of opting for just one aspect of it when it occurs in the New Testament. What we can say, by way of summary, is that this 'righteousness of God' is revealed in the gospel and is associated with God's action in justifying sinners.

Righteous

The adjective 'righteous' or 'just' (Hebrew ṣaddîq; Greek dikaios) is very widely used in the Old Testament. In the first place it describes the LORD. Because righteousness belongs to his very nature, it is a characteristic of God to be righteous. 'Righteous are you, O LORD, and your laws are right' (Psalm 119:137). It is the testimony of the psalmist that 'the LORD is righteous in all his ways' (Psalm 145:17). He is righteous when he punishes sin, as the returned exiles confess: 'In all that has happened to us, you have been just'. (Nehemiah 9:33). In saving those who call upon him in their distress, 'The LORD is gracious and righteous' (Psalm 116:5). He is true to his nature and to the terms of the covenant which he has made with his people.

'Righteous' is also the way of referring to the godly. Proverbs and Psalms provide the majority of instances. The righteous are those who are characterised by 'righteousness'. They are in a right standing before God and seek to do what is right. They are the humble poor, the meek, who have a reverence for God which is the beginning of wisdom. In the context of legal disputes, the righteous are those who are innocent before the law and therefore are to be acquitted by the judge (Deuteronomy 25:1).

In the New Testament, dikaios ('righteous/just') is found in similar contexts. Jesus addresses God as 'righteous Father' (John 17:25). God is righteous in his judgments and righteous and true in his ways (Revelation 15:3; 19:2). 'The righteous' or 'the just' are those godly people who stand in a right legal position before God, whose trust is in the Lord's promises and who seek to live lives that conform to God's law (Matthew 1:19; 13:17; Luke 1:6; Acts 10:22). The New Testament discloses the gospel mystery of sinners being constituted righteous as a result of God's justifying grace (Romans 5:19) and of Jesus Christ the righteous one suffering in the place of the unrighteous in order to bring them to God (1 Peter 3:18).

To justify

The verb dikaioō is used in the Greek Old Testament to translate the various forms of the Hebrew verb ṣādaq. In the simple stem (qal) the verb means 'to be righteous' or 'to be vindicated'. It is used in this sense particularly in the book of Job. In the D stem (*piel*) it means 'to justify' in a demonstrative sense (i.e. 'to demonstrate to be righteous'). Elihu is angry with Job 'because he justified himself rather than God' (Job 32:2). In other words, he felt that Job should have been showing God to be righteous rather than himself. The verb is also found in the H stem (*hiphil*) and means 'to justify' in the declarative sense (i.e. 'to declare righteous'). It is used in this sense in such legal contexts as Exodus 23:7 where God declares 'I will not justify the wicked'. In Deuteronomy 25:1, judges are directed to 'justify the righteous and condemn the wicked'. Proverbs, likewise, has this sense in 17:15: 'He who justifies the wicked, and he who condemns the righteous are both alike an abomination to the LORD'.

It is this latter meaning that is significant when we come to the use of *dikaioō* in the New Testament, particularly in Paul's letters. The contrast between 'to justify' and 'to condemn' that we see in the Old Testament passages is present in Romans 8:33-34 where Paul brings to a grand climax the absolute security and safety of those justified by God's grace: 'It is God who justifies. Who is he who condemns?' Matthew 12:37 presents a similar contrast: 'For by your words you will be justified, and by your words you will be condemned'. It is a legal declaration. There is no way the verb could have the meaning of 'to make righteous'. The contexts clearly indicate that the one judging is not infusing any righteousness into people, he is simply declaring them to be not guilty and therefore acquitted. There can be no mistake that in these texts the Greek word for 'justify' can only mean 'to be cleared of blame' and 'to be declared not guilty'.

While the declarative meaning predominates in the New Testament, there are cases where *dikaioō* has the demonstrative sense of 'to show to be righteous'. We read of the lawyer who felt he needed to 'justify himself' by asking Jesus the question 'who is my neighbour?' (Luke 10:29). He wanted to 'show himself righteous'. At the end of Matthew 11:19 Jesus remarks that 'wisdom is justified by her children'. Again, the meaning is that wisdom is 'shown to be righteous' rather than 'declared to be righteous'. It is important to bear in mind this meaning of the verb when we consider the statement in James 2:24, where it is often suggested that James is contradicting Paul. Instead of using the word in Paul's declaratory sense 'to declare righteous' James could well be saying that a person is 'shown to be righteous' by his works and not simply by his faith.

Our study of the 'right-' or 'just-' word-groups and our survey of divine justification in the Bible prepare us for what has to be tackled in the remainder of the book. As we examine Rome's teaching on justification and the ecumenical efforts to remove this one remaining doctrinal stumbling-block to unity, as well as the recent evangelical attempts to revise our understanding of this important doctrine, we must bear in mind that they would all claim to be working from the biblical text. The question is whether they are being faithful to the whole of Scripture or not. But before we consider these issues we must first present the teaching of the Reformers and their successors, for it is their perception of the subject that is under attack today.

Notes

1. G. C. Berkouwer, *Faith and Justification*, Eerdmans, 1954, p. 17.

2. The following word studies have been consulted and although their conclusions cannot always be accepted they have proved helpful: D. Hill, *Greek Words and Hebrew Meanings: Studies in the Semantics of Soteriological Terms,* Cambridge, 1967; B. Przybylski, *Righteousness in Matthew and His World of Thought,* Cambridge, 1980; J. A. Ziesler, *The Meaning of Righteousness in Paul: A Linguistic and Theological Investigation,* Cambridge, 1972.

Cf. also R. Y. K. Fung, 'The forensic character of justification', *Themelios,* Vol. 3, No.1, 1977, pp. 16-21; J. Piper, *The Justification of God: An Exegetical and Theological Study of Romans 9:1-23,* Baker, 2nd edition 1993, pp. 103-150; J. Reumann, *"Righteousness" in the New Testament,* Fortress Press, 1982.

3. Cf. D. J. Moo, *Romans 1-8,* Moody, 1991, pp. 351, 355.

4. N. H. Snaith, *Distinctive Ideas of the Old Testament,* London, 1944, p. 90 and 'Righteous, Righteousness' in *A Theological Word Book of the Bible,* ed. A. Richardson, SCM, 1950, p. 202; D. B. Knox 'Righteousness' in *The New Bible Dictionary,* ed. J. D. Douglas, IVP, 1962, p. 1097.

5. Cf. the German scholar H. Cremer who seems to have been the first to describe 'right-

eousess' as a 'concept of relation referring to an actual relationship between two persons and implying behaviour which corresponds to, or is true to, the claims arising out of such a relationship' (quoted by W. Eichrodt in *Theology of the Old Testament,* Vol. 1, SCM, 1961, p. 240). Cf. also G. Von Rad, *Old Testament Theology,* Vol. 1, Oliver and Boyd, 1962, pp. 370-371.

6. Cf. Snaith, 'Righteous, Righteousness', pp. 202-204.

7. Cf. L. Morris, *The Epistle to the Romans,* IVP/Eerdmans, 1988, p.101.

8. Cf. Ziesler, *The Meaning of Righteousness in Paul:* pp. 36-39.

9. G. J. Wenham, *Genesis 1-15,* Word Bible Commentary, Vol. 1, Word, 1987, p. 330.

10. S. K. Williams, 'The "Righteousness of God" in Romans', *Journal of Biblical Literature 99,* 1980, p. 261 note 64.

11. S. K. Williams, p. 262.

Part 2

Evangelicals and Rome

6 Justification and the Evangelical Protestant Position

The uneasy peace that existed in the western church of the sixteenth century was shattered by a monk who was prepared to defy the pope and the emperor. At the heart of Martin Luther's rebellion was a spiritual transformation which arose out of his appreciation of the biblical truth that God justifies the ungodly, not by their good works but solely through reliance on Jesus Christ. From then on, the truth concerning justification by faith dominated his thinking. If the other Reformers were not as vocal as Luther on this crucial issue, it was not because they did not consider it to be of central importance. John Calvin, for instance, in his *Institutes of the Christian Religion,* devotes more space to justification than to almost any other doctrine.[1] As he introduces the subject he reminds his readers that 'this is the main hinge on which religion turns' and therefore 'we devote the greater attention and care to it. For unless you first of all grasp what your relationship to God is, and the nature of this judgment concerning you, you have neither a foundation on which to establish your salvation nor one on which to build piety toward God.'[2]

Early Protestant Statements
The great Protestant Confessions of Faith and Catechisms that arose during the sixteenth century are one in drawing attention to this fundamental gospel truth. Article 4 of the Augsburg Confession of 1530 on justification reads:

'Also they teach that men cannot be justified [obtain forgiveness of sins and righteousness] before God by their own powers, merits, or works; but are justified freely [of grace] for Christ's sake through faith, when they believe that they are received into favour, and their sins forgiven for Christ's sake, who by his death hath satisfied for our sins. This faith doth

God impute for righteousness before him.' *(The brackets are original)*

Good works are treated in great detail in Article 20 where, again, it is stressed that 'our works cannot reconcile God, or deserve remission of sins, grace, and justification at his hands, but that these we obtain by faith only, when we believe that we are received into favour for Christ's sake, who alone is appointed the Mediator and Propitiatory, by whom the Father is reconciled.'[3]

The French Confession of Faith of 1559 includes this statement in Article 18:

'We therefore reject all other means of justification before God, and without claiming any virtue or merit, we rest simply in the obedience of Jesus Christ, which is imputed to us as much to blot out all our sins as to make us find grace and favour in the sight of God.'[4]

Article 11 of the Thirty-Nine Articles of the Church of England (1571) is based on similar words found in the earlier Forty-Two Articles of 1553. It reads:

'We are accounted righteous before God, only for the merit of our Lord and Saviour Jesus Christ by faith, and not for our own works or deservings. Wherefore, that we are justified by faith only, is a most wholesome doctrine, and very full of comfort...' Its closing words refer to the Homily on Justification (or 'Salvation' as it is later called) for a larger treatment of the subject.[5]

Question 60 of the Heidelberg Catechism (1563) asks: 'How art thou righteous before God?

Answer. Only by true faith in Jesus Christ; that is, although my conscience accuse me that I have grievously sinned against all the commandments of God, and have never kept any of them, and that I am still prone always to all evil, yet God, without any merit of mine, of mere grace, grants and imputes to me the perfect satisfaction, righteousness, and holiness of Christ, as if I had never committed nor had any sin, and had myself accomplished all the obedience which Christ has fulfilled for me, if only I accept such benefit with a believing heart.'[6]

The Second Helvetic Confession, a revision of Bullinger's confession, was approved by the Swiss Reformed cities in 1566. In chapter 15 a full statement 'of the true justification of the faithful' is given. 'To justify...does signify to remit sins, to absolve from the fault and the punishment thereof, to receive into favour, to pronounce a man just...But we are justified - that is, acquitted from sin and death - by God the Judge, through the grace of Christ alone, and not by any respect or merit of ours...God, therefore, is merciful unto our sins for Christ alone, that suffered and rose again, and does not impute them unto us. But he imputes the justice of Christ unto us for our own; so that now we are not only cleansed from sin, and purged, and holy, but also endued with the righteousness of Christ...it is God alone that justifieth us, and that only for Christ, by not imputing unto us our sins, but imputing Christ's righteousness unto us.'[7]

The Medieval Church

How a person could be right with God was a matter of great concern to Luther. The church of his day was in confusion over the issue. There was much talk among the theologians about grace and about God's initiative in salvation. To the ordinary churchgoer, however, salvation was seen to be very much in the hands of the church to dispense and something that a person could earn through doing various good works. This was not a case of popular piety being at odds with the church authorities. From pope to parish priest such opinions were encouraged for they helped swell the papal coffers and provided local clergy with added income. Prayers and masses for the dead on payment of a fee were believed to reduce the amount of time needed to be purified from all sin. In England, Cardinal Wolsey promised 'one hundred days of pardon releasing of penance in Purgatory' to anyone who contributed towards the rebuilding of the church at Rickmansworth.[8] A plenary indulgence bought from the pope would, so it was claimed, release a soul from the fires of purgatory, a place more feared than hell. Souls languished there, according to Thomas More, 'sleepless, restless, burning and broiling in the dark fire one long night of many days, of many weeks and some of many years...' and they cry out to the living for more prayers and masses to be said.[9] These, along with the benefits of making pilgrimages to sacred sites, were the more obvious and glaring indications that the church preached a religion of works.

In addition, the whole sacramental system, which the church performed for its members from the cradle to the grave, gave the impression that only by participating in these rites and ceremonies could a person ever be finally accepted by God. The Fourth Lateran Council of 1215 and the Council of Florence, 1438-1445, not only emphasised the power of the priest but the power of the sacraments and good works for gaining acceptance before God. 'Not only virgins and those practising continence merit the attainment of eternal blessedness but married persons also, who are acceptable to God through true faith and good works.' 'Through baptism we are spiritually reborn; through confirmation we grow in grace and are strengthened in faith...we are sustained by the divine food of the eucharist. But if we become sick in soul through sin, we are healed spiritually through penance, and healed spiritually as well as physically...through extreme unction.'[10]

The Reformers

The Reformers, on the other hand, stressed from the Bible that human beings were quite incapable of doing anything toward their salvation. Salvation is God's work, the result of God's unmerited favour. The views of such men as Luther and Calvin on the subject of justification can be itemized in the following way:

1 Justification is a legal declaration made by God that believing sinners are righteous. 'Therefore, we explain justification simply as the acceptance with which God receives us into his favour as righteous men. And that it consists in the remission of sins and the imputation of Christ's righteousness.'[11] It is a pronouncement concerning their right standing before God. The Reformers correctly understood the verb 'to justify' to mean 'to declare righteous' and not 'to make righteous' as Augustine of Hippo and the medieval Schoolmen supposed. Outside of Christ sinners are guilty, but in Christ they are declared righteous. A definite distinction was made between justification on the one hand and regeneration and sanctification on the other. This was a clear departure from the teaching of Augustine and the medieval church, who regarded justification as an

all-embracing concept.[12] Though the Reformers showed that the initial inward change of regeneration with which repentance and faith are associated and the on-going process of renewal and development in righteous living to which sanctification refers are intimately linked to justification, they insisted that this sanctification work should never be confused with it.[13] It is guilty sinners whom God pardons and pronounces righteous, immediately they trust Christ.

2 This new legal status which sinners have in Christ is due entirely to the work of Christ. It is not Christ plus any righteousness which God may find sinners or saints performing. They are declared righteous *solely* on the basis of Christ's atoning death, whereby all their sins were imputed to Christ who fully satisfied divine justice, and Christ's spotless righteousness imputed to them. Thus Calvin wrote, 'The Son of God, utterly clean of all fault, nevertheless took upon himself the shame and reproach of our iniquities, and in return clothed us with his purity.'[14] Luther expressed it so beautifully in these words:

'Lord Jesus, you are my righteousness, just as I am your sin. You have taken upon yourself what is mine and have given to me what is yours. You have taken upon yourself what you were not and have given to me what I was not.'[15]

3 The Reformers also stressed that it is through faith in Jesus Christ that sinners are justified. For them, saving faith is not merely the faith of assent to the facts of the gospel or a willingness to accept what the church believes, but a personal reliance on the Lord Jesus Christ. Justification, however, is not based on faith. It is based on Christ and received through faith. Luther was also quick to emphasise that it is through faith *alone* that sinners are declared righteous. He was, and still is, criticised for adding 'alone' to his German New Testament translation of Romans 3.28. His reply was to the effect that the sense of the passage demanded it. Both he and Calvin point out that, in the very same part of Romans, Paul goes on to stress that works do not justify. If it is not faith plus works that justifies then it must be by faith alone.[16]

4 Although the Reformers stressed that good works have no part to play in justification, they did show how important these were in the life of the believer. They insisted, however, that the good works of believers are not meritorious but are the fruit and signs of justification. They do not merit salvation; they do not help to gain final acceptance on the day of judgement.[17] In fact, Calvin says, 'we have not a single work going forth from the saints that if it be judged in itself deserves not shame as its just reward'. 'Let a holy servant of God, I say, choose from the whole course of his life what of an especially noteworthy character he thinks he has done...Undoubtedly he will somewhere perceive that it savors of the rottenness of the flesh.'[18]

5 Because the Reformers looked to Jesus Christ alone they could be assured that they were accepted by God. Christian assurance is not confidence in oneself and one's own abilities: it comes from relying entirely on the grace of God in Christ. Already the Christian has passed from death to life and will not be condemned. Such assurance is most noticeable in the wording of the wills that people from all classes of society made prior to death. Those who still clung to the old religion of the pope committed their souls not only to God but to Mary and the saints, and requested that prayers and masses be said for their souls to bring a speedy end to their time in purgatory. Money was often left for this specific purpose. On the other hand, those who embraced the gospel of justification by faith alone expressed absolute certainty in Christ and his death to save them. In London, the famous English chronicler, Edward Hall, wrote out his will in 1546, yielding his soul to its 'maker and redeemer by whose passion, and not by my deserts, I trust only to be saved, for He hath washed away my sins, I doubt not, by His precious blood'.[19]

In summary, the teaching of the Reformers emphasised that a person is justified by grace *alone*, through faith *alone*, in Christ *alone*, to God's glory *alone*. By insisting on these points, they had not invented a new doctrine but rediscovered an old truth. The Reformers went back to the Bible for their understanding of this as they did for other matters of faith and practice.

Not a New Teaching

In his masterly treatment of justification James Buchanan staunchly defends the Protestant position against the Roman allegation that it was unknown for fourteen hundred years and was a new thing introduced for the first time by Luther and Calvin. He shows that the doctrine of justification 'was so thoroughly discussed in the writings of the Apostles... that their immediate successors had no occasion to treat it as an undecided question... They found it an established and unquestioned article of the common faith, and they assumed and applied it in their writings, without thinking it necessary to enter into any formal explanation or proof of it.'[20] Alister McGrath in his history of the subject states that 'For the first three hundred and fifty years of the history of the church, her teaching on justification was inchoate *(undeveloped)* and ill-defined. There had never been a serious controversy over the matter'.[21] At this time the attention of the church was directed toward other important elements of the faith that were being denied, which resulted in the great Christological and Trinitarian debates and creeds.

The following examples show that after the Apostolic period, there were those in the church who continued to hold a biblical view of justification. In his Letter to the Corinthians, Clement of Rome writes concerning the patriarchs that 'they all therefore were glorified and magnified, not through themselves or their own works or the righteous doing which they wrought, but through His will. And so we, having being called through His will in Christ Jesus, are not justified through ourselves or through our own wisdom or understanding or piety or works which we wrought in holiness of heart, but through faith, whereby the Almighty God justified all men that have been from the beginning; to whom be the glory for ever and ever. Amen.'[22]

From about the middle of the second century A.D. we have the Letter to Diognetus in which the author expresses the amazing kindness and love of God in the gospel. God planned everything with his Son and at the right moment showed his goodness and power. 'He hated us not, neither rejected us, nor bore us malice, but was longsuffering and patient, and in pity for us took upon Himself our sins, and Himself parted with His own Son as a ransom for us, the holy for the lawless, the guileless for the evil, the just for the unjust, the incorruptible for the corruptible, the immortal for the mortal. For what else but His righteousness would have covered our sins? In whom was it possible for us lawless and ungodly men to have been justified, save only in the Son of God? O the sweet exchange, O the inscrutable creation, O the unexpected benefits; that the iniquity of many should be concealed in One Righteous Man, and the righteousness of One should justify many that are iniquitous!'[23]

There is, however, evidence from a very early date that the biblical truth concerning justification was obscured and false ideas entered which gained momentum as the medieval period advanced. T. F. Torrance has shown that many of the early Christian writers, as witnessed for instance in the Didache, Barnabas, the Shepherd of Hermas and Ignatius, did not adequately appreciate the significance of God's grace. He concludes that 'religion was thought of primarily in terms of man's acts towards God, in the striving towards justification, much less in terms of God's acts for man which put him right with God once and for all.'[24]

On the other hand, Augustine of Hippo (354-430) dealt a thorough blow to Pelagianism by emphasising the absolute sovereignty of God, human bondage to sin, the grace of God toward helpless sinners and by insisting that justification is the result of God's grace not man's merits. However, because he interpreted the verb 'to justify' in his Latin Bible as 'to make righteous' this led him to believe that justification meant that God made us inwardly righteous. Throughout the medieval period justification was thus always associated with the inner transformation of the individual. Even so, there were theologians and preachers who, although they adopted teachings and practices which were not biblical, continued 'to hold the truth in substance, and in a state of comparative purity, as contrasted with its subsequent corruption' by scholastic theology.[25]

Jerome (c. 347-420), for instance, in his comments on Paul's letters to the Romans and 2 Corinthians, remarks that, 'When an ungodly man is converted, God justifies him through faith alone, not on account of good works, which he possessed not; otherwise, on account of his ungodly deeds, he ought to have been punished...Christ, who "knew no sin", the Father "made sin for us," that, as a victim offered for sin was in the Law called "sin", so likewise Christ, being offered for our sins, received the name of "sin", that "we might be made the righteousness of God in Him" - not our righteousness, nor in ourselves.'[26]

Bernard of Clairvaux (1090-1153), despite his misguided support of the Crusades and his Mariolatry, has this to say, 'What can all our righteousness be before God? Shall it not, according to the prophet, be viewed as "a filthy rag"; and if it is strictly judged, shall not all our righteousness turn out to be mere unrighteousness and deficiency? What, then, shall it be concerning our sins, when not even our righteousness can answer for itself? Wherefore, exclaiming vehemently with the prophet, "Enter not into judgment with thy servant, O Lord!" let us flee, with all humility, to mercy, which alone can save our souls...Whosoever, feeling compunction for his sins, hungers and thirsts after righteousness, let him believe in Thee, who "justifiest the ungodly"; and thus, being justified by faith alone, he shall have peace with God...Thy Passion is the last refuge, the alone remedy. When wisdom fails, when righteousness is insufficient, when the merits of holiness succumb, it succours us.'[27]

The 12th century Bible scholar, Herveus, commenting on Hebrews 10:38, speaks in God's name and says, 'and every just one of mine is justified by faith, not by the works of the law. For he who is justified by the works of the law is not mine, but his own just person, because he is justified not by me but by himself, and he glories not in me but in himself. But he who is justified by faith is my just one, because he is justified by the gift of my grace, and he attributes the fact that he is justified to my grace and not to himself.'[28]

It is clear from the Bible and the early period of the church that the Reformers, in insisting on justification by faith alone, were not presenting a new teaching. Nevertheless, just as there was a time for systematising the Bible's teaching on the doctrine of Christ and the Trinity due to error and heresy, so the Reformation was the period for rediscovering and clarifying the biblical understanding of justification. As a result, there has been a large measure of unanimity among the main Protestant churches in their definition of justification.

Later Protestant Confessions

The Anglican position is set out in the Thirty-Nine Articles which has been quoted above, and they refer to the fuller presentation of the subject in the *Homily of Salvation*. The Wesleyan Methodists of the 18th century accepted the Thirty-nine Articles and further light was thrown on the subject through the sermons and hymns of the Wesley brothers.[29] The Savoy Declaration of 1658 (Congregational), the Baptist Confession of 1689 and the 1823 Calvinistic Methodist (or Presbyterian Church of Wales) Confession of Faith, all contain a full statement of the subject, closely following the wording of the Westminster Confession of Faith which was first adopted by the Presbyterians in 1649. It is worth quoting the first two paragraphs of this latter document:

'Those whom God effectually calleth he also freely justifieth; not by infusing righteousness into them, but by pardoning their sins, and by accounting and accepting their persons as righteous: not for any thing wrought in them, or done by them, but for Christ's sake alone: not by imputing faith itself, the act of believing, or any other evangelical obedience, to them as their righteousness; but by imputing the obedience and satisfaction of Christ unto them, they receiving and resting on him and his righteousness by faith: which faith they have not of themselves; it is the gift of God.

Faith, thus receiving and resting on Christ and his righteousness, is the alone instrument of justification; yet is it not alone in the person justified, but is ever accompanied with all other saving graces, and is no dead faith, but worketh by love.'[30]

Evangelical Hymns

The hymns of the Protestant churches also draw attention to this evangelical faith. Martin Luther's hymn 'From deep distress I cry to

Thee', based on Psalm 130, has these lines:

Our pardon is Thy gift; Thy love
And grace alone avail us;
Our works could ne'er our guilt remove,
The strictest life would fail us;
That none may boast himself of aught,
But own in fear Thy grace hath wrought
What in him seemeth righteous.
And thus my hope is in the Lord
And not in mine own merit; ...[31]

From the Methodist Revival of the eighteenth century comes Charles Wesley's famous hymn 'And can it be' which includes the verse:

No condemnation now I dread;
Jesus, and all in Him, is mine!
Alive in Him, my living Head,
And clothed in righteousness divine,
Bold I approach the eternal throne,
And claim the crown, through Christ my own.

The following hymn was used extensively both in the Church of England and Nonconformist chapels when it was first composed by Augustus Toplady:

A debtor to mercy alone,
Of covenant mercy I sing;
Nor fear, with Thy righteousness on,
My person and offering to bring;
The terrors of law and of God
With me can have nothing to do;
My Saviour's obedience and blood
Hide all my transgressions from view.

Horatius Bonar, 'the Prince of Scottish hymn writers', also emphasises the truth of justification in his hymn 'Thy works not mine, O Christ', from which these lines are taken:

Thy righteousness, O Christ,
Alone can cover me;
No righteousness avails
Save that which is of Thee:
To whom save Thee, who canst alone
For sin atone, Lord, shall I flee?

This is the evangelical Protestant position.

English Reformers, Puritans and Methodists
William Tyndale, the English Bible translator, set out his view on justification in *The Parable of the Wicked Mammon* (1528): 'That faith only before all works and without all merits, but Christ's only, justifieth and setteth us at peace with God, is proved by Paul in the first chapter to the Romans'.[32] In *The Obedience of a Christian Man* (1528) he writes, 'I say that no man is so great a sinner, if he repent and believe, but that he is righteous in Christ and in the promises'.[33] Bishop Hugh Latimer, burnt in 1555 under the reign of Queen Mary, in a sermon on the Lord's Prayer encourages believers not to let their sins keep them from praying. 'Our Saviour maketh them nothing: when we believe in him, it is like as if we had no sins. For he changeth with us: he taketh our sins and wickedness from us, and giveth unto us his holiness, righteousness, justice, fulfilling of the law, and so, consequently, everlasting life: so that we be like as if we had done no sin at all; for his righteousness standeth us in so good stead, as though we of our own selves had fulfilled the law to the uttermost. Therefore our sins cannot let us, nor withdraw us from prayer: for they be gone; they are no sins; they cannot be hurtful unto us. Christ dying for us, as all the scripture, both of the new and old Testament, witnesseth..."He hath taken away our sorrows."'[34]

The Puritan preachers and writers from the end of the sixteenth and on into the seventeenth century laid great emphasis on the subject. A whole volume of John Owen's works is given over to expounding it in great detail.[35] In the eighteenth century the most outstanding preacher of the day in England was George Whitefield. In one of his sermons on justification, *The Lord our Righteousness* (Jeremiah 23:6) we can sense the passion and earnestness of his preaching: 'And think you, O sinners, that you will be able to stand in the day of judgment, if Christ be not your righteousness! No, that alone is the wedding-garment in which you must appear. O Christless sinners, I am distressed for you! the desires of my soul are enlarged. O that this may be an accepted time! that the Lord may be your righteousness! For whither would you flee, if death should find you naked? Indeed, there is no hiding yourselves from his presence. The pitiful fig-leaves of your own righteousness will not cover your nakedness, when God shall call you to stand before him. Adam found them ineffectual, and so will you. O think of death! O think of judgment! Yet a little while, and time shall be no more; and then what will become of you, if the Lord be not your righteousness.'[36]

Thus the Confessions of Faith and the doctrinal statements of the main-line Protestant denominations bear witness to the biblical teaching on justification as rediscovered by the Reformers of the sixteenth century. The writings of the Puritans in the seventeenth century and the preaching of the leaders of the Evangelical Awakening in the eighteenth century also testify to their grasp of this important subject and their desire to make it known to the people. In addition, through the hymns of Luther, Watts, Wesley and others, the people were taught to express in song and as a part of worship the wonderful truth of justification by faith alone.

19th and 20th Century Evangelical Protestants

From the nineteenth century we have this comment on Romans 3:25 by Principal David Brown (1803-1897), one of the most brilliant theologians Scotland has ever produced: 'Glorious paradox! "Just in punishing," and "merciful in pardoning," men can understand; but "just in justifying" the guilty, startles them. But the propitiation through faith in Christ's blood resolves the paradox, and harmonizes the seemingly discordant elements. For in that "God hath made Him to be sin for us who knew no sin," *justice* has full satisfaction; and in that "we are made the righteousness of God in Him," *mercy* has all her desire.'[37]

During the latter half of the same century on London's South Bank, Charles Haddon Spurgeon (1834-1892) constantly preached justification by faith alone. In 1857 at the Music Hall, Royal Surrey Gardens, the young preacher told his large congregation, 'Christ takes our sins, we take Christ's righteousness; and it is by a glorious substitution and interchange of places that sinners go free and are justified by his grace. "But," says one, "no one is justified like that, till he dies." Believe me, he is. ...If that young man over there has really believed in Christ this morning...he is as much justified in God's sight now as he will be when he stands before the throne.'[38]

Turning finally to the twentieth century, there have been well-known evangelical commentators, theologians and preachers who have all expressed the truth concerning justification in the traditional Protestant sense. John Murray in his treatment of justification points out: 'We thus see that if we are to find the righteousness which supplies the basis of the full and perfect justification which God bestows upon the ungodly we cannot find it in anything that resides in us, not in anything which God does in us, nor in anything which we do. We must look away from ourselves to something which is of an entirely different sort in an entirely different direction...It is in Christ we are justified.'[39]

In summing up Paul's doctrine of justification, Herman Ridderbos regards it as 'an imposing and carefully integrated whole'. The righteousness of God 'is revealed in the great redemptive event of Christ's death and resurrection, in which God as Judge has manifested his righteousness, both judging and acquitting. And as the redemptive gift of God, it is given to those who are in Christ by faith. It consists for them, therefore, in imputation by grace, as a free gift, and not in the accounting of man's own works as merit. In that sense it can be said that faith is reckoned for righteousness, namely, as the means, on the ground of the obedience and righteous act of the One, to come to justification unto life and to peace with God through our Lord Jesus Christ (Rom. 5:1, 18, 19).'[40]

The truth concerning justification is expressed by J. I. Packer in these words: 'Justification has two sides. On the one hand, it means the pardon, remission, and non-imputation of all sins, reconciliation to God, and the end of his enmity and wrath...On the other hand, it means the bestowal of a righteous man's status and a title to all the blessings promised to the just: a thought which Paul amplifies by linking justification with the adoption of believers as God's sons and heirs.'[41]

Two sentences from more recent evangelical scholarly expositions of Romans express the matter succinctly. First of all, there is this statement from John Stott: 'Justification (its source God and his grace, its ground Christ and his cross, and its means faith alone, altogether apart from works) is the heart of the gospel and unique to Christianity.'[42] Then Douglas Moo makes this apt comment: 'While justification effects for the believer a new and permanent status, justification itself is a once-for-all act by which God acquits the sinner.'[43]

Dr. Martyn Lloyd-Jones consistently preached justification by faith alone throughout his long ministry at Westminster Chapel, London. Towards the close of his sermon on Philippians 3:9 these words ring out, 'If I am in Christ, God regards me as guiltless; not only that, God regards me as one who has kept the law fully. Christ has kept it and I am in Christ. I receive all the benefits of his perfect life and atoning death exactly as I am. That is the doctrine: "Just as I am without one plea" - with nothing, nothing at all, indeed to start to do anything is a denial of the doctrine. You can do nothing, Christ has done everything...We must realise that if we lived to be a thousand years old we would be no more righteous in the sight of God then than we are now. You may grow in grace, but on your death bed your only hope will be the righteousness of Christ.'[44]

Conclusion

The traditional evangelical Protestant position on the subject of justification is thus quite clear. Every human being is a sinner. Jews and Gentiles alike are sinners. They are in rebellion against God and have broken the law which reveals God's righteous character. By that righteous standard they are guilty and condemned, and will be sentenced by the divine Judge on the final day of judgment. No one on the basis of their works belongs to the class of the righteous. Being righteous himself, God cannot be expected, then, to justify sinners. Yet despite this, the amazing truth revealed in the gospel is that God has provided a way to justify sinners that meets his own righteous requirements. God's justifying action is his declaration that the guilty sinner is acquitted, pronounced not guilty, given a full pardon, and judged to be in a right standing and relationship before God and his law.

This astounding judgment is made on account of Christ's representative activity on behalf of sinners. He lived the righteous life, kept all the covenant demands and endured the covenant curse as the federal head of a new righteous humanity. The righteous are those sinners who realise their own poverty and need, and who rely entirely on Christ as their Saviour and are united to him. Jesus has satisfied the divine wrath on account of their sins and his guiltless, righteous life is reckoned or imputed to them. They are no longer under condemnation and are assured that on the day of judgment they will be vindicated and blessed for ever. It is through faith alone that they are justified. Their faith in Christ is not regarded as a meritorious work, but as the means whereby they embrace his person and work. In the matter of justification, faith is the empty hand which receives Christ and his righteousness. That faith through which alone they are justified nevertheless produces the good works which God has prepared in advance for them to do (Ephesians 2:10). Such works contribute nothing to their justification but show the genuineness of their professed faith.

Notes

1. Cf. W. Stanford Reid, 'Justification by faith according to John Calvin', *Westminster Theological Journal*, Vol. XLII, Spring 1980, No.2, pp. 290-307.

2. Calvin, *Institutes of the Christian Religion*, Book 3, chapter xi, para. 1. (Battles edition, Westminster Press, Vol. 1, p. 726).

3. P. Schaff, revised by D. S. Schaff, 'The Evangelical Protestant Creeds', *The Creeds of Christendom, Vol.III*, Baker reprint, 1983, pp. 10, 20.

4. Schaff p. 370. For the view that in this French confession 'justification is nothing more than pardon', cf. A. Clifford in *Evangelical Quarterly vol.58, No.3*, July 1986 pp.

195-206, 'John Calvin and the Confessio Fidei Gallicana'. That Calvin himself regarded justification as more than forgiveness is clear from the quotations from the *Institutes* presented in this chapter. Though the early Reformers do not refer to the 'active' and 'passive' obedience of Christ imputed to the believer they do believe in the concept. Compare also the quotations from Luther and Latimer.

5. G. Bray, *Documents of the English Reformation,* James Clarke, 1994, p. 291.

6. Schaff, *Creeds,* p. 326f.

7. Schaff pp. 862-864.

8. Quoted by Susan Brigden, *London and the Reformation,* Oxford, p. 31f.

9. Thomas More, *The Supplication of Souls,* 1529; quoted by A. G. Dickens, *The English Reformation,* Batsford, 1964, p. 5f.

10. J. H. Leith, *Creeds of the Churches,* John Knox Press, revised 1973, pp. 56-61.

11. Calvin, *Institutes,* Bk 3, ch. xi, para. 2. (Battles Vol. 1, p. 727).

12. Cf. A. McGrath, *Iustitia Dei,* Vol.1, Cambridge, 1986, pp. 31ff.

13. Calvin, *Institutes,* ch. xi, para. 15. (Battles, Vol.1, pp. 745-6).

14. Calvin, *Institutes,* Bk.2, ch. xvi, para.6 (Battles, Vol.1, p. 510).

15. *Luther's Works,* Vol.48, *Letters I,* Fortress Press, 1963, pp. 12f.

16. Calvin, *Institutes,* Bk.3, ch.xi, para. 19. (Battles, Vol.1, pp. 748f.)

17. *ibid.* ch. xiv, para.20.

18. *ibid.* ch. xiv, para.9.

19. Quoted by Bridgen, *London and the Reformation,* p. 381.

20. James Buchanan, *The Doctrine of Justification,* Banner of Truth, 1961, p. 97.

21. McGrath, *Iustitia Dei,* p. 23.

22. Clement of Rome 'To the Corinthians', para. 32, J. B. Lightfoot, *The Apostolic Fathers,* Baker Books, 1956, p. 26.

23. The Epistle to Diognetus, para. 9, Lightfoot, p. 256-7.

24. T. F. Torrance, *The Doctrine of Grace in the Apostolic Fathers,* Oliver & Boyd, 1948, p. 133. Cf. P. E. Hughes, 'Justification by Faith: Distortions of the Doctrine', *Evangelical Quarterly,* Vol. 24, No.2, 1952, pp. 78-90.

25. Buchanan, p. 111-112. For the views of Augustine and Pelagius cf. A. E. McGrath, *Justification by Faith: What it means for us today,* Zondervan, 1988, pp. 33-45. Cf. also C. P. Bammel, 'Justification by Faith in Augustine and Origen', *Journal of Ecclesiastical History,* Vol. 47 No. 2, April 1996, pp. 223-235.

26. Buchanan, p. 109.

27. Buchanan, pp. 110-111.

28. Quoted by P. E. Hughes, *A Commentary on the Epistle to the Hebrews*, Eerdmans, 1977, p. 436 (from *Patrologia Latina*, ed. by J. P. Milgne, 217 vols., 1844-1855).

29. Though John Wesley had reservations concerning the doctrine of imputed righteousness, due to his fear of antinomianism, and did not teach it, his followers certainly sang it! 'In Him complete we shine; His death, His life, is mine; Fully am I justified, Free from sin, and more than free, Guiltless, since for me He died; Righteous, since He lived for me.' Quoted by Buchanan, p. 194.

30. Chapter XI. Of Justification.

31. Translated by Catherine Winkworth. These and the other lines from hymns are taken from *Christian Hymns*, Evangelical Movement of Wales, 1977.

32. Tyndale's *Doctrinal Treatises*, Parker Society, Cambridge, 1848, p. 46f.

33. Tyndale's *Doctrinal Treatises*, p. 198. For further discussion of Tyndale, cf. M. E. Dever, 'William Tyndale and Justification by Faith: "Answer to Sir Thomas More"', in *Building on a Sure Foundation*, Westminster Conference Papers, 1994, pp. 7-34; C. R. Trueman, *Luther's Legacy*, Clarendon Press Oxford, 1994, pp. 92-94.

34. Sermons of Hugh Latimer, Parker Society, Cambridge, 1844, p. 330.

35. Owen's *Works*, Vol. 5, Banner of Truth reprint. For a study of justification and the Puritans cf. J. I. Packer, 'The Doctrine of Justification in Development and Decline among the Puritans' in *Among God's Giants*, Kingsway, 1991, pp. 196-214.

36. *Select Sermons of George Whitefield*, Banner of Truth, 1958, p. 134.

37. D. Brown, *Romans*, Handbooks for Bible Classes and Private Students, eds. A. Whyte & J. Kelman, T. & T. Clark, p. 37.

38. Spurgeon, *New Park Street Pulpit*, Vol. 3, 1857, Banner of Truth reprint, p. 157.

39. J. Murray, *Redemption Accomplished and Applied*, Banner of Truth, 1961, p. 126.

40. H. N. Ridderbos, *Paul: an outline of his theology*, Eerdmans, 1975, p. 178.

41. J. I. Packer, 'Justification' in W. A. Elwell, *Evangelical Dictionary of Theology*, Marshall Pickering, 1985, p. 594.

42. J. R. W. Stott, *The Cross of Christ*, IVP, 1986, p. 190; *The Message of Romans (The Bible speaks Today)*, IVP, 1994, p. 118.

43. D. J. Moo, *Romans 1-8, The Wycliffe Exegetical Commentary*, Moody, 1991, p. 306.

44. D. M. Lloyd-Jones, *The Life of Peace, Studies in Philippians 3 and 4*, Hodder and Stoughton, 1990, p. 66

7 Justification and Rome's Present Position

Not only are there Protestants who assume that Rome has changed its position on justification but representatives from the Roman communion often speak as if there is now no difference between the opposing parties. The fact of the matter is, however, that Rome has not changed on this crucial subject since the Council of Trent's decrees in the 16th century. A moderate Jesuit theologian, in an interview published in *Christianity Today* in 1986, said to his evangelical questioner, 'We do not greatly disagree on the way in which the individual comes to justification: through the grace of Christ accepted in faith.' When asked to elaborate he replied: 'The response to Luther was made official at the Council of Trent...In its "Decree on Justification", the council described the process of justification and insisted that it is through faith that one is justified.[1]

Here lies the confusion in people's minds over this subject. What is wrong with the Jesuit theologian's statement? In the first place, though justification is said to be through grace, Christ and faith, the missing factor is the little word 'alone'. It is this which makes all the difference in the world between the Roman and Protestant positions. Secondly, justification is described as a 'process'. For Rome justification is a process within the individual, which means that the person is being continually put right with God. This process ends with the final verdict on the day of judgment. The Protestant position is that it is not a process but a judicial act of God outside of the individual in which the person who trusts Christ is pronounced right with God here and now, at the very beginning of the Christian life, correctly anticipating the final verdict. Thirdly, appeal is made to the Council of Trent, whose 'Decree on Justification' was specifically drawn up to counter Protestant teaching. That Decree is still the definitive statement on the subject of justification for Roman Catholics.

The Council of Trent

The Council of Trent, which sat intermittently from December 1545 to December 1563, was set up to address the glaring abuses in the church and to define doctrine, particularly in the light of Lutheran teachings. It was at Session VI, 13 January 1547, during the first period of the Council's work, that the decree on justification was finally read out and unanimously adopted. Prior to this, there had been six solid months of debate and discussion of various draft proposals. The leaders of the Council were in no doubt concerning the vital importance of the subject. Cardinal Cervini, who was chairing the proceedings at this time, impressed upon the assembled company the great responsibility resting on them. It was not a subject that the Church had been called on to treat in any detail before and few theologians had written on the subject. Luther's doctrine of justification by faith alone, he stressed, was at the root of most of his 'errors' concerning the sacraments, indulgences and purgatory.[2] Reporting to Rome the papal legates wrote: 'The significance of this Council in the theological sphere lies chiefly in the article on justification, in fact this is the most important item the Council has to deal with'.[3]

Three issues caused the most trouble to the delegates and took up the lion's share of the time. There was the question over what contribution, if any, a person made in preparation for justification. This involved the complicated doctrine of merit that had evolved during the medieval period. Secondly, it was argued very forcefully by Cardinal Seripando, General of the Augustinian Order, and supported by about eight other prelates, that the subject of imputed righteousness should be included in the decree. Thirdly, there was the matter of assurance. While all condemned Luther's view, differences existed between those who allowed for no certainty other than by special revelation and those who saw the sacraments as a basis of certainty.

In the final decree on justification, for the first time in the history of such Councils, positive teaching on the subject is presented. This is set out in sixteen chapters and then follows the customary canons anathematizing the holders of error. Thirty-three errors relating to justification are highlighted and denounced, the highest number of any of the decrees. These canons were not thought of as appendages to the doctrinal chapters. On the contrary, the chapters were meant to be read in the light of the canons. The sixteen doctrinal chapters are divided into three parts corresponding to what they saw as the three stages in the process of justification. A similar order is followed in the canons. Part one (chapters 1-9) is concerned with 'initial' justification. Interestingly, the Council looked at the subject from the point of view of an adult unbeliever coming to accept the Christian Faith and covered such topics as original sin and free will, prevenient grace and human cooperation, the nature and causes of justification, faith, merit, and assurance. This 'initial' justification is associated with baptism and defined in terms of an alteration of a person's nature as well as his status.

Part two (chapters 10-13) covers the so-called 'second' justification. The concern is with the advance of righteousness in the one who has been justified. Protestants would have placed much of the teaching found here under the heading of sanctification. As it is, a person cooperates with God's grace towards the final justification of the judgment day by putting to death his fleshly members and presenting them as 'instruments of righteousness unto sanctification' and observing the commands of God and the church. The canons lay stress on the necessity and possibility of observing God's commands, the importance of works as well as faith, while denouncing the gift of perseverance and rash presumption based on the doctrine of predestination.

Part three (chapters 14-16) deals with the subject of falling from the grace of justification through 'mortal' (i.e. 'deadly') as opposed to 'venial' (i.e. 'light', 'everyday') sin and being restored again through the sacrament of penance. The closing words of the final chapter stress that not to 'faithfully and firmly' accept the Council's teaching on justification means that a person 'cannot be justified'. The canons underline this with their list of anathemas. In other words, anyone who embraces the Protestant doctrine of justification by grace alone through faith alone is condemned to everlasting hell.[4]

The decrees of the Council were confirmed by the Pope in 1564. Since that time the Roman church has not officially considered the question of justification. It was not even dealt with by Vatican II. In 1566, shortly after Trent, the first definitive Roman Catechism appeared. The second authoritative Roman Catechism was published in 1992 with an English translation best-seller in 1994.[5] This recent document shows beyond all doubt that official Roman teaching on the subject of justification has not changed in the slightest since the 16th century.

The New Roman Catechism

Before we set out Rome's teaching on justification from the new Catechism, a few cautionary words are in order. It is noticeable that there are many quotations and references from the Bible. In this the Catechism follows the trend set by Trent in its decree on justification. This may lead the unwary to think that the teaching presented is biblical, but in reality the Bible is being used to support a theology that is unbiblical.

Again, as with Trent so in the Catechism, there are some statements with which Protestants can wholeheartedly agree. Certain expressions are found which can make Rome's position sound right and appealing to evangelicals. James Buchanan in his important work on the doctrine of justification felt it necessary, even in the middle of the nineteenth century, to give a warning not to be taken in by some of the well-guarded and cautious statements in the Trent decree. Trent, it must be remembered, was concerned to condemn Pelagianism as well as to counteract the teachings of Luther. The Pelagian heresy taught that human beings had the capacity to save themselves. The Fall did not make them powerless to act. They could raise themselves up and achieve salvation by their own good works. Trent therefore rightly spoke of the powerless state of human beings as a result of the Fall, of the need for the grace of God and the merits of Jesus Christ. All this, however, was effectively 'neutralized by other erroneous principles', so the result was 'an amalgam of some truth mixed with much error.'[6]

The same caution needs to be applied to the recent Catechism. It must be admitted that at a time when Roman Catholic and Protestant theologians are reinterpreting and denying basic Christian truths the Catechism strongly defends such essential elements of the gospel as the divinity of Jesus Christ, his virgin birth, his bodily resurrection and ascension, the future judgment, heaven and hell and the doctrine of the Trinity. One reviewer claims that 'there are excellent reasons for thinking that this document reflects the public defeat of more liberal trends within Roman Catholicism.'[7] When it comes to the subject of justification it stands, like Trent, against the Pelagian heresy. Take this statement for instance: 'Our justification comes from the grace of God. Grace is favour, the free and undeserved help that God gives us to respond to his call to become children of God, adoptive sons, partakers of the divine nature and of eternal life.' They also quote with approval this statement of Augustine: 'the justification of the wicked is a greater work than the creation of heaven and earth, because "heaven and earth will pass away but the salvation and justification of the elect...will not pass away."'[8] The evangelical can warm to such words and yet, as will be shown below, other statements appear which are contrary to biblical truth and nullify the gospel of God's justifying grace.

What then is Rome's up-to-date teaching on justification?

1 According to Rome, justification is an activity of the Holy Spirit in which the sinner's inner being is changed. The Catechism article on grace and justification quotes Trent: 'Justification is not only the remission of sins, but also the sanctification and renewal of the interior man' and the article goes on to emphasise that it 'entails the sanctification of his whole being'.[9] Justification, we are told has two aspects: there is the initial response to the grace of God in turning away from sin and receiving the forgiveness which God offers; and at the same time there is 'the acceptance of God's righteousness through faith in Jesus Christ'. In reference to forgiveness, justification 'detaches man from sin which contradicts the love of God, and purifies his heart of sin.' As for the acceptance of 'righteousness' (or 'justice') this is said to mean 'the rectitude of divine love. With justification, faith, hope and charity are poured into our hearts, and obedience to the divine will is granted us'.[10] It is thus made abundantly clear that justification is used in an unbiblical way to mean regeneration, renewal and sanctification in addition to the forgiveness of sins. Rather than justification referring exclusively to a change in the status of a sinner it has become a word which particularly draws attention to a change in the sinner's inner state. In the Catechism's article on Baptism this same point is made that

'The Most Holy Trinity gives the baptized *sanctifying grace* the grace of justification', which involves three elements: 1) it enables them to believe in God, 2) it gives them 'the power to live and act under the prompting of the Holy Spirit' and 3) it allows them 'to grow in goodness through the moral virtues.'[11] That is not justification according to the Bible. Justification itself does not do anything in us. It is a judicial act of God outside of ourselves and concerns our status before God. By so confusing justification with regeneration and sanctification the door is open for a religion of salvation by good works.

2 Trent condemned the Reformers' position that the sinner was declared righteous on the basis of a righteousness outside of himself - what Luther called 'the alien' righteousness of Christ imputed to the believer. The Catechism does not enter into debate, or present opposing views. It does not refer to imputed righteousness. Neither is there any reference to justification being a divine judicial act declaring the sinner to be righteous in God's sight. It merely reiterates the position set out at Trent. Justifying righteousness is 'the acceptance of God's righteousness through faith in Jesus Christ' which is understood as the righteousness of divine love. It is a righteousness that 'makes us inwardly just by the power of his mercy'. Though it speaks of God's righteousness coming through faith in Jesus Christ, there is no belief in the merits of Christ's perfect righteousness being reckoned to the believer. 'Clothed in his righteousness divine' is not something about which Rome can sing. As a result, it leads to the position where the believer's justification does not rest solely on the sufficiency of Christ's work. The door is left ajar for human activity to be thought important and necessary in order to be fully right with God.

3 The Catechism keeps very close to Trent in describing the place of faith in connection with justification. God's grace and man's free will are seen as cooperating. Faith is 'an act of the intellect assenting to the divine truth'.[12] The Holy Spirit precedes and preserves this assent and perfects the initial free response with 'charity'. Faith is not seen as personal reliance on Christ and what he has done. Indeed, in line with

what has already been said about Rome's understanding of justification, the faith of assent when supernaturally supplemented with 'charity' is an indication of the inner change which justification initially makes. 'With justification,' as was quoted earlier, 'faith, hope and charity are poured into our hearts.' This is so different from the Reformers' biblical understanding of faith. Archbishop Cranmer's *Homily of Salvation* published in 1547 makes it clear that faith is not seen as a virtue within ourselves: '...although we have faith, hope, charity, repentance, dread and fear of God, within us; and do never so many works thereunto; yet we must renounce the merit of all our said virtues...'[13]

4 The real means by which justification is obtained, is not, as we have seen, through trust in Jesus Christ but through the sacrament of baptism. Baptism is described as 'the sacrament of faith'. Faith, as understood by Rome, has a place, but it is through the sacrament of Baptism that justification is granted.[14] It 'is conferred in baptism'. Baptism 'conforms us to the righteousness of God'. The Catechism teaches that 'through the Holy Spirit, Baptism is a bath that purifies, justifies and sanctifies.'[15] This shows the indispensable involvement of the church in the justification of sinners. Even in the initial stages of Rome's view of justification, human activity through the church sacraments is strongly in evidence. This is not all.

5 The so-called 'Sacrament of Penance' is also associated with justification. It is instituted above all 'for those who, since Baptism, have fallen into grave sin, and have thus lost their baptismal grace...It is to them that the sacrament of Penance offers a new possibility to convert and to recover the grace of justification.' 'Grave sin' is 'mortal' or 'deadly' sin for it places a person back where he was before baptism, in danger of eternal punishment. The Catechism, like Trent, continues to refer to Penance as 'the second plank [of salvation] after the shipwreck which is the loss of grace.'[16]

The Catechism teaches that there are two essential elements to this 'sacrament': there is man's action, through the work of the Spirit, of contrition, confession, and satisfaction; there is also God's action through the Church. By the Church is meant the Roman bishops and priests: they act on behalf of God and Christ in forgiving sins and determining 'the manner of satisfaction'. Penance thus involves going to Rome's priests to repent, confess and to receive forgiveness and to be told what one has to do in order to expiate sin. In order to regain full spiritual health the repentant sinner must do 'something more to make amends' for his sins. Such satisfaction for sins can consist of prayers, sacrifices, works of mercy, voluntary self-denial, etc.[17] All this unbiblical teaching arises from a wrong view of justification. This is the position that Luther was in before he had his eyes opened to the truth of justification. He could not get assurance that he had done enough to be right with God. Again, this understanding of justification places the person in absolute dependence on the Church. The Catechism is clear on the matter: 'Reconciliation with the Church is inseparable from reconciliation with God.'[18]

6 It is under the heading of Penance that the Catechism also deals with other non-biblical subjects such as indulgences, purgatory, and the treasury of merit.[19] On the subject of merit, the summary statement reads: 'No one can merit the initial grace which is at the origin of conversion. Moved by the Holy Spirit, we can merit for ourselves and others all the graces needed to attain eternal life....'[20] Any spare merit we may attain goes into the treasury of merit. This treasury is made up first and foremost of the prayers and good works of Mary which are 'truly immense, unfathomable and even pristine in their value before God'. Also contained there are the prayers and good works of the saints.[21] For the Reformers the good works of believers are never spoken of as meritorious. They refer to them as the fruit and signs of justification. John Calvin in his commentary on the words in 1 Corinthians 1:13, 'Was Paul crucified for you?' shows how the verse 'wrecks the wicked invention of the Papists, which they use to try to bolster up their system of indulgences' and speaks of the treasury of merit as 'that counterfeit treasury of the Church, which, they teach, is dispensed by indulgences'. With devasting logic he argues that 'they

make the martyrs partners with Christ in winning our salvation'.[22]

Everyday or 'venial' sins, so Rome teaches, are not like 'mortal' or 'deadly' sins; they are not as serious and do not bring eternal punishment. Though they are forgiven, the Catechism says it is still necessary to be purified from these sins through temporal punishment. This punishment may be here on earth or after death in purgatory. An indulgence is said to free a person in part or wholly from temporal punishment depending on whether it is a plenary or partial indulgence. 'An indulgence is obtained through the Church who..... intervenes in favour of individual Christians and opens for them the treasury of the merits of Christ and the saints to obtain from the Father of mercies the remission of the temporal punishments due for their sins.' 'Since the faithful departed now being purified (i.e. in purgatory) are also members of the same communion of saints, one way we can help them is to obtain indulgences for them, so that the temporal punishments due for their sins may be remitted.'[23] This is Rome's official teaching at the end of the twentieth century. Though the Catechism pays lip service to the merits of Christ's death,[24] it is clear that neither a sufficient nor complete satisfaction for sins has been made on the cross.

7 Because it is possible to lose one's justification, there can be no assurance of salvation. Post-baptismal sins can either bring about a loss of justification altogether, and expose people to the danger of hell, or they can at least make it necessary to do something extra to make amends in this life and after death to pass through the fires of purgatory before reaching heaven. It is not at all surprising then that the Catechism has nothing to say about assurance or certainty of salvation. It does refer to the hope of obtaining the joy of heaven, which is 'God's eternal reward for good works accomplished with the grace of Christ'.[25] Again, in this it is being true to Trent. While the Reformers rested in the promises of God for salvation, Trent criticised their 'ungodly' confidence. It attacked what it saw as a cock-sure attitude, an all too common criticism still made by those who have no understanding of the gospel. If assurance is understood as being based on one's own effort in cooperation with God through the church's administrations there

would be no ground for confidence. The gospel revealed in the Bible, as the Reformers saw so clearly, indicates that assurance of one's justified state does not mean confidence in one's personal faith and one's activity in doing what the church requires, but that it is a complete dependence on the grace and activity of God in Christ.

In summing up the present position of Rome on this crucial subject it is important to stress that there has been no shift whatsoever from the definitive statement made at Trent. The Roman Catholic view of justification involves two main stages: an initial activity which includes the sacrament of baptism and then a process throughout life which includes the 'sacrament of penance' and after death in the fires of purgatory. In the end the Roman position is a reliance on oneself and the clergy of the Roman Church. Though justification is said to be by God's grace it is also by human activity. Though it is through Christ's merit it also involves human merit. It is administered by the Roman Church first through baptism and can be renewed again through penance. Though Rome's doctrine of justification is meant to bring glory to God in reality it bolsters human pride and glorifies the Roman system.

Notes

1. 'America's Catholics: What They believe - Catholic Doctrine According to Jesuit Theologian Avery Dulles', *Christianity Today*, 7th November 1986, pp. 26-27.
2. J. Waterworth, *The Canons and Decrees of the Council of Trent*, Dolman, 1848. p. ci.
3. H. Jedin, *A History of the Council of Trent*, Vol.2, Nelson, 1961, p. 171.
4. For a critique of Trent on justification cf. P. H. Eveson 'The Council of Trent and Modern views of Justification' in *Building on a Sure Foundation*, Westminster Conference Papers, 1994, pp. 35-42. Also McGrath, *Iustitia Dei*, Vol.2, pp. 54-97.
5. *Catechism of the Catholic Church*, Geoffrey Chapman (Cassell imprint), 1994.
6. J. Buchanan, *The Doctrine of Justification*, Banner of Truth reprint, 1961, p.155f.
7. A. E. McGrath, 'Do we still need the Reformation?' in *Christianity Today*, 12th December, 1994, p. 29.
8. *Catechism*, pp. 433-434.
9. *ibid.* pp. 432, 434.
10. *ibid.* p. 433.

11. *ibid.* pp. 286-287.

12. *ibid.* p. 39.

13. 'The Homily of Salvation' in *Miscellaneous Writings and Letters of Thomas Cranmer*, Parker Society, Cambridge, 1846, pp. 128-134.

14. *Catechism*, p. 286.

15. *ibid.* p. 280.

16. *ibid.* p. 325.

17. *ibid.* p. 328.

18. *ibid.* p. 325.

19. *ibid.* pp. 331-333.

20. *ibid.* p. 439.

21. *ibid.* p. 332.

22. Calvin's Commentaries, *The First Epistle of Paul to the Corinthians*, trans. J. W. Fraser, eds. D. W. & T. F. Torrance, Eerdmans/St Andrews Press, 1960, p. 29.

23. *Catechism*, p. 331, 333.

24. *ibid.* p. 433: 'Justification has been merited for us by the Passion of Christ who offered himself on the cross as a living victim, holy and pleasing to God, and whose blood has become the instrument of atonement for the sins of all men.'

25. *ibid.* p. 404.

8 Justification and Unity

Evangelicals and Roman Catholics Together

In 1994 the evangelical world was presented with a document entitled *Evangelicals and Catholics Together: The Christian Mission in the Third Millennium*. It was drawn up by eight Protestants, under the leadership of Charles Colson, founder of the Prison Fellowship, and seven Roman Catholics, headed by the Roman Catholic priest R. J. Neuhaus, a former Lutheran pastor. In addition, it was endorsed by twelve more Protestants, including such well-known figures as J. I. Packer, Os Guinness, Mark Noll and Bill Bright, and by thirteen more Roman Catholics such as Cardinal O'Connor and the Jesuit bishop Carlos Sevilla.[1]

The document recognises that evangelicals and Roman Catholics have much in common. Despite certain disagreements and differences in doctrine and practice, 'Evangelicals and Catholics are brothers and sisters in Christ' who share a common faith in Jesus as Lord and Saviour and affirm together that they are 'justified by grace through faith because of Christ'. They also share values crucial to the well-being of society. They condemn the practice of proselytizing or 'sheep stealing' and 'of recruiting people from another community for purposes of denominational aggrandizement', while at the same time they defend 'the legal freedom' to do so. The call, however, is to a new commitment not only to work together on social and cultural issues but also to witness together in preparation for Christ's return. Whether it be in 'great Christian expansion' or in 'persecution and apparent marginalization' they affirm that 'we are in this together'. Difficult and long-standing problems 'must not be permitted to overshadow the truths on which we are, by the grace of God, in firm agreement'. They see the present as a time of opportunity and responsibility 'for Evangelicals and Catholics to be Christians together in a way that helps prepare the world for the coming of him to whom belongs the kingdom, the power, and the glory forever.'

In the light of much adverse criticism, a number of the original signatories and backers came together and faced their critics at a meeting held on 19th January 1995 at Fort Lauderdale, Florida. By the end of the day the evangelical leaders of the accord agreed a five-point statement, designed to 'elucidate' their own position.[2]

The new statement says that cooperation between evangelicals and 'evangelically committed Roman Catholics' on common concerns does not mean they endorse the Roman Catholic 'church system' or 'doctrinal distinctives'. They affirm their own belief in 'the historic Protestant understanding of salvation by faith alone (*sola fide*)' which they spell out as 'the substitutionary atonement and imputed righteousness of Christ, leading to full assurance of eternal salvation.' While viewing all who profess to be Christian, whether Protestant, Roman Catholic or Orthodox, 'with charity and hope', they add 'our confidence that anyone is truly a brother and sister in Christ depends not only on the content of his or her confession but on our perceiving signs of regeneration in his or her life.' Again, although they reject proselytizing as defined in the original document, they add 'we hold that evangelism and church planting are always legitimate, whatever forms of church life are present already.'

Some of the critics have applauded this second statement while others are less than happy. John MacArthur, the pastor of the independent Grace Community Church in Sun Valley, California was glad that Colson and Packer had the opportunity to clarify 'what is clarified there'. But he feels that 'it still doesn't go as far as I would have hoped.' He firmly believes that the evangelical signatories of the original document should 'recant'. Roman Catholicism should be recognised as 'another religion'.[3]

One of the evangelical men to back *Evangelicals and Catholics Together*, as we have seen, was Dr. Jim Packer who issued a statement of his own in *Christianity Today* prior to the Fort Lauderdale meeting, entitled 'Why I Signed It'. In it he makes clear his opposition to Rome while at the same time justifying cooperation with Roman Catholics not only in social witness but also in evangelism.[4] The document he says, 'affirms positions and expresses attitudes that have been mine for half a lifetime.'

He gives three reasons for maximizing 'mission activity in partnership with Roman Catholics'. First, we must recognize that 'good evangelical Protestants and good Roman Catholics - good, I mean, in terms of their own church's stated ideal of spiritual life - are Christians together'. This 'mutual acknowledgment brings obligations', one of these obligations is 'that God's family here on earth should seek to look like one family by acting as one family'. This means that 'where there is fellowship in faith, fellowship in service should follow....So togetherness in mission is appropriate.' To cherish an isolationist spirit is sin. Secondly, the present situation 'cries out for an alliance of good evangelical Protestants with good Roman Catholics (and good Eastern Orthodox, too)'. While a coalition already exists among evangelicals in North America to resist the post-modernist theologies that have affected both Protestantism and Roman Catholicism, there would be a stronger stand for truth if it were in closer step with 'the parallel Catholic coalition that has recently begun to grow.' He believes that propagating the basic faith together is timely. Thirdly, we need to recognize that 'mission ventures involving evangelicals and Catholics side by side, not only in social witness but in evangelism and nurture as well, have already emerged'. He gives three examples: battling together on the abortion issue; 'Billy Graham's cooperative evangelism'; and 'charismatic get-togethers'.

There are many aspects of the accord between evangelicals and Roman Catholics and of Packer's clarifying statement which are disturbing but none more so than the affirmation concerning justification. 'We affirm together that we are justified by grace through faith because of Christ. Living faith is active in love that is nothing less than the love of Christ.' It would appear from this that there is no fundamental disagreement between evangelicals and Roman Catholics on this crucial issue. The differences between Roman Catholics and evangelicals which are listed later do not include the subject of justification. This is incredible when it is generally admitted that this was the great divide at the time of the Reformation and is still the major doctrinal sticking-point between Rome and Protestants. Kenneth Kantzer, one of the senior editors of *Christianity Today*, commented, 'Justification by faith is mentioned as a common commitment as though it had never been a matter of serious disagreement.'[5]

This statement on justification is quite acceptable to all Roman Catholics, whether they would describe themselves as evangelical or traditional. It is very similar to the definition given at the beginning of the last chapter by the Jesuit theologian. It is the position of Trent and the recent Roman Catechism. Rome affims that justification is by grace. It has no problem with the need for faith which is 'active in love'. Rome also believes that the meritorious cause of justification is the work of Christ on our behalf. Where lies the problem? It is, as we have previously emphasised, over the little word 'alone'. A whole world of difference results when 'alone' is added to each of the words 'grace', 'faith' and 'Christ'. This is not a question of agreeing to disagree over some secondary issue. The heart of the gospel is at stake.

If this is so, how can 'good evangelical Protestants and good Roman Catholics', to use Packer's words, cooperate in evangelism? Though the evidence available suggests that there is a significant number of Roman Catholics who do not accept the authority of all the official Roman teaching and may privately embrace some evangelical views, this does not necessarily mean they appreciate the essence of the gospel. It may also be true that there are many 'real Christians' who for one reason or another are remaining within the Roman Catholic Church.

Nevertheless, it must be pointed out that among the 'real Christians' and 'good Roman Catholics' there are people like R. J. Neuhaus, the chief Roman Catholic instigator of this accord. From being a Lutheran pastor he has converted to Rome and become one of its priests. He seems to like what he sees in evangelicalism and wants to cooperate with evangelicals, yet has recently gone on oath to accept all the unre-formed teachings of Rome. In America, there has been a disturbing number of converts to Rome from within the evangelical constituency in recent years.[6] It is clear that they do not appreciate the heart of the gospel.[7] How then can there be unity in preaching the gospel and nurturing young believers with such people as Neuhaus, who have openly embraced a system of belief that runs counter to all that historic evangelicalism stands for?

Though Colson, Packer and the other evangelical participants have clarified their position with regard to justification, they in no way want to detract from what they originally affirmed. This must mean that while they personally believe that justification is by grace *alone* through faith *alone* because of Christ *alone* they have deliberately agreed to leave this out in the interests of working more closely together. What kind of evangelicalism is that? They say they are firmly committed to the Protestant understanding of salvation and see Rome's teaching as cutting across Paul's doctrine of justification, and yet they are prepared to agree to a Roman Catholic statement concerning justification, in the interests of social, cultural and evangelistic ends.

United action by individuals across political and religious lines for the good of society has always been encouraged. We have no quarrel with that. What is unacceptable is evangelicals and Roman Catholics working together in mission as a kind of para-church organization, to maintain Christian traditions and culture, to battle for truth, to engage in evangelism and to advance the kingdom of Christ. Colson and Packer are encouraging a new generation of evangelicals to assume that justification by faith *alone* is not that important and that Roman Catholics merely belong to a different Christian denomination. The sad truth is that Roman Catholics are joined up to what can only be described as 'another religion' - something which, in the end, the Reformers came to see.

It is less than consistent for the evangelical supporters of the accord to state in one breath that they believe the historic Protestant position on justification and then to affirm with Roman Catholics a deliberately weakened statement. Each party to the agreement is being allowed to understand the statement according to its own particular position, whether Protestant or Roman. There is no recognition that in the very matter of justification the two positions are diametrically opposed. We have to ask the evangelicals about the strength of their commitment to the evangelical Protestant truth. The doctrine of justification cannot be left vague in 'interfaith accord' with Roman Catholics. What is more, there is no concern to encourage the Roman Catholic partners to the agreement to embrace the gospel truth concerning justification rediscovered by the Reformers. But as John

Armstrong the Director of Reformation and Revival Ministries urges, 'I owe it to God and to my [Catholic] friend to 'speak the truth.' I also owe it to him to do it 'in love.'[8]

It needs to be recalled that men like Luther, Latimer and Calvin, to name but a few, grew up in a church where the Trinity, the virgin birth of Christ, the importance of his atoning sacrifice, the grace of God, and the power of the Holy Spirit were believed. Nevertheless, these men were never taught the key element in the gospel, the truth concerning the biblical doctrine of justification. It is not impossible that such a situation could arise again, especially as the doctrine is so little understood and preached, and as evangelical leaders are allowing a truncated version of it to be the basis for united evangelistic activity.

Remember the situation that existed between Jew and Samaritan when our Lord was on earth and his outspoken criticism of the Samaritan religion. Surrounded as they were by a multiplicity of gods, it would have been in the interests of Jew and Samaritan to have cooperated together on moral, cultural and religious issues of the day, seeing they both believed in one creator God, accepted the Mosaic law, saw the need for sacrifice at a central sanctuary, and looked forward to a promised deliverer. They had so much in common! Jesus, however, makes it very clear that the Samaritans do not belong within that stream of divine revelation out of which the Saviour will come (John 4:22). After making such uncompromising statements to the woman of Samaria, Jesus then directed her to himself, of Davidic Jewish line. He is the reality to which the shadowy Jerusalem, and not the heretical Gerizim, worship pointed. In a similar way evangelicals need to be more outspoken in their criticism of Roman Catholicism, and far from uniting with individual Roman Catholics in evangelism and encouraging them in their false religion and view of justification, they should be pointing them to the gospel truth concerning justification by faith alone and all that that means in practice.

Instead of evangelicals drawing attention to the errors of Rome and urging 'brothers and sisters' in that religious system to come out, the Evangelical-Catholic accord denounces 'sheep-stealing'. 'It is neither theologically legitimate nor a prudent use of resources for one Christian community to proselytize among active adherents of another Christian community.' No wonder Neuhaus is quoted as saying that 'appropriate parties at the Holy See' gave the initiative their 'strongest encouragement'.[9] If such a statement, endorsed by evangelical heavy-weights, can become accepted worldwide it would call a halt, for instance, to the massive drift from Rome into the evangelical churches of South America. At the same time, Rome itself, which is not party to the agreement, can continue to woo evangelicals and other Protestants into its fold. 'It is with mounting conviction' reported *The Times* on May 30, 1995, 'that today's Catholics pray for the conversion of England. The conversion of the Establishment, crucial to their goal, is already well advanced.'

Charles Colson is adamant that the situation today demands more than Christians merely working together with others as citizens in political alliances. A distinctively Christian witness is needed to fight against secularism, New Age spirituality and theological liberalism. Writing in *Christianity Today* he states, 'At root, it is a battle for truth - and to fight effectively we need a distinctive Christian presence and world-view.' He goes on to argue that 'our best weapon is the distinctiveness of Christian truth, expressed in unity by all true believers.'[10] This is all very well and good if there is a clear statement setting out what the Christian truth is and on which all the participants are agreed. But if there is uncertainty and confusion over such a vital element of the gospel as God's justifying grace then how can they battle for the truth? What is more, is Colson suggesting that evangelical Protestants should work alongside Roman Catholics to maintain the kind of 'Christian' culture seen in countries where the Reformation truths have been suppressed for many centuries? Awful idolatrous practices, encouraged by the Roman establishment, dominate those societies which have not known the doctrine of justification by faith alone. Are we to ask evangelical missionaries in Italy and Spain, for instance, to support a culture where idols of Mary are often paraded through the streets? Would they now be better employed if they pulled out of these 'Catholic' countries and went across the Mediterranean to North Africa?

The Reformers did not think in the way some modern evangelicals are expressing themselves, nor did the evangelicals of the eighteenth century. At the time of the Reformation, the Pope and the Reformers were well aware of the growing might of Islam, in the form of the Ottoman Empire. Did the Reformers compromise on the doctrine of justification in order to unite with Rome against the common enemy? No! Did the evangelicals of the eighteenth century feel it necessary to unite with Roman Catholics to fight the deists? No! They strongly denounced Roman doctrine and looked to the Lord for success in preaching the gospel. It was revival in the church which killed off the effects of deism and set in motion a great advance in evangelical Christianity worldwide resulting in social and moral by-products for the good of societies.

Packer sees this Evangelical-Roman Catholic alliance as a grassroots ecumenical action out of which can grow a relationship of trust. It is in this atmosphere that he believes the differences and disagreements on doctrine and practice between the Roman and Protestant churches can be more fully and candidly addressed.[11] Such 'unofficial' cooperation is now being more widely appreciated as the best way to progress towards the goal of Christian unity. This is something that we shall return to at the end of the chapter.

Prior to these evangelical moves, two notable documents on the subject of justification appeared, the result of 'official' dialogue between Protestants and Roman Catholics. They are included here not only for their importance to the ecumenical debate on justification but as examples of the kind of language that present-day theologians are using to produce such joint statements and the evangelical response to them.

Lutherans and Roman Catholics Together

After six years of discussion the United States Lutheran-Roman Catholic dialogue group published, in 1983, a comprehensive document entitled *Justification by Faith*.[12] It is in two parts. Part Two prints the sixteen background papers. The agreed statement appears in Part One, which is divided into three chapters. Chapter one deals very competently with the history of the doctrine. In chapter two there is reflection on and interpretation of the various elements of the doctrine that have produced misunderstanding and differences of opinion, such as forensic justification, the sinfulness of the justified, the sufficiency of faith, merit, satisfaction for sins, and the criteria for testing authentic Christianity. All this is done by setting them in the light of the different concerns and patterns of thought in the two traditions. This is very cleverly done so that, despite the differences which are freely admitted, what is highlighted is a growing consensus over fundamental concerns and beliefs. An effort is made in chapter three to think jointly over the differences that remain by looking briefly at the biblical data on justification, and then by summarizing and reflecting on the 'convergences in biblical exegesis and theological understanding.'[13]

Despite their differences, both Lutherans and Roman Catholics are said to be bearing witness in their different contexts and statements to a basic consensus on the gospel. They make the following affirmation:

'Our entire hope of justification and salvation rests on Jesus Christ and on the gospel whereby the good news of God's merciful action in Christ is made known; we do not place our ultimate trust in anything other than God's promise and saving work in Christ.'[14]

They admit that such an affirmation 'is not fully equivalent to the Reformation teaching on justification', but by its insistence that reliance for salvation should be placed entirely on God, they claim that 'it expresses a central concern of that doctrine'. Yet at the same time 'it does not exclude the traditional Catholic position that the grace-wrought transformation of sinners is a necessary preparation for final salvation.'[15] What is this but a compromise in the direction of Rome?

In addition, they were able to formulate twelve points of agreement where previously there has been misunderstanding. Among them is this statement: 'Justification, as a transition from disfavor and unrighteousness to favor and righteousness in God's sight, is totally God's work. By justification we are both declared and made righteous. Justification is, therefore, not a legal fiction. God, in justifying, effects what he promises; he forgives sin and makes us truly righteous.' This again is a far cry from the Reformation teaching, but very acceptable to Rome. The word 'transition' is itself an ambiguous term in this context.

In so far as it suggests a process of change, the meaning, as we saw in the last chapter, runs counter to the Protestant position. Justification is not a transition from unrighteousness to righteousness but a judicial act of God pronouncing the unrighteous to be immediately righteous in God's sight. But even if 'transition' simply means 'change of position' the definition makes it clear that justification includes an inward state of righteousness as well as an outward change of status.

In his study of the document, Dr. Alister McGrath, the noted Oxford don who is an authority on justification, helpfully draws attention to the way it acknowledges the quite different approaches to the doctrine by the two traditions while at the same time it argues 'that they are complementary and convergent, rather than contradictory and divergent'.[16] Like *Evangelicals and Catholics Together*, the Lutheran-Roman Catholic statement emphasises that differences can exist between the two parties in the way they view and express justification but in reality they are all bearing witness to the one gospel. This will not do. The message which it conveys is that, though Protestants disagree with Roman Catholics in their confessional statements on justification, it does not really matter any more. As McGrath puts it, this document affirms that Protestant and Roman confessions are all 'legitimate ways of attempting to safeguard the same crucial insight' that 'the ultimate foundation of our justification' lies in God's action in Christ.[17] This is just not sufficient. Despite all the effort to present a common statement, the great doctrine of the Reformers has been compromised and it has lost its cutting edge.

Anglicans and Roman Catholics Together

The Second Anglican-Roman Catholic International Commission (ARCIC II) was set up to resolve some of the outstanding doctrinal differences that still divide the two communions. It was recommended that they first consider the doctrine of justification, as it was widely believed that unless there was the prospect of agreement on this issue there could be no 'full doctrinal agreement' between the two church organizations. After three years' work an agreed statement was published in 1987.[18] It is not an authoritative declaration by either

Rome or Canterbury but simply a joint statement by the Commission for reflection by the churches they represent. The same applies to the previous document from the United States which we have considered.

The title of this Agreed Statement, *Salvation and the Church*, is significant in itself and immediately draws attention to the ecumenical nature of the document. If there is to be any doctrinal agreement on the subject of justification without loss of face by either party, it would be necessary to consider it in the wider context of salvation and of the church. It is true, of course, as the document indicates, that justification is one of a whole cluster of doctrines associated with salvation. Likewise, it is not improper to study justification in the context of the church, for the church, as the statement rightly maintains, 'is the community of those who believe in Jesus Christ and are justified through God's grace'. However, the way in which justification is set out and dealt with results in a very inadequate treatment of the subject. A new synthesis is achieved where past differences are viewed as misunderstandings and all are really meaning much the same thing. McGrath criticises it for being 'reluctant to address the real disagreements' between classical Anglicans and Rome.[19]

The Agreed Statement is set out under four heads: 'Salvation and Faith', 'Salvation and Justification', 'Salvation and Good Works' and 'The Church and Salvation'. It is striking that in only one of the subtitles does the actual term 'justification' appear which conveys the impression that justification is being reduced in importance. This is confirmed when justification is made to look insignificant by being placed last in a list of ten items under the all-embracing term 'salvation'. The Statement admits that some terms are more important that others but it refuses to regard any one term as the controlling concept. 'They complement one another'. This effectively demotes justification from the place it occupied for the Reformers. What is more, in the Preface explaining their choice of title, the two co-chairmen write that the doctrine of justification 'can be properly treated only within the wider context of the doctrine of salvation as a whole. This in turn has involved discussion of the role of the church in Christ's saving work'. As Hywel Jones, the first Principal of the London Theological Seminary, has pointed out, 'To claim that justification can only be *properly* treated when it is connected with all the other constituent elements of salvation on the one hand and with the church on the other is tantamount to denying that it can be properly treated by *itself* as a distinct theological entity, which is 'obviously ridiculous'. This would be to deny the validity of former theological work in this area. Dr. Jones goes on to stress that the Bible not only treats justification within the wider context of salvation and the church but 'In places it speaks of it *as if there were no other element in salvation and as if there were no such organism/organisation as the church.*'[20]

When the Agreed Statement eventually comes to discussing what justification means, it does so in the context of sanctification. Biblical warrant for dealing with these two subjects together is said to be I Corinthians 6:11, 'But you were washed, you were sanctified, you were justified in the name of the Lord Jesus Christ and by the Spirit of our God'. This is quite inadmissible, because Paul there uses both sanctification and justification in a positional sense. The Christian has a sanctified as well as a justified status. That is why the Corinthian believers can be called saints.[21] However, this is not how the Statement understands sanctification and the use of the biblical reference in this context only adds to the confusion. Sanctification (seen as God's activity within a person's life recreating and renewing) and justification (seen as God's pronouncement of acquittal) are not 'two aspects of the same divine act' as the Agreed Statement suggests, although they are 'indissolubly linked'. We shall return to this important subject in chapter eleven.

At first sight it is very encouraging to have justification described as 'a divine declaration of acquittal' and to be informed that 'Instead of our own strivings to make ourselves acceptable to God, Christ's perfect righteousness is reckoned to our account.' This is deceptive, for the document keeps on emphasising the place of the inner divine activity of making righteous in association with justification. 'God's grace effects what he declares: his creative word imparts what it imputes. By pronouncing us righteous, God also makes us righteous'. The result of this confusion is, as Hywel Jones puts it, 'that our righteousness and our works become mingled with Christ's righteousness and faith. This is fatal for the biblical doctrine of justification.'[22] John Henry Newman, the Anglican clergyman who converted to Rome in the last century and was made a Cardinal, used the creative word idea to link imputed and imparted righteousness. Relying heavily on Newman, Hans Küng, the radical Roman Catholic theologian, follows the same line of argument when he writes in his work on justification, 'Unlike the word of man, the word of God does what it signifies.'[23]

Turning briefly to ARCIC II's view of the church in relation to justification, McGrath regards this section of the report as by far the weakest. It is most unacceptable to be told that salvation in all its aspects, including justification, 'comes to each believer as he or she is incorporated into the believing community'. From the biblical perspective it is God who justifies not the church. Baptism is referred to by the Roman Catholic expression 'the sacrament of justification' but what that means is not spelt out. In paragraph 22 there is an oblique reference to what is involved in the Roman sacrament of penance. But Rome's teaching on penance is not specifically considered, even though, as was seen in the last chapter, it is a vital ingredient in its understanding of justification. The associated subject of indulgences, so closely related to penance, is also ignored in this document.

Here then is an agreement on justification which marginalises the subject, merges it with sanctification and makes it dependent on the church. While it accepts the biblical meaning of justification with one breath, it takes away from it at the next. The document pinpoints four areas of difficulty: faith, justifying righteousness, good works and the role of the church in salvation. As a result of their discussions the members of the Commission are able to affirm that the above-mentioned difficulties need no longer be matters of dispute. This is 'justification by unity' as the heading to *The Times* editorial perceptively put it.[24]

It is sad but not surprising to find a number of influential Anglican evangelicals welcoming the Agreed Statement. Michael Baughen, former vicar of All Souls, Langham Place, London and until 1996 Bishop of Chester wrote at the time, 'most evangelicals in the Church of England will welcome [it] with warmth' and he recommends it for containing excellent statements about justification.[25] One of the members of the Commission that produced the document is the Anglican evangelical, Julian Charley, who naturally warmly commends it. He speaks of this agreement as the result of 'a process of convergence' that had been taking place for some decades. He reminds readers that it is in the nature of ecumenical agreed statements that you cannot expect to get what you personally want. 'What matters is that nothing is said or omitted that compromises your fundamental faith.'[26] We believe that ARCIC II does compromise the truth concerning justification by faith alone. What is more, can one say that agreement has been reached when subjects like indulgences are ignored?

McGrath, Justification and Unity

Alister McGrath, an expert in historical theology, is an Anglican evangelical who has written many learned articles and books on justification and related themes. We have already drawn attention to his pertinent comments in the present chapter. His knowledge and grasp of the subject and of the issues involved is impressive. From his considerable output it is possible to build up a picture of his own personal preferences and beliefs on justification within the context of the ecumenical debate.

It is McGrath's opinion that the doctrine of justification should be allowed to develop a meaning that is much broader than the biblical usage. In his two-volume history of the doctrine of justification, *Iustitia Dei,* he begins by making a distinction between the *concept* of justification as used by Paul and the *doctrine* of justification as formulated by the church. The *concept* or idea of justification, he argues, is one of many used in the Bible and particularly by Paul 'to describe God's saving action towards his people'. The *doctrine* of justification as developed by the theologians has acquired a meaning in Protestant as well as Roman theology that is 'virtually independent of its biblical origins and concerns the *means by which man's relationship to God is established*'.[27] In another place he writes, 'In dogmatic theology...the concept of justification has come to mean the restoration of man's broken relationship with God - a meaning which is best illustrated from the brilliant Tridentine definition of the term.'[28] The passage which he quotes is from chapter four of Trent's decree on justification. It describes the justification of the sinner 'as being a translation from that state in which man is born a child of the first Adam, to the state of grace and of the adoption of the sons of God through the second Adam, Jesus Christ, our Saviour.'[29]

McGrath is right to distinguish between the Bible's use of justification and what it came to mean for the medieval church and the Council of Trent. It would be wrong, however, to lump historical Protestant theology with that of Roman. The Reformers brought people back to the biblical and Pauline use of the term. They correctly understood it to mean God's declaration that the guilty sinner is acquitted and judged to be in a right legal position before God and his law. Rome turned its back on this biblical position and instead, at Trent, codified the inaccurate medieval teaching which continues to lead it to accept other false and unbiblical ideas.

In his more popular book *Justification by Faith: What it means to us Today*, Dr. McGrath argues for the development of a doctrine of justification from the original biblical idea, in order to appeal to the needs of the present generation.[30] He is encouraged to go beyond the New Testament statements on the subject by appealing to what has happened in the history of theology to the term 'atonement'. From its more narrow biblical usage as the word for 'reconciliation', it has come to stand, in systematic theology, for the whole subject of what Christ accomplished through his death.

McGrath uses this illustration to expand the meaning of justification by taking on board elements associated with the Roman view. He argues that, while the biblical concept is about the removal of condemnation and the establishment of a right status and relationship with God, the doctrine can designate the whole matter of what a person must do in order to have a life-transforming encounter with God through Christ. He keeps on referring to justification as a transforming experience. 'Justification changes us, initiating a new relationship with God that is charged with a creative power to transform us'. Or again, 'In justification God offers to dwell within us as his temple' and he quotes

the lines from Cardinal Newman's famous hymn, *Praise to the Holiest in the Height*:
'God's presence, and his very self
And essence all-divine'.
He claims, without giving any references, that both the Old and New Testaments 'regard justification as a transformational experience'.[31]

With this understanding of justification he proceeds to show its contemporary significance from the 'existential', 'personal' and 'ethical' dimensions. In other words, justification now stands for authentic existence, 'the abolition of our alienation from our authentic mode of existence.'[32] It is about 'the transformation and fulfilment of our persons through an encounter with *the* Person who underlies personality itself.'[33] 'We are *made* children of God through our justification as an act of free grace - and now we must act in accordance with this transformation.'[34]

With all due respect to Dr. McGrath, his arguments for widening the meaning of justification are unconvincing and his definitions are actually dangerous to the evangelical or gospel truth. The dedicated preacher concerned to present the truth of justification by faith in today's world has no right to impose his own meanings onto the term in order to make it relevant. Biblical terms are not like pieces of plastic that can be made to bend at will to suit a particular need. McGrath reasons that the Reformers, in proclaiming the doctrine of justification in legal terms, were drawing upon the 'experiences, hopes, and fears of their own day and age.' The doctrine of justification, he states, must be 'liberated' from 'the forms of theological expression used in the sixteenth century'.[35]

On the contrary, in using legal terminology the Reformers were being more faithful to Paul than medieval or modern scholarship. McGrath, one feels, has also been too much influenced by the latest trends in Pauline scholarship which see justification in relational rather than legal terms.[36] What is more, his argument that a term like 'justification' should be allowed to evolve in a way similar to the word 'atonement' is not sound. 'Justification', unlike the word 'atonement', has already had a long history of fierce debate in the church over its precise meaning. It must also be pointed out that there is a biblical *doctrine* of justification not merely a biblical *concept*. We need to preach this biblical doctrine in as pure a way as we can, working hard at showing its relevance and importance without compromising its meaning.

McGrath's definition of justification using transformational language reminds us of Rome's position. He has, as we have seen above, described the Council of Trent's definition of justification as 'brilliant'. In an article in the *Evangelical Quarterly* he presents a definition that is very similar. His doctrine of justification as distinct from the Pauline doctrine is put in these terms: 'We are dealing with the turning of the godless man against his godlessness; with his transformation from man without God to man with God, for God, and before God; with his transition from *homo peccator* [sinful man] to *homo iustus* [righteous man]; with his transition from nature to grace.'[37] As a statement concerning conversion the definition is fine and cannot be faulted, but as a definition of justification it is unbiblical and agreeable to Rome. It merges regeneration, justification and sanctification and opens the door to all the disagreeable features of Rome's religion.

As he draws attention to the strengths and weaknesses of both the Lutheran-Roman Catholic and the Anglican-Roman Catholic statements of agreement, McGrath's sympathies lie clearly with the former document. This is so not only because it treats the subject in a more detailed and scholarly fashion and does not, like ARCIC II, gloss over the difficulties, but because it takes an existential approach to theological truth. ARCIC II, on the other hand, is criticized for its propositional approach.

In the Lutheran-Roman statement, Protestant and Roman views of justification are recognised as contradictory at a propositional level, but accepted as complementary at an existential level. In other words, the Protestant view of an imputed righteousness and the opposing Roman view of an imparted righteousness are affirming in their own separate ways that 'it is God in Christ alone whom believers ultimately trust'.[38] ARCIC II, however, in gently conceding that the Reformers were correct on the forensic meaning of the verb 'to justify', puts itself on a collision course with Trent. The previous document avoids such confrontation. It does not say one is right and the other wrong. Neither does it underestimate the differences or speak of accepting the two contradictory statements as saying the same thing, which, clearly, they are not at the propositional level. What the document does is to look beyond what each opposing view is saying (at the propositional level) for a more basic insight common to both (at the existential level). The heart of the division between Rome and the Reformers is thus resolved by suggesting that both positions are legitimate ways of drawing attention to the same essential idea of God's saving work in Christ. This is the approach which McGrath seems to favour in order to get agreement on justification. Whichever view is more faithful to Scripture is not the final concern. The basic idea is the same: 'something happens that initiates a creative encounter' through which a person is forgiven and renewed.[39]

A noticeable anti-propositional attitude has begun to creep into modern evangelicalism. Anthony Thiselton, for instance, goes so far as to regard 'propositional' as an unfortunate term which 'I would like to see banned from discussion as a chameleon word'.[40] If this is the case, then it would mean, as Christopher Bennett crisply puts it, 'the death of proper doctrinal definition, discussion and debate'.[41] If we cannot speak in propositional terms then it means we cannot define anything or say that anything is wrong. We are back with Alice in Wonderland and any statement can mean what you want it to mean.

McGrath's opinion of the World Council of Churches as a 'discredited and outmoded' organization is not an indication that he has no time for ecumenism. That will be obvious from what has already been said. His sympathies lie, however, with the more 'unofficial' efforts. He reports on the increasing numbers of individual Roman Catholics who 'are being drawn to evangelicalism *while generally remaining publicly loyal to their church.*'[42] He expects this 'unofficial' ecumenism to grow in extent and influence and, although he is careful to add that he is merely reporting not defending or criticising, he seems to favour evangelicals and Roman Catholics joining ranks. He writes, 'Whatever the differences between evangelicals and Catholics may be - and these differences should neither be denied nor underplayed - the possibility that the two groups could form a coalition working for doctrinal orthodoxy and moral renewal at every level of society is inviting.'[43]

Concerning his own views on unity with Rome, Dr. McGrath is very careful not to give too much away. However, his desire to see justification develop a meaning which goes beyond the biblical usage certainly leads him to look favourably at those who search for a basic idea common to both Protestant and Roman positions on justification. The trouble is that the preciseness of the biblical teaching on the subject, so clearly perceived by the Reformers, is in danger of being lost. This is something which cannot be allowed to happen: the essence of the gospel is at stake. We need to be on our guard lest some from a new generation of evangelical scholars, who are highly respected and doubtless with the best of motives, should imperceptibly move us away from the biblical doctrine of justification rediscovered by the Reformers.

Notes

1. The statement is published by R. J. Neuhaus' New York City-based organization, 'Religion and Public Life'. A critical review of the statement is found in the *Modern Reformation* magazine published by 'Christians United for Reformation'.

2. Cf. *Christianity Today*, March 6, 1995, pp. 52-53, 'Evangelicals Clarify Accord with Catholics'.

3. ibid. p. 53.

4. Cf. *Chrsitianity Today*, December 12, 1994, pp. 34f.

5. K. S. Kantzer, 'Should Roman Catholics and Evangelicals Join Ranks?', *Christianity Today*, July 18, 1994, p. 17.

6. Cf. J. Armstrong (editor), *Roman Catholicism*, Moody, 1994, pp. 220-222. Also P. Madrid (editor), *Surprised by Truth: Eleven Converts give the Biblical and Historical Reasons for becoming Catholic*, Basilica Press, 1994.

7. Cf. J. H. Gerstner, 'Rome NOT Home', in *Justification by Faith Alone* (editor D. Kistler), Soli Deo Gloria, 1995, pp. 176-177, 182 concerning Scott Hahn a former Presbyterian educated at Gordon-Conwell who has defected to Rome.

8. J. Armstrong, *Roman Catholicism*, p. 317.

9. Quoted in *Christianity Today*, May 16, 1994, 'Interfaith Accord. Evangelicals, Catholics Pursue New Cooperation.'

10. Cf. *Christianity Today*, November 14, 1994, p. 136, 'Why Catholics are Allies'.

11. *Christianity Today*, December 12, 1994, p. 37.

12. *Justification by Faith. Lutherans and Catholics in Dialogue VII*, Augsburg Publishing House, 1985.

13. *ibid*. p. 49.

14. *ibid*. p. 16.

15. *ibid*. p. 72.

16. A. E. McGrath, *ARCIC II and Justification: an Evangelical Anglican Assessment of 'Salvation and the Church'*, Latimer Studies 26, 1987, p. 34; 'What shall we make of Ecumenism?', in J. Armstrong, *Roman Catholicism*, p. 207.

17. Latimer Studies p. 35.

18. *Salvation and the Church: An Agreed Statement by the Second Anglican-Roman Catholic International Commission*, Catholic Truth Society and Church House Publishing, 1987.

19. Latimer Studies p. 44.

20. H. R. Jones in *Evangel*, Summer 1987, 'Five Views of ARCIC II', p. 15.

21. Cf. D. Peterson, *Possessed By God: A New Testament Theology of Sanctification and Holiness*, Apollos/IVP, 1995, pp. 40-47.

22. H. R. Jones, *Gospel and Church*, Evangelical Press of Wales, 1989, p. 99. In another agreed Common Statement (1995), this time between representatives of the Anglican and Lutheran churches across northern Europe, the following confession is made: 'We share a common understanding of God's justifying grace, i.e. that we are accounted righteous and are made righteous before God only by grace through faith because of the merits of our Lord Jesus Christ, and not on account of our works or merits....' *What We Agree In Faith* para. 32c quoted in *Ecumenical Digest*, Summer 1995, British Evangelical Council. Here again, justification and sanctification are merged.

23. J. H. Newman, *Lectures on Justification*, Longmans & Green, 1874, pp. 87-89, 109-111; H. Küng, *Justification*, Burns & Oats, 1981, pp. 212-213.

24. Quoted by H. R. Jones, *Gospel and Church*, p. 102.

25. *The Times*, March 21, 1987.

26. J. Charley, *Evangel*, Summer 1987, 'Five Views of ARCIC II', pp. 9, 11.

27. A. E. McGrath, *Iustitia Dei: a history of the Christian doctrine of justification*, Vol.1, Cambridge, 1986, pp. 2-3.

28. A. McGrath, 'The Article by which the Church stands or falls', *Evangelical*

Quarterly Vol.58, p. 211.

29. 'Canons and Decrees of the Council of Trent', Sixth Session, chapter IV, in *Creeds of the Church*, J. H. Leith (editor), pp. 409-410.

30. A. E. McGrath, *Justification by Faith. What it means to us today*, Academie/ Zondervan, 1988, pp. 10-17.

31. *ibid.* pp.142-147; cf. also McGrath in the *Evangelical Quarterly* Vol.58, p. 211.

32. McGrath, *Justification by Faith*, p. 92.

33. *ibid.* p. 113.

34. *ibid.* p. 117.

35. *ibid.* p. 10-12.

36. Cf. 'Righteousness, Righteousness of God' in *Dictionary of Paul and his Letters*, G. F. Hawthorne, R. P. Martin, D. G. Reid (editors), IVP, 1993, pp. 834-837. Also D. Moody, *The Word of Truth*, Eerdmans, 1981, pp. 325-328. 'A return to biblical exegesis requires a translation that denotes relationship rather than legalistic declaration' p. 326.

37. McGrath in the *Evangelical Quarterly* Vol.58, p. 211; also cf. *Iustitia Dei*: p. 2.

38. *Justification by Faith. Lutherans and Catholics in Dialogue VII*, §158, p.72.

39. Latimer Studies 26, p.142.

40. A. C. Thiselton, 'Authority and Hermeneutics: Some Proposals for a More Creative Agenda' in *A Pathway into the Holy Scripture*, eds. P. E. Satterthwaite and D. F. Wright, Eerdmans, 1994.

41. C. J. L. Bennett, 'Justification and ARCIC II' in *The Banner of Truth* 297, June 1988, p.11.

42. A. McGrath, *Evangelicalism and the Future of Christianity*, Hodder & Stoughton, 1994, p. 182.

43. *Christianity Today*, Dec.1994, p. 33.

Modern Revision

9 The Wright Position

Some evangelical scholars are of the opinion that all who have gone before them have, in varying degrees, misread the New Testament concerning the whole issue of justification. In particular, they claim that neither the Protestant nor the Roman understanding is fair to the apostle Paul's teaching on the subject.

One of these evangelicals is Dr. N. T. Wright, a leading New Testament scholar, who has taught at Cambridge, McGill and Oxford universities and is now Dean of Lichfield cathedral. He is a prolific writer and can ably communicate his views both at a popular and academic level. His doctoral thesis at Oxford (1980) was entitled *The Messiah & the People of God. A Study of Pauline Theology with Particular Reference to the Argument of the Epistle to the Romans.* His first significant piece on justification came to public attention in 1980 in a Fount paperback entitled *The Great Acquittal* which was edited by Gavin Reid. The chapter by Tom Wright was headed 'Justification: The Biblical Basis & its Relevance for Contemporary Evangelicalism'. Prior to that, a lecture that he gave to the Tyndale Fellowship was published in the *Tyndale Bulletin 29*, (1978) entitled 'The Paul of History & the Apostle of Faith'. These two writings contain the substance of his thinking on justification. Since then he has expressed his views on the subject in two important lectures: one in 1987 at the Latimer House Open Day lecture in Oxford, *Justification in the NT and in ARCIC II*; and the other, the 1994 Tyndale Biblical Theology Lecture, 'Justification by Faith: Can we get it right now?' In addition, the *New Dictionary of Theology*, edited by Ferguson & Wright (1988), has articles by him on 'Justification' and 'Righteousness'. More recent scholarly works include a collection of essays under the heading *The Climax of the*

Covenant (1991) and a series of volumes entitled *The NT & the People of God.*[1]

What is Wright's view of justification? He would agree with McGrath that the church has developed an understanding of justification that is different from the biblical idea (see previous chapter). But unlike McGrath, he criticises the way in which the biblical concept has been developed. According to Wright, the Pauline texts have been misused by later generations in order to support the church's thinking. His great desire is to see the church get back to the biblical understanding of the term as he perceives it. We shall set out his position under the following headings:

First Century Judaism

According to Wright we shall not understand Paul and justification until we appreciate the first century Jewish world. Contrary to popular and former scholarly opinion, Wright believes that it is wrong to think of Judaism in Paul's day as a legalistic religion in which the Jew tried to earn righteousness and merit God's favour by good works. The Jews thought of themselves as God's people, members of a covenant community. God, in his love, had chosen their forefathers to be a special holy nation, had given them his law, and had provided the means of atonement for their sins through the sacrificial system. It did not look in the first century as if they were God's people and Wright claims that Jews of that time still thought of themselves as living under the curse of exile. They were, therefore, looking to God to vindicate his oppressed people on the judgment day.[2]

Actually, justification had a present as well as a future dimension for the Jew. From his researches Wright argues that present justification was a secret thing and depended on remaining true to the covenant community. Future justification would be public and consist of vindication and victory for the community. It was anticipated in the present by those who were loyal to the covenant. This did not mean that the faithful Jew had to keep the law completely in order to be vindicated. If he sinned then atonement, cleansing and forgiveness were offered through the various rituals set out in the law. Both future and present justification depended on 'the divine covenant faithfulness'.[3]

Wright goes on to add that the debates within the Judaism of the day focussed on who exactly would be vindicated in the age to come. The big question was 'What are the badges of membership that mark one out in the group that is to be saved, vindicated, raised to life (in the case of members already dead) or exalted to power (in the case of those still alive)?' Each rival group within Judaism, whether Pharisees, Essenes, Zealots, etc., had its own interpretation of what true covenant membership involved and therefore of who would be justified on the last day. They all held to the law but each group had its distinctives, and these distinctives, such as loyalty to community rules for the Essenes or keeping the law according to the tradition of the elders among the Pharisees, became the important markers for group members to demonstrate covenant membership and to be assured of arriving safely in the new world to be ushered in by God.[4]

The conclusion which Wright advances is that for first century Judaism justification in the present is all about showing in advance who belongs to the covenant community before the end comes. 'Covenant membership in the present was the guarantee (more or less) of "salvation" in the future.' Belonging to one of the sects within Judaism and maintaining valid membership of it became the important thing. The justification to come, 'will consist of the victory of the sect'.[5]

Paul's criticism of Judaism

From what has been said above, it follows, according to Tom Wright, that Paul is not attacking Judaism because it is legalistic. Wright believes that Paul is against Israel boasting in her national superiority and of attempting 'to confine grace to one race'. Israel is wrong and missing out because she is pursuing the law in the wrong way. Paul's criticism of Israel is not that she is treating the law as a means of salvation or to earn merit, but as a charter of automatic national privilege. She is guilty of the idolatry of national privilege.[6] The righteousness that Paul criticises in Romans 2:17-29, 9:30-10:13, Galatians 2-4 and Philippians 3:1-9 is not self-righteousness (i.e. 'legalism' or 'works-righteousness') but what he calls 'national righteousness', 'the belief that fleshly Jewish descent guarantees membership of God's true covenant people'. When Paul charges the Jews with boasting, he is not accusing them of being legalists who boast that they have kept the law in order to gain favour with God. They are boasting, rather, in the fact that *they* have God's law. Possessing the law and doing it indicates that they are God's chosen people. 'For the Jew, possession of the law is three parts of salvation: and circumcision functions not as a ritualist's outward show but as a badge of national privilege.'[7]

Taking Romans 2:17-29 as one example of Paul's criticism of the Judaism '*as its advocates present it*', Wright makes four brief points. 'First, Paul's basic charge against the Jews is that of boasting.' But it is not the boast of a legalist. They are boasting in God (v. 17) claiming that God is the God of the Jews only and not of the Gentiles (cf. 3:29-30). They are also boasting in the law (v. 23), not because they are trying to keep it to earn salvation, but because possession of the law marks them out as members of the chosen people. Secondly, Paul accuses them not of legalism but of sin, of breaking the law. Thirdly, Paul does not speak against the law itself, for it is actually God's law (cf. ch. 7). 'Paul has not a word to say against the law itself, but only against its abuse - and its abuse is not legalism but "national righteousness", the attempt to use the fact that God has entrusted the Jews with his oracles (compare 3:2) as a foundation for permanent and automatic Jewish privilege' (compare 3:27-31). Finally, 'Paul's attack on Jewish trust in the law and circumcision as badges of national privilege does not abolish the idea of the "true circumcision" which keeps the law from the heart'. The last verses of Romans chapter 2 present in outline Paul's 'theology of the church as the true Israel, the people of God'.[8]

Justification, then, according to Wright, is to be seen as a polemical doctrine whose target is not the usual Lutheran one of the legalist trying to get right with God through keeping the law, but the Pauline one of the proud nationalist. Justification by faith declares that the way is open for all, not just Jews, to be members of the family of God.[9]

Law and Works of the law

Wright understands the term 'law', when used by the apostle Paul, not as an abstract generalized entity, but as a reference to the Mosaic law (Torah), given to Jews and Jews only, which relates to Gentiles simply in that it forms a barrier to keep them out of the covenant. In Colossians 2:14 he takes the 'written code' to stand for the Mosaic law which stood over-against Jews and Gentiles in different ways. 'In Paul's view, it shut *up* the Jews under sin and shut *out* the Gentiles from the hope and promise of membership in God's people.'[10] According to Wright, Paul considers that the law was given to the nation Israel in order to convict her of sin, Adam's sin. The purpose of this was 'that Israel should be cast away in order that the world might be redeemed'.[11] Christ is 'the secret goal' of the law so that Israel's rejection of Christ and her abuse of the law were one and the same thing. Israel's rejection of Jesus as Messiah is the logical outworking of her misuse of the Torah by treating it as a charter of national privilege. The law itself is a good thing. It is not abolished because it was a bad thing, but now that it has reached its goal in Christ its reign is ended. In a paradoxical way the law is still 'the boundary marker of covenant membership' ('the righteousness that is by the law', Romans 10:5), for it is fulfilled not, as the Jews thought, by the boundary markers which kept Jews separate from Gentiles but by faith. The law is fulfilled 'when Christ is preached and believed'.[12]

Paul's polemic against "works of the law", Wright argues, 'is not directed against those who attempted to *earn* covenant membership through keeping the Jewish law (such people do not seem to have existed in the 1st century) but against those who sought to *demonstrate* their membership in the covenant through obeying the Jewish law.'[13] On this understanding, when Paul uses the phrase 'works of the law' he is not thinking of legalistic works to gain merit and salvation but of those aspects of the law that were done to clearly demonstrate evidence of membership in the covenant ('doing the things that mark Israel out') and to keep 'Jews separate from Gentiles'. These 'works of the law' or 'badges' included such items as the Sabbath, dietary laws and circumcision.[14]

The curse connected with those doing the works of the law, is the curse of exile/death. In Deuteronomy the covenant presents blessing/life or curse/death. It also shows that Israel will make the wrong choice and will therefore suffer the final curse, that of exile (Deuteronomy 27-29). Deuteronomy 30 then speaks of hope and restoration after exile. The Jews, according to Wright, still considered themselves to be in exile because they were under foreign domination. Their return from Babylon had not brought about that 'independence and prosperity which the prophets had foretold'.[15] They were looking for the end of the exile in terms of 'a cleansed Land, a rebuilt Temple, an intensified Torah.' For Paul the exile had come 'to its cataclysmic end when Jesus, Israel's representative Messiah, died outside Jerusalem, bearing the curse, which consisted of exile at the hands of the pagans'.[16] For Gentile believers to embrace the law (Torah), would mean embracing Israel's national way of life. But because Israel as a nation is under the curse for her failure as a nation to keep the Torah, all who come under the Torah now are under this national curse.

Paul's argument in Galatians and Romans

Before proceeding further, it will help at this point to have some idea of Wright's overall view of Galatians and Romans. At the start it is important to bear in mind that he considers both letters to be dealing not with individual sin and salvation but with Jews and Gentiles as groups of people and with the big issue concerning who are the people of God. 'It is a measure of how far the church has travelled from Paul's vision that Romans has often been read as a book about individual salvation rather than as a treatise on the nature of the people of God.'[17] Secondly, the books are not written to oppose legalism. 'The real problem is not "legalism" as usually conceived within traditional Protestant theology, but rather the question of whether one has to become a Jew in order to belong to the people of God'.[18]

What then is the purpose of these two books according to Wright? Galatians is written to convince converted pagans that they have nothing to gain by becoming Jews. Romans, on the other hand, is written to convince Christians from a mixed background that they do indeed inherit all the blessings of Israel yet at the same time to warn them not to lapse into anti-Semitism. While the issue in Galatians is how to avoid the risk of embracing Judaism, what Wright terms 'philo-

Judaism' (i.e. a love for the Jewish religion), in Romans the issue is how to avoid the risk of 'anti-Judaism'.[19] Instead of being tempted toward Judaism these Roman ex-proselytes of Judaism were thankful for being relieved of the burden of the Mosaic law, were in danger of rejoicing in its death and of thinking that Christianity was for non-Jews.

The message of Galatians, according to Wright, is that the law brings the curse because Israel as a nation has not kept it. 'I do not mean by this that individual Jews do not keep it fully...Rather, Israel as a whole has failed in her task of being the light to the nations, of being the seed of Abraham through whom the nations of the world would be blessed'.[20] The curse of the law, as was pointed out in the previous section, means the death of exile. Individual Jews who failed to keep the law did not need 'to languish for long under the awful threat of either exclusion from the covenant people or, for that matter, eternal damnation'.[21] Remedy lay in repentance and the whole ceremonial system which God in his grace had provided. Because the nation of Israel has failed to keep the perfect law, the law cannot be the means through which she can retain membership of the covenant or be the means of bringing blessing to the Gentiles. This is what is meant in Galatians 2:16 where Paul writes, 'by observing the law no-one will be justified' (i.e. reckoned among God's people). Paul also argues that the Old Testament itself, using Genesis 15:6 and Habakkuk 2:4 alongside of Leviticus and Deuteronomy, indicates that God had in mind all along that faith not the law would accomplish the task of marking out the covenant family of God. 'Clearly no-one is justified (reckoned within the covenant family) before God by the law, because "the righteous will live by faith"' (Galatians 3:11).[22]

How then can the blessing of Abraham come to Jews when they are under the curse of the law or to Gentiles when those responsible for bringing the blessing have failed? The answer lies in the death of Jesus the Messiah. He, as Israel's representative, has taken on himself Israel's curse and exhausted it (Galatians 3:13-14). Jesus died 'as the King of the Jews, at the hands of the Romans whose oppression of Israel is the present, and climactic, form of the curse of exile itself'. The crucifixion of the Messiah is 'the *quintessence of* the curse of exile, and its climactic act'.[23] So the context demands, according to Wright, that the first person plurals in the verse 'Christ redeemed us from the curse of the law by becoming a curse for us' (Galatians 3:13), refers to Jewish people only. It is not a general statement concerning the atonement applicable to all who belong to Christ.[24] The same is true of Galatians 2:19-20. Paul is not seeking to draw attention to his own 'experience'. The first person singular references concern Israel. It is 'Paul's theological, not psychological, autobiography' that is included in this picture.[25]

As for Romans, Wright believes the apostle is concerned that the church understands the theology of his missionary endeavours. Paul wants to make Rome a base for missionary work in the west, much as he had originally used Antioch in the east, and therefore it is essential that he has their full support. Wright suggests that the situation in Rome is the mirror-image of what he met in Antioch. The church in that city had been tempted to keep the distinctions between Jew and Gentile. There was an 'inner-circle' of Jewish Christians who were urging Gentile believers to get circumcised in order to join them. In Rome, Paul is worried lest a largely Gentile church which is 'relishing its status as the true people of God' will have no interest in ethnic Jews, and will not only regard those who believe as second-class members of the church, but those outside the church as beyond hope. So, according to Wright, Paul argues for the total equality of Jew and Gentile within the church and a mission to Gentiles that would always include Jews within its scope.[26]

The gospel reveals God's faithfulness to his covenant promises to Abraham. 'God is faithful in calling Gentiles and Jews alike, on the basis of faith in the crucified and risen Jesus Christ, into true membership of Abraham's family'.[27] The family of Abraham is defined by faith in Jesus Christ (Romans 3:21-4:25). 'Over against the Jewish exclusivism attacked in Romans 2:17ff, stands the Christian assurance of Romans 5:1-11: *we* (the worldwide, believing, missionary church) boast in God through our Lord Jesus Christ, through whom we have received the reconciliation.'[28] The Roman church was a 'mirror opposite of the Galatian situation'. It consisted largely of ex-proselytes who were 'thankful to be relieved of the burden of Torah - and who were in danger of rejoicing too happily over its apparent demise'.[29] Paul therefore defends the Torah in chapter 7 and attacks anti-semitism in chapter 11. Romans 7:13-25, like Galatians 2:19-20, is not Paul's own personal experience but a reference to Israel. 'Sin has now been concentrated in Israel.'[30] Wright claims that the Torah has 'the divinely intended function of drawing sin on to Israel, magnifying it precisely within the people of God (7:13-20)', in order that in God's purposes it might be 'drawn on to Israel's representative and so dealt with on the cross (8:3)'.[31] The death of Jesus the Messiah at the hands of pagans 'lies at the heart of the revelation of God's covenant faithfulness and justice in 3:21ff.' He is 'the climax of the covenant'. The cross brings to an end 'Jewish national privilege' as well as 'the process of concentrating *sin* within Israel'. It also means that he has fulfilled God's purpose for Israel so that the Gentiles can be welcomed into the covenant family.[32]

There is, of course, more that could be added, but enough has been given to show the drift of Wright's position concerning these two Pauline epistles. To his mind it is clear that Romans and Galatians have been misread down the centuries! Paul's argument in both is not so much about how the individual is put right with God. It is much more about who belongs to the covenant community. Rather than being treatises about individual salvation, they are books about the nature of the people of God.

Justification/Righteousness

Wright sees justification as a legal term but, as most scholars today agree, it is Hebrew lawcourt imagery that provides the setting for its understanding. It is a declaration of status before the court that a person is in the right. The standard of judgment in the Old Testament is the law of God. But the law in the Old Testament is connected to God's covenant with his people Israel. Thus the judge who pronounces the person in the right, i.e. 'righteous', does so according to the standard of the covenant law of God. In God's dealings with Israel, for God to act righteously means that he acts according to the covenant he made with them. God's righteousness is God's faithfulness to his covenant. For Judaism at the time of Jesus, to have righteousness meant to belong to the covenant and to have the law (Torah) and to wait in hope for God finally to vindicate or justify them in the sight of their enemies that they really are God's people. The scandal of the cross is that it puts an end to all this. Galatians 2:21 is translated: 'If covenant membership (i.e. 'righteousness') were through the Torah, Christ died in vain.'[33]

It is important to Wright's whole thesis that the 'righteous' word group is 'best rendered in terms of "membership within the covenant."'[34] 'Righteousness' is a covenantal word. God's righteousness is not the medieval idea of God's distributive justice 'in which he rewards virtue and punishes vice' and which Luther found so terrifying. 'Luther's alternative...was in some ways equally misleading', for it 'placed greater emphasis upon the status of the human being'. God's righteousness is his faithfulness to the covenant. It is what God is doing to fulfil his covenant. His people's righteousness is covenant member status given by God, 'with all the overtones of appropriate behaviour'.[35] Justification is, therefore, God's declaration that certain people are within the covenant. It is a matter of covenant membership. In the context of the gospel 'it is God's declaration, in the present, that those who believe the gospel are in the right, are members of the covenant family'. 'This declaration', says Wright, 'is in turn closely correlated with baptism, in which one becomes a member of that family in its historical life'.[36]

Wright also notes the close link in Paul between justification and resurrection. Resurrection is, as in contemporary Jewish thought, the ultimate 'justification'. 'Those whom God raises from death...are thereby declared to be his covenant people' (cf. Romans 8:11). Present justification is discussed in Romans 3:21-26 and is 'simply the advance announcement' of the future justification spoken of in 2:1-16.[37]

Wright reasons that if the believer's righteousness is his status as a covenant member, there is no need for a verb like 'to impute' (or for that matter 'to impart') to describe how 'one lot of righteousness' gets from A to B. God is not giving his own personal righteousness to the defendant. Justification refers to the status which results when the Judge righteously declares in the defendant's favour. So there is no need for a theology of imputed (Protestant) or imparted (Roman) righteousness. Paul does not use the phrase 'righteousness of Christ', but speaks only of the obedience of Christ, and the faith of Christ.[38] Thus Wright is able to conclude that Romans chapter 8, for instance, 'demonstrates that justification by faith is not a legal fiction, imputing something to man which he does not really possess; nor is it a process, imparting to man a quality he did not have before...Justification is the correct and proper anticipation, in the present, of the righteous verdict which will be delivered on the last day, when death will have swallowed up all that now remains of our sinful nature and when we shall stand before God in the full likeness of his risen and glorified Son'.[39]

The Basis of Justification

Tom Wright declares that the basis of justification is the grace of God given to undeserving sinners. This grace is revealed in God's covenant promises which reach their climax in the work of Jesus Christ and the Spirit. It is because of the work of the Son and the Spirit that God rightly declares Christian believers to be members of the covenant family. Both Christ and the Spirit redefine the people of God.[40]

The question Tom Wright must answer is: how can justification be on the basis of the work of the Son *and* the Spirit?

In relation to the Son, he says that the basis of justification is the representative death and resurrection of Jesus. In his earlier works Wright maintains that justification 'presupposes an objective dealing with sin'.[41] Sin is universal and 'God can only be in covenant with human beings if that sin is dealt with, and this has been achieved by God himself in the death of his Son...Jesus takes on himself the curse which would have prevented God's promised blessing finding fulfilment'. Romans 3:24-26, 5:8-9 and Galatians 3:10-14 are used in support.[42] 'In Gethsemane, and on the cross itself, Jesus obeys the Father's saving purposes by drinking the cup of the wrath of God, so that his people may not drink it'.[43]

In more recent works Wright has spelt out what this means. Jesus is the one who fulfils Israel's vocation. Israel was called to be the light of the world, God's agent in the healing of the world.[44] What Israel failed to be and do, Jesus as Israel's representative accomplishes. Jesus saw

Israel's destiny ending not in final vindication but in doom at the hands of the Romans, as God's judgment on his wayward people unless they repented. In summoning Israel to repent, it was 'not so much of petty individual sins, but of the great national rebellion, against the creator, the covenant God.'[45] Drawing on Jewish apocalyptic belief concerning the great tribulation, Wright shows that Jesus believed himself to be the one to meet the judgment in the place of Israel. He took Israel's dark night of curse and exile and at the same time took the hatred and all the worst that paganism could do.[46] 'The Messiah has come where Israel is, under the Torah's curse (that is what Wright understands by 'under the law' in Galatians 4:4), in order to be not only Israel's representative but Israel's *redeeming* representative...He *is* Israel, going down to death under the curse of the law, and going through that curse to the new covenant life beyond'.[47] He fulfils Israel's destiny and by doing so saves the world. At the same time, Wright argues, paganism's great longing to worship something within this world is fulfilled; it is satisfied in Jesus, a human being who can be worshipped without detracting from the worship of the one true God. He sees the cross as the victory of weakness over strength, love over hatred. It consisted 'in Jesus' allowing evil to do its worst to him...He bore the weight of the world's evil to the end and outlasted it.[48]

Likewise, the resurrection is 'God's declaration that Jesus, and hence his people, are in the right before God' (cf. Romans 4:24-25).[49] The resurrection is restoration after the curse of exile. What God was expected to do for Israel at the end, he did for Jesus. God stepped into history, raised Jesus from the dead and vindicated him above his enemies. He did not act to end the space-time universe but acted in the middle to inaugurate the end time which the people of God were waiting for. So what Israel expected for herself at the end has happened in advance to Jesus as Israel's representative.[50] At another level, the death and resurrection of Christ is a victory over paganism. The resurrection of Jesus, 'functions as the divine proclamation to the whole world that evil has in fact been dealt with'.[51]

And how can justification be also on the basis of the work of the Spirit? Concerning the Spirit, Wright says the basis of justification is faith.

The verdict awaited on the last day is issued in the present on the basis of faith. This faith is the evidence of the work of the Spirit. It is the evidence of a renewed heart, of that true circumcision, which is inward and spiritual, that the person is a Christian and that the believer is already a member of the covenant.[52]

In order to understand Wright's logic concerning faith it is important to remember his definition of justification, that it is God's declaration of membership of God's covenant people. The people of God are now no longer characterised by possessing and doing the law or by membership of the Jewish race, but by faith. Instead of Jewish race with its badges of circumcision, kosher laws, etc. being the sign of membership of the people of God, faith is the sign, the badge. Faith is not a work. It is not what a person must do in order to get into the covenant family. It is the sign that a person is already in. It is the evidence of grace in the heart, evidence of the work of the Spirit, and it is the fulfilment of the law. Faith is described in terms of its object. It is a 'Christ-shaped' faith. This is the boundary-marker now, not Jewish race. True Christian faith is the confession that Jesus is Lord and that God has raised him from the dead. In this sense God justifies on the basis of faith. When God sees faith he rightly declares the believer to be in the right, to be a member of God's covenant family.[53] The 'faith' which is insufficient and which James opposes in 2:19 is 'bare Jewish monotheism'.[54] In order to draw attention to the unique status and nature of the Christian confession which marked off the Christian communities from their pagan and Jewish neighbours, Wright proposes using 'belief' rather than 'faith'. 'It is justification by *belief*, i.e. covenant membership demarcated by that which is believed.'[55]

These are the main points in Tom Wright's reconstruction of Paul's teaching on justification. While not agreeing with him on every detail, there are other well-known scholars who take a similar line. James Dunn, professor of divinity at Durham, does so in his two-volume commentary on Romans.[56] In a little work called *The Justice of God*, Dunn summarizes the new perspective on Paul, which he and Wright have embraced, by calling attention to two assumptions that four centuries of Protestant exposition have made. First, it is assumed that the Judaism of Paul's day is a prime example of a legalistic religion analagous to the medieval church's teaching on merit. Secondly, it is taken for granted that Paul was liberated from a guilt-ridden conscience. Both the idea of meriting salvation and the problem of a guilt-ridden conscience are said to be preoccupations of Western culture.[57]

Don Garlington, a lecturer at the Toronto Baptist Seminary and a former student of James Dunn, has also been influenced by this new perspective. In his survey of Paul's argument in Romans 1:1-3:8 Garlington concludes that 'the mentality against which he argues is not that of a "legalistic" works-righteousness method of salvation, but one which would confine (eschatological) salvation to the members of a specific group - Israel'. Commenting on Romans 9:30-10:13 he writes, 'Israel has preferred to maintain her own righteousness, i.e. a righteousness peculiar to herself (= national righteousness) as defined by the Sinai covenant ... instead of submitting to the righteousness of God in Christ'.[58]

In the following chapter an attempt will be made to assess this modern revision of our understanding of Paul and of Judaism, particularly as most ably presented in the writings N. T. Wright.

Notes

1. 'The Paul of History & the Apostle of Faith' in *Tyndale Bulletin 29* , 1978, pp. 61-88; 'Justification: The Biblical Basis & its Relevance for Contemporary Evangelicalism' in *The Great Acquittal,* ed. Gavin Reid, 1980, pp. 13-37; 'Justification in the NT and in ARCIC II', Latimer House Open Day Lecture, 1987, (Tape Recording); 'Justification' & 'Righteousness' in *The New Dictionary of Theology*, eds. Ferguson & Wright, IVP, 1988; *The Climax of the Covenant*, T. & T. Clark, 1991; *The NT & the People of God-Vol.I Christian Origins & the Question of God*, SPCK, 1992; 'Justification by Faith: Can we get it right now', Tyndale Lecture, 1994.
Wright uses many of his conclusions in *New Tasks for a Renewed Church,* Hodder & Stoughton, 1992. In the USA it appears as *Bringing the Church to the World,* Bethany House, 1992.

2. *The New Testament & the People of God,* vol.1, SPCK, 1992, p. 270.

3. *ibid.* p. 337.

4. *ibid.* p. 335.

5. *ibid.* pp. 334, 337.

6. *The Climax of the Covenant*, p. 240.

7. 'The Paul of History...', p. 65.

8. *ibid.* p. 82.

9. *ibid.* p. 71.

10. *The Epistles of Paul to the Colossians & Philemon*, Tyndale NT commentaries, (New Series), IVP, 1986, p. 113.

11. *The New Testament and the People of God*, p. 406.

12. ibid. pp. 240-245.

13. Cf. article on 'Justification' in *New Dictionary of Theology*, p. 360.

14. *The Climax of the Covenant*, pp. 150, 240.

15. *ibid.* p. 141.

16. *The New Testament and the People of God*, p. 406. Cf. *The Climax of the Covenant*, pp. 144-148.

17. *The Climax of the Covenant*, p. 252.

18. *ibid.* p. 173.

19. *ibid.* p. 252.

20. *ibid.* p. 155.

21. *ibid.* p. 145.

22. *ibid.* p. 155, 148-150.

23. *ibid.* p. 151.

24. *ibid.* p. 138.

25. *ibid.* p. 197f.

26. *ibid.* p. 234.

27. Wright, 'A new Tübingen school? Ernst Käsemann and his commentary on Romans', *Themelios*, vol. 7, No. 3, 1982, p. 14.

28. Wright, 'Towards a biblical view of universalism', *Themelios*, vol. 4, No. 2, 1979, p. 58.

29. *The Climax of the Covenant*, p. 195.

30. *ibid.* pp. 196-200. Cf. Wright's unpublished thesis *Messiah and the People of God*, pp. 93-96, 145-148 for the view that 'I' in Romans 7:7-25 refers to Israel.

31. *The Climax of the Covenant*, p. 39.

32. *ibid.* p. 242.

33. *ibid.* p. 242.

34. *ibid.* p. 148.

35. *The New Dictionary of Theology*, p. 592. Cf. N. T. Wright, '"That we might become the righteousness of God": Reflections on 2 Corinthians 5:21', in Pauline Theology, Vol. II, ed. D. M. Hay, Augsburg Fortress, 1993, pp. 200-208.

36. *The Climax of the Covenant*, p. 214.

37. *ibid.* p. 203. Wright also shows that resurrection is the restoration or return after the curse of exile. Just as the exile came to an end when Jesus, the representative Messiah, died, so the return from exile began with Jesus, who emerged from the tomb on the third day. Cf. *The New Testament and the People of God*, p. 406.

38. Cf. 'Justification in the NT and in ARCIC II', Latimer House Open Day Lecture 1987 in answer to a question on imputed righteousness (Tape Recording).

39. *The Great Acquittal*, p. 27.

40. ibid. pp. 16-17; *The Climax of the Covenant*, p. 255.

41. *The Great Acquittal*, p. 16.

42 *The New Dictionary of Theology*, p. 359-360.

43. *The Great Acquittal*, p. 16.

44. *Bringing the Church to the World*, Bethany House, 1992, p. 92.

45. *Who was Jesus?*, SPCK, 1992, p. 101.

46. *Who was Jesus?* pp. 100-103; *Bringing the Church to the World*, p. 93.

47. *The Climax of the Covenant*, pp. 151-152.

48. *Bringing the Church to the World*, p. 93.

49. *The New Dictionary of Theology*, p. 360.

50. *The New Testament and the People of God*, p. 406.

51. *Bringing the Church to the World*, p. 102.

52. *The Great Acquittal*, p. 16; *The New Dictionary of Theology*, p. 360.

53. *The Climax of the Covenant*, pp. 36, 167, 244-245.

54. *The New Dictionary of Theology*, p. 360.

55. *The Climax of the Covenant*, pp. 2-3.

56. *Romans*, 2 vols., Word Biblical Commentary, 1988; cf. also *Jesus, Paul and the Law: Studies in Mark and Galatians*, SPCK, 1990.

57. J. D. G. Dunn & A. M. Suggate, *The Justice of God: A fresh look at the old doctrine of justification by faith*, Paternoster Press, 1993, pp. 13-16.

58. D. B. Garlington, 'The Obedience of Faith in the Letter to the Romans. Part II: The Obedience by faith and Judgment by Works', *Westminster Theological Journal* Vol.53, Spring 1991, pp. 56, 63.

10 Is Wright Right?

N. T. Wright is a very stimulating speaker and writer and there is much that can be profitably gleaned from his studies. His interpretation of the Pauline texts is arguably the strongest challenge to the traditional Protestant approach that has yet appeared. Coming from someone who treats Scripture seriously and who claims an evangelical, Reformed attachment, his views need to be considered most carefully. Is he right in his understanding of the situation Paul is addressing? Is he right in his interpretation of Paul's teaching on justification? We will respond to his position under six headings and then point to seven dangers connected with it.

1. First century Judaism and Paul's criticism of it
In his understanding of Palestinian Judaism in the time of Paul, Wright has accepted the main conclusions of E. P. Sanders, whose book *Paul and Palestinian Judaism*, written in 1977, has revolutionized New Testament scholarship.[1] Briefly, Sanders' thesis is that Judaism of the first century was not a religion of 'works'. It is 'completely wrong' to think of Rabbinic religion as a religion of legalistic works-righteousness. He criticises those scholars, like Strack-Billerbeck, who have relied too heavily on fifth century Jewish sources for their view of first century Palestinian Judaism. The material Sanders uses is limited to the early Rabbinic (Tannaitic) literature, the Dead Sea Scrolls, and the Apocryphal and Pseudepigraphical writings. From this background he shows that the Judaism of Paul's day can be described as 'covenantal nomism', which involved obedience to the law within the context of God's gracious covenant. Salvation depended on God's covenant with them, his electing love, his provision of atonement for their sins and his promise of salvation or vindication for all faithful Israelites. Obedience to the law was not a means of winning God's favour but a demonstration of their response to God's grace and served to maintain their covenant relationship. Their keeping of the law showed their distinctiveness as the people of God. Obedience to the law was not thought of as the way of 'getting in' to the covenant relationship but the way of

'staying in' it. Similarly, when Sanders comes to discuss Paul's doctrine of justification by faith he again emphasises that Paul was not attacking Judaism because it was legalistic. This false view of Judaism has arisen, so Sanders argues, as a result of 'the retrojection of the Protestant-Catholic debate into ancient history, with Judaism taking the role of Catholicism and Christianity the role of Lutheranism'.[2]

Wright's assessment of this thesis is very positive: 'Despite some criticisms that have been launched, it seems to me thus far completely correct as a description of first-century Judaism'.[3] James Dunn would utter similar sentiments. Not everyone will share their confidence in accepting Sanders' view of Palestinian Judaism in the time of Paul, although there is enough in what Sanders says to make it plausible. In so far as the Judaism of the Second Temple was in line with the religion of Moses, it certainly was not a religion of merit to earn acceptance before God. The grace of God is evident in the case of Noah, in the call of Abram, and in God's free, unconditional love for Israel (Deuteronomy 7:7-8). There is also evidence from the first century A.D. to support the view that some Jews of the time had an understanding of the grace of God who had chosen Israel to be a special people, and that good works were done out of gratitude and merely demonstrated that they were in the covenant.[4]

This is not, however, the whole story. There are hints outside the New Testament that legalism was more widespread than Sanders would have us believe. Although there is no mention of a 'treasury of merits' or of 'balancing merits against demerits', analogous to the Roman Catholic doctrine of merits, in Palestinian Jewish literature of the period,[5] Professor Don Carson of Trinity Evangelical Divinity School argues that 'it does not appear to be improper to speak of "merit theology"...even if such theology is extended considerably only in later generations'. Sanders 'consistently downplays the strength of the merit theology which the rabbis do accept'.[6] It is also clear, even from what Sanders says, that although entry into the covenant was by grace, 'staying in' and attaining the life of the world to come was strongly based on merit. It is quite clearly a faith plus works theology.[7] It is against such Jewish ideas that Paul maintains that 'a man is justified by faith apart from observing the law' (Romans 3:28). He also insists that not only 'getting in' but 'staying in' is all of grace and none of merit, 'Are you so foolish? After beginning with the Spirit, are you now trying to attain your goal by human effort?' (Galatians 3:3). In Romans 5:2 Paul shows that those who are 'in' continue to stand in grace. As R. H. Gundry concludes, 'For Paul, then, getting in and staying in are covered by the seamless robe of faith as opposed to works, with the result that works come in as evidential rather than instrumental'.[8]

Carson also criticises Sanders for failing 'to come to grips with the diluted value' of such words as 'grace' and 'mercy' in inter-testamental literature. Grace is often in response to merit rather than being free and unconditional. He proves his point with many examples from the same Jewish sources that Sanders uses. These often say that God chooses Abraham and other saints of the period because they are more worthy than others. In the literature of the rabbis 'there is an increasing dependence on personal merit as an approach to God' and again Abraham is singled out as one whose merits are especially powerful.[9] When Israel sinned in the desert by worshipping the golden calf, it was the merits of the Patriarchs which saved them, according to the rabbis. It was only when Moses prayed 'Remember your servants Abraham, Isaac and Jacob' (Exodus 32:13) that God listened and they were not exterminated. [10]

It is true that the Qumran community held a strong belief in divine predestination and the grace of God. This did not prevent them, however, from believing that good works possessed atoning efficacy and helped toward their religious standing. Mark Seifrid, Assistant Professor of New Testament Interpretation at the Southern Baptist Theological Seminary, Louisville, following the initial work done by his teacher Don Carson, has examined carefully the evidence of the Qumran Scrolls in Cave One[11] and comments that 'One could only be clean from sin by belonging to the community and observing their strict regulations'.[12] The yearly examination and ranking of community members according to their 'understanding and deeds' also indicates that 'the community consciously linked religious standing to the deeds of the individual'.[13]

Seifrid has also investigated *The Psalms of Solomon*, a pseude-pigraphal work of eighteen psalms originally dating from between 74 to 40 BC. He concludes that these psalms do not 'include mercy in the face of impiety, but mercy because of piety'.[14] Saving value is attached to the behaviour of the 'pious'. Like the Qumran community 'They too know of an atonement through deeds of repentance...and a saving righteousness gained by works'.[15] Josephus, the first-century Jewish historian, though he often refers to God's grace, regards it as something to be earned by obedience to God. Speaking of Ezra's plans, Josephus comments that the fact 'they turned out well for him was, I think, due to God, who judged him worthy of obtaining his desires because of his goodness and righteousness'.[16] Carson comments: 'Merit theology is sufficiently developed in Josephus to produce statements attributing assorted blessings to the merits of the patriarchs or of Moses.[17]

Sanders himself is forced to admit that the apocryphal book of 4 Ezra is an exception to his thesis. In it, one is faced, as he puts it, with 'a religion of individual self-righteousness...in short, we see an instance in which covenantal nomism has collapsed. All that is left is legalistic perfectionism.'[18] John Stott remarks, 'If one literary example has survived, may there not have been others which did not survive?'[19] Indeed, the evidence that has been presented suggests that there was a much wider acceptance of legalism among Jews of Paul's day than Sanders or Wright admit. In their effort to correct a false view of Judaism they have moved too far in the opposite direction.

Again, it should be remembered that despite official traditional teaching, the natural thinking and practice of the average worshipper is more works than grace orientated. The Council of Trent and the modern Roman Catechism, as we saw in chapter seven, can speak in terms of grace and faith but in reality and practice the Roman religion is one of salvation by works. Even Protestant churches, with their confessional statements emphasising that a person is saved not by his own good works but by grace, have been unable to prevent many of their members from trusting in the value of their own works to put them right with God on the last day.

Neither is the whole business of trying to earn salvation and

Part 3: Modern Revision

acceptance a characteristic of the Western world. Nothing could be further from the truth. There is ample testimony, from all over the world to this natural human tendency to look to one's good works to gain divine approval or to supplement God's work. Sanders, Wright and others are ignoring what the Reformers saw only too clearly. Why should Paul be so insistent that we are not saved by works but by the grace of God if there was no problem in this area of grace versus works? This emphasis by the apostle, it should be noted, is not confined to Romans and Galatians. In Ephesians 2:8-9 he writes, 'it is by grace you have been saved, through faith... not by works'. The Pastoral Epistles reveal the same concern. Timothy is told that God 'has saved us and called us to a holy life - not because of anything we have done but because of his own purpose and grace' (2 Timothy 1:9). Again, Paul reminds Titus that God 'saved us, not because of righteous things we have done, but because of his mercy...justified by his grace' (3:4-7). Such passages are a reminder to Christians not to allow their faith to degenerate to a works orientated religion. Stott makes this perceptive comment concerning Sanders: 'As I have read and pondered his books, I have kept asking myself whether perhaps he knows more about Palestinian Judaism than he does about the human heart.'[20]

If the views of Sanders concerning Palestinian Judaism of the first century are suspect in certain important respects, then it is well to ask of Wright, 'Is it *only* Jewish national pride that Paul is criticising?' 'Is "my own righteousness" in Philippians 3 *only* a statement about Paul's former life as a Jew boasting of his national privileges?' 'Is "their own righteousness" in Romans 10:3 speaking *exclusively* of the Jews priding themselves in their Jewishness which guarantees them covenant membership?' To answer these questions it is necessary to take into account what is said about 'works of the law'.

2. Law and Works of the Law
Wright presents much that is helpful on the subject of the law. A vast amount of scholarly literature has been written about it in recent years and he makes good use of it. We agree that Paul in Galatians and Romans is thinking particularly of the Jewish Torah, the law of

130 The Great Exchange

Moses, not law in general. There are exceptions and Romans 2:14 and Galatians 5:23 are among them, but these only go to highlight the fact that Paul uses law 'more often and most basically of the Mosaic law'.[21]

Douglas Moo, Associate Professor of New Testament at Trinity Evangelical Divinity School, has also argued that 'law' is not used by Paul to mean 'legalism'.[22] What is more, the law is for Paul 'a single indivisible whole'.[23] Paul does not neatly segregate the law into moral, ceremonial and civil. If he had such distinctions in mind, he could have argued in Galatians that circumcision (regularly regarded as being 'ceremonial' by those who use these categories) is now no longer required, for it is not part of the moral law. On the contrary, Paul emphasises the unity of the law (cf. Galatians 5:3 'I declare to every man who lets himself be circumcised that he is required to obey the whole law'.) The threefold distinction between moral, ceremonial and civil law was unknown to the Jews of the first century A.D. It was introduced in the Middle Ages, accepted by Calvin and has been popular in Reformed circles ever since. Useful though it is in systematic theology, it cannot be sustained from the New Testament. This is not to deny that the Bible reveals that some laws are more basic and important and express principles which govern the other laws.[24] But there is no disagreement with Wright that 'law' refers to the Mosaic law, that it is not used to mean 'legalism' and that the common threefold distinction that is made cannot be supported.

It must be admitted that a good deal of Protestant exegesis has taken Galatians 3:15-4:7 to mean that Paul was talking only on a personal level of how an individual comes to faith through first experiencing the effects of the law. The law is a 'schoolmaster' to bring individuals to Christ (3:24). Wright is correct in pointing out that Paul's great concern in this passage is to demonstrate the purpose of the law in salvation history. The apostle speaks of a time before the coming of faith when believers under the old Sinai covenant were held prisoner by the law, but 'now that faith has come we are no longer under the supervision of the law' (3:23, 25). 'Faith' is here used of the coming of Christ. The age of the law gives way to the age of the gospel which fulfils the promise to

Abraham and is associated with that moment in God's plan when he sent his Son (4:4).

Having said this, we need not get into an either/or position. In Galatians, Paul seems to oscillate between the communal and the individual. At one moment he is thinking of the people of God in the context of the history of God's saving purposes (salvation history), at another he has the believer's personal experience in mind. In some passages there may even be two levels of interpretation. F. F. Bruce, for instance, considers that '"the coming of faith" ... may be understood both on the plane of salvation-history and in the personal experience of believers.'[25]

It is also true to say that the keeping of the law certainly marked off the Jew from the Gentile and kept them separate. The law divided humanity. In a brilliant exegesis of Galatians 3:15-20 Wright explains that though the law points to the one family of God it was not possible for the Mosaic law to bring about the one family of God. G. J. Wenham in his commentary on Leviticus has drawn attention to the way the law taught and constantly reminded Israel in major and minor matters of life that she was different, that she was a holy nation set apart for God.[26] The law was meant to keep Israel apart. God ordained that it should separate Israel off from the rest of the nations. But it did not shut out the Gentiles completely in the way that Wright seems to imply. Not only do we find Gentiles becoming members of God's covenant people in the Old Testament period, such as Rahab of Jericho and Ruth the Moabitess, but also Gentiles were converting to Judaism in the Inter-testamental period to become God-fearers and Jewish proselytes (cf. Matthew 23:15; Acts 2:11). Josephus gives an account of the conversion to Judaism of King Izates in which the king was pressed into being circumcised by a certain Jew named Eleazar.[27] Mark Seifrid also notes how Josephus in *Contra Apionem* gives a warm welcome to Gentiles wishing to come into the household of Moses and fails to see how Wright can describe such a welcome as 'going so far and no further'.[28]

It is over the meaning of the Pauline phrase 'the works of the law' (NIV 'observing the law') that disagreement enters. It is quite inadmissible for Wright and Dunn to limit the phrase to certain kinds of works such as the food laws, circumcision and the Sabbath. There is no justification for narrowing the meaning to include only those aspects of the law that clearly separated Jews from Gentiles. This restricted meaning is not a new idea but one advanced by Pelagius and others in the Early Church period and was later roundly condemned by Calvin. 'Let them now babble if they dare, that these statements apply to ceremonies, not to morals. Even schoolboys would hoot at such impudence. Therefore, let us hold as certain that when the ability to justify is denied to the law, these words refer to the whole law.'[29]

It has been convincingly shown by Douglas Moo that 'works of the law' must not be restricted to laws which particularly marked off Israel from others.[30] Neither is it right to confine Paul's phrase to 'works done in the flesh' or to what is termed legalism, although this is nearer the truth.[31] Outside Paul's letters the exact phrase has, to date, only been found in one other source, in a Dead Sea Scroll fragment 'Florilegium' from Qumran cave four, where it signifies obedience to the Mosaic law in general.[32] Other similar expressions have been found in Jewish literature 'all of which' says Moo, 'clearly denote actions done in obedience to the law'. The term 'works' also has essentially the same meaning as 'works of the law' in those polemical passages of Romans (cf. 3:20, 28; 4:2-6; 9:12) and Galatians (cf. 3:10-13). 'Works' are good actions and 'works of the law' are 'simply what we might call "good works" defined in Jewish terms'.[33] Paul's point is that no good works, not even the observing of the Mosaic law, can put the person doing them in a right position before God. He is insisting that no one can be justified by any kind of law-work or human activity, for the simple reason that no one can perform perfect obedience.[34] If the Jews with the best law in the world cannot obtain justification through it no one can.

It seems clear that these 'works' and 'works of the law', which are actions done in obedience to the law, were in some way regarded as meritorious or had some saving value. In Romans Paul stresses, against the Jewish theology of the day, that we are justified not by faith plus works but by faith alone. If Abraham, who lived long before the law separating Israel from the Gentiles was introduced, had been justified by works, then it would have meant that his work deserved payment.

God would have been obliged to reward him. It is merit theology that Paul is attacking in Romans 4:4-5 . Works have no part in justification. God is under no obligation to justify. It is a free, gracious act of God toward those who have no work, who are in fact 'wicked'. There can therefore be no boasting in one's own efforts. To the Galatians who were being tempted to believe that they needed to top up faith with works (i.e. become Jews) in order to be fully justified, Paul tells them in no uncertain terms not to be so foolish. 'All who rely on observing the law are under a curse' (3:10), because no one is able to do all the law to such perfection that merit is gained before God.[35]

Even supposing that 'works of law' do refer especially to those 'boundary markers' or 'badges' such as circumcision, they were not mere national identity markers. A good case has been made out by Seifrid for believing that circumcision was understood in ethical terms.[36] Gentiles who converted to Judaism were seen by Jews to be turning from idols to serve the one true God and their circumcision was the sign of this. The case of King Izates demonstrates this clearly. His circumcision was an indication that he had truly conformed to the Law. Circumcision served not merely as a mark of national identity but of faith and piety.[37]

In addition, some of these so-called 'badges' or evidences of national identity were used to segregate Jew from Jew, depending on the group within Judaism to which they belonged. Rival groups existed in Judaism as Wright himself shows.[38] Each group had its distinctive 'works' which demonstrated their membership of the group. The Qumran writings, for instance, show that only those following the practices characteristic of the community were in the covenant. They are the people of God. It seems clear that the idea of *ethnic* identity markers has given way to *ethical* and religious markers that divide the Qumran community from other Jews. 'Salvation and forgiveness come only to those who have taken on the practices of the community.'[39] Such 'works of the Torah' marked them out as morally superior to other Jews, never mind Gentiles. This is well on the way to being a religion of works as well as of pride in one's own group.

This brings us back to our main contention that, notwithstanding the necessary correctives that have been made by Sanders, Wright and others, Palestinian Judaism was more legalistic than these modern scholars think. What is more, to restrict the definition of 'works of the law' in any way, as Moo comments, '*can* have the effect of opening the door to the possibility of justification by works'. Not even good works done from the right motive or by God's enabling grace can justify a person.[40] At Romans 3:20 Paul concludes that no one will be declared righteous before God on the basis of observing the law, 'rather, through the law we become conscious of sin'. This is, as John Stott puts it, 'the climax of Paul's argument not just against Jewish self-confidence, but against every attempt at self-salvation ... what the law brings is the knowledge of sin, not the forgiveness of sin. In spite of the contemporary fashion of saying that Luther got it wrong, I think he got it right'.[41]

3. Sin

Wright and Dunn reject the idea that Paul lived with an anguished conscience under the law prior to faith in Christ. In this they are following the conclusions of the Lutheran scholar Krister Stendahl who, in an article first published in 1963, criticised the traditional view of the apostle. It had read back into Paul, he argued, the western church's own preoccupation with a guilty conscience. He claims that, unlike Augustine and Luther, Paul had a 'robust conscience' before his conversion, in contrast to the West's 'introspective conscience'.[42]

It may well have been the case, however, that Paul's conscience was dulled by his religious self-satisfaction. He was able to say concerning the righteousness which is in the law that he was blameless. (Philippians 3:6) Like the rich young ruler questioned by Jesus, Paul could have replied that he had kept all ten commandments from his youth upwards. Not until his self-righteousness was specifically challenged did he begin to realise he had a conscience. Many, like Paul before his conversion, thought themselves righteous because they had never had the implications of God's law spelled out to them. When John the Baptist, and later Jesus, came preaching repentance, even people like the Pharisees were stirred in their consciences, some confessing their sins, others remaining stubbornly obstinate.

Again, when people are confronted with the stunning presence of the righteous and holy God they are brought to confess their sinfulness. This was the case with Peter as he suddenly began to appreciate the awesome divine glory of Christ: 'Go away from me, Lord; I am a sinful man!' (Luke 5:8). Likewise, when Isaiah saw the glory of the Son of God he said, 'Woe to me...I am ruined! For I am a man of unclean lips' (6: 1-5). Surely this is what must have happened to the apostle Paul when he came face to face with the risen glorified Lord Jesus Christ on the Damascus road. James Dunn, following the view of Stendahl, sees the Damascus Road experience 'not as a conversion as such, but as a calling - a commissioning ...to take the Gospel to the Gentiles'.[43] But surely it was both: a conversion as well as a commissioning. As he looks back upon that conversion in Philippians 3:3-9 he speaks of it in terms of justification by faith alone in Christ alone putting 'no confidence in the flesh'. In 1 Timothy 1: 12-15 Paul refers not only to his call to be a minister of the gospel but to his conversion and he makes this significant confession in verse fifteen: 'Christ Jesus came into the world to save sinners - of whom I am the worst'.

It is not only national sin that Paul is speaking of in Galatians and Romans but individual human sin. 'We have already made the charge' says Paul in Romans 3:9, 'that Jews and Gentiles alike are all under sin'. That this statement is not to be taken merely in a national sense but as a truth which applies to every individual within each nation is clear from Paul's quotation from the Psalms which immediately follows: 'There is no-one righteous, not even one' (Rom. 3:10).

What is more, the trend by Wright and others to regard Paul's first person references as a stylistic device to mean Israel in passages like Galatians 2:19-20 and Romans 7:7-25 flies in the face of strong evidence to the contrary.[44] When Paul uses 'I' he is generally referring to himself. He might, occasionally, in a short hypothetical construction use the first person where no personal reference is intended, as in Romans 3:5 (first person plural), but never in such a long passage as Romans 7.[45] Dunn, who takes a radically different line to Wright on Romans 7, has to admit that in Romans 7:14-25 some reference to Paul himself cannot be excluded. He comments that the character of the verses as 'personal testimony is too firmly impressed upon the language to be ignored'.[46] We would submit that while the whole passage from verses 7-25 may in a secondary sense be taken to mean the experience of 'everyman' or of Israel, it is first and foremost a reference to Paul himself.

It may be, however, that the tenth commandment concerning covetousness, which Paul draws attention to in Romans 7:7-11, is quoted to emphasise the internal nature of the law and the sinful desires that lurk within the human heart. Paul's pre-conversion conscience was probably not as 'robust' as is suggested. External conformity to the law is one thing but the law on covetousness was a reminder to him of the filthiness of the human heart. Paul later reminds the Colossians of the inward sins of 'lust, evil desires and greed, which is idolatry. Because of these the wrath of God is coming' (3:5-6). Neither the rich young ruler nor Saul of Tarsus would have regarded themselves as idolators. Yet it was this sin of covetousness which was brought to the attention of both the young man and Saul (cf. Mark 10:21-22; Romans 7:7).

In Galatians 2:18 Paul changes from 'we' (meaning Jewish believers like Paul and Peter, cf. 2:15-17) to a hypothetical use of 'I', in which he applies to himself a charge that is really directed against anyone who tries to build up again what they have formerly destroyed. On the other hand, the emphatic 'I' in verse 19 is used representatively of all *believers* including the apostle. F. F. Bruce comments that the emphatic 'I' suggests that Paul 'knew in a special way what it meant to die to law' and certainly by the end of verse 20 'it is difficult not to recognize the intense personal feeling in his words'.[47] To think of Galatians 2:19-20, therefore, as a reference to Israel is imposing a quite unnatural interpretation on to the text.

The sin of the Jew consists not only in boasting of his Jewish national privileges but in self-righteous boasting of his moral superiority. In the parable of the Pharisee and the tax collector it is not a boasting in Jewish ethnic privilege that we see but self-righteous assurance in a moral superiority gained by works of the law as understood according to the tradition of the elders. It is the repentant tax collector, having nothing to plead but God's mercy, who is justified. The Pharisee, with all his religious and social advantages, is not justified. In the Old Testament the righteous are often described as poor and needy sinners. This is quite the opposite to the kind of language used by the Pharisee in the parable and by Saul the Pharisee before his conversion. Paul did not become truly aware of the nature of sin until he met up with the Lord.

Augustine, Luther and every evangelical preacher worthy of the name, have all had a healthy and necessary preoccupation with sin for precisely the same reason as Paul. It is biblical. The Old Testament is full of it and Paul presents a list of verses in Romans 3:10-18 to support what he himself has been proving in Romans 1:18-3:9. John the Baptist and Jesus were constantly drawing Jewish attention to sin, not merely to national sin but to individual human sins which were symptomatic of the sinful nature of the human heart. To those aware of their sin and need Jesus was gentle and called them to him. His harshest comments were kept for those who thought themselves righteous, clean and needing nothing. Unless people are made aware of their sin they will not appreciate their need to be justified by God's grace.

There are passages in the Old Testament ignored by Wright and Dunn which should at least be considered when seeking to interpret those statements by Paul concerning 'one's own righteousness'. The 'righteousnesses' of which Isaiah 64:6 speaks ('all our righteous acts are like filthy rags') are not Jewish ethnic badges: they are all the good deeds they thought they had done. If they were relying on them to demonstrate their covenant membership Isaiah says, 'Forget it!' They are like dirty rags. This is in line with Deuteronomy 9:4-6. God gave Israel the land of Canaan not because of their righteousness or integrity but 'on account of the wickedness of these nations' - the nations that were presently occupying it. Righteousness is here contrasted with wickedness. 'My righteousness' and 'your right-eousness' suggest an attitude of moral and religious superiority which merits some benefit. Such an understanding of these phrases from the Jewish Scriptures provides a much better background to Paul's 'my own righteousness' and 'their own righteousness' than the views expressed by Wright, Dunn and Garlington. 'National righteousness' is not the whole picture or even the most important part of the picture.

4. Curse

As we saw in the last chapter Wright argues that Paul accepted a belief among Jewish writers of the time that the Jewish people were still experiencing the curse of exile as set out in the covenant curses of Deuteronomy 27. If they were still under the curse, this raised the difficulty of how God's promise to Abraham concerning Gentile blessing could ever be fulfilled. In Galatians 3:6-14, where the promise to Abraham and the curses of the covenant are quoted (3:8; 3:10), Paul shows how Christ has resolved the problem. According to Wright, 'the covenant has reached its climax in the death of Messiah'. On this understanding Galatians 3:13 means that Christ has redeemed 'us' Jews who were under the curse. The curse of exile being ended, blessing can now flow to the Gentiles (3:14).

This is certainly a very radical treatment of the passage. Division of opinion does exist over whether the first person plural means all Christians or Jewish Christians,[48] but to suggest that it is a reference to the Jewish nation who are still suffering the curse of exile is quite breath-taking. There are a number of factors which tell against this understanding of the passage.

For one thing, it is a debatable point whether the Jews generally saw themselves as still under the curse of the exile. It seems only to have been a minority view. But even if that were the case, preaching a gospel concerning the crucified Christ now risen who had brought to an end Israel's exile, would hardly have made the cross an offence and an occasion of stumbling for the Jew. The curse which Christ took is first and foremost the wrath of God on account of human sin.

It is not the most natural way of reading the passage. While differences remain as to whether the 'us' in Galatians 3:13 means all Christians or Jewish Christians, there has been general agreement that it refers to Christians. We would go further and point out that the 'we' of verse 14b ('so that by faith we might receive the promise of the Spirit') surely includes the Gentiles of verse 14a ('that the blessing of Abraham might come to the Gentiles through Christ Jesus'). This would suggest that the 'us' in verse 13 has Gentile as well as Jewish believers in mind.

The wider context suggests that the reference in verse 13 is neither to Jews nor to Jewish believers only but to believers generally. In verse 1 Paul commences with a reference to his preaching of the cross and its powerful effects on the Galatians and follows this up in verses 2 to 5 with a reference to their experience of the Spirit. These are the very matters which are brought together again in verses 13 and 14. To bring in a reference to Israel and the curse of exile seems quite out of place.

Besides the quotations from Genesis 12:3 and Deuteronomy 27:26, Paul uses two other verses from the Old Testament, namely, Habakkuk 2:4 and Leviticus 18:5. It is significant that both of them refer to individuals within the nation: 'the righteous' person, the remnant within Israel, and 'the man who does these things'. As Wright correctly observes, a common feature of both quotations is the word 'life', which is 'the chief blessing of the covenant, as death is its chief curse (Deuteronomy 30:15).' The life/death theme at the close of the Pentateuch leads us back to the beginning, to Genesis 2, to the tree of life and the warning that disobedience leads to death. In using these two quotations Paul emphasises that justification is by faith and not by works. It is the one who is righteous by faith who will live. Justification is associated with faith alone. The curse of death is the result of trying to observe the law in order to be justified. No sinful human being can keep the law perfectly. When Paul, in the very next verse declares that 'Christ has redeemed us from the curse of the law, being made a curse for us' (verse 13) it is the curse of death that springs to mind not the curse of exile.

Then again, the quotation in verse 13 from Deuteronomy 21:23 ('Cursed is everyone who is hung on a tree') provides the most natural understanding of the curse in this context. It does not refer to the curse of exile for the nation Israel but to individuals within Israel who are guilty of a capital offence. In the final analysis it then points to Christ who bears the just punishment which all sin deserves. In the words of Ardel Caneday, 'Deuteronomy 21:22-23 prepares for and anticipates Christ's curse bearing upon the cross. The corpse of the covenant-breaker is hung "upon the tree" as a gruesome sign that he is an object of curse. He is suspended between heaven and earth, exposed to the vengeance of God to propitiate his wrath'.[49] The leaders in the sin of Baal Peor were killed and, in accordance with the requirement of Deuteronomy 21:22-23, their bodies exposed 'in broad daylight before the Lord, so that the Lord's fierce anger may turn away from Israel' (Numbers 25:5; cf. also 2 Samuel 21:6-14). Such incidents from the Old Testament anticipate and point forward to the curse that Christ endured on the cross. Other New Testament writers also allude to Deuteronomy 21:23 when they describe the cross as a 'tree' in Acts 5:30; 10:39; 13:29; 1 Peter 2:24. Such passages suggest wide debate between the followers of Jesus and non-Christian Jews over whether one who was 'hung on a tree' in crucifixion, cursed by God, could be the Messiah.

Isaiah is describing this same curse situation in chapter 53 of his prophecy when he writes, 'he was despised, and we esteemed him not...we considered him stricken by God, smitten by him, and afflicted' (vv3-4). Though Isaiah speaks of the exile and the return in chapter forty and elsewhere, that is not how he describes the sufferings of the Servant of the Lord. The people, on account of whose sins he suffered, are those not only from Israel but from 'many nations' (52:15). The Suffering Servant bears the sins of many. 'The Lord has laid on him the iniquity of us all' (53:6). He bears the awful punishment which sin deserves: 'the punishment that brought us peace was upon him' (53: 5). This is the context for understanding the death of Christ and his propitiatory sacrifice in Romans 3:24-25 and Galatians 3:10-13.

If, as Wright expresses it, Messiah comes under the curse of the law in order to be Israel's 'redeeming representative', this leaves us with the impression that in Paul's theology the Messiah does not directly die for the sins of Gentiles. It becomes a secondary issue arising out of Messiah's concern to exhaust the curse on Israel. Ronald Fung, in his criticism of similar views proposed earlier by Duncan and Donaldson, argues that 'the Gentiles must themselves be redeemed from the curse before they can receive the blessing of Abraham.' Though the Gentiles do not possess the Mosaic law, they do have 'the equivalent of the law within their hearts and consciences and are in principle subject to its curse' (cf. Romans 2:12-15).[50]

5. Justification/Righteousness

Recent scholarship generally understands these terms against the background of God's covenantal relationship with his creatures and particularly his chosen people.[51] Wright accepts these findings and has a very simple solution to the problem surrounding the meaning of the terms. He maintains that God's righteousness is his faithfulness to his covenant. His people's righteousness is covenant member status given by God and justification is God's declaration that believers are covenant members. This, as Wright acknowledges, is a controversial point and, in the light of our discussion of the 'right' word group and Paul's use of the terms, it is surely wrong to force every reference into this mould. For instance, the expression 'the righteousness of God' could refer to God's righteous character. This meaning is very suitable in Romans 3:26 and is supported by Douglas Moo, Cranfield and Lloyd-Jones.[52] In Romans 1:17, on the other hand, it can be thought of as God's gift of a right legal status, or God's righteous activity in being faithful to the covenant. Indeed, it may be Paul's short-hand way of including more than one idea. John Stott even suggests that the phrase means at one and the same time God's attribute, activity and gift![53]

Is it an acceptable insight to consider justification in terms of God's declaration of covenant membership? In Galatians and Romans it is certainly true that one of Paul's concerns is to show who belongs to the covenant community. We applaud Dr. Wright for pressing home this point. It is quite another matter to make this the only concern and to define justification in these terms. To do so is to ignore or fail to do justice to other references. Paul speaks not only in a general way of Jew and Gentile together as the children of Abraham and members of the covenant, but in very personal terms of Christ's love for him and of being right with God. Can Wright be allowed to give justification an entirely new meaning simply because this is what he claims it means in the context of the covenant?

It is true, as we have shown in the previous chapter, that Wright mentions the legal background to the term 'justification' and that it is the Hebrew lawcourt scene in particular that is in mind. However, it is a particular aspect of this background, namely the covenant concept, which is used by Wright to understand the Pauline texts. This is not wrong in itself but what happens is that a subtle shift takes place in the meaning of justification whereby the word is no longer associated with that which is right in God's estimation, with God's broken law, with God's justice and the punishment of sinners. All the emphasis falls on covenant community status, on God's pronouncement of a person's legal status within the righteous community. This is not the emphasis in the biblical understanding of God's justification of sinners.

In the final analysis the justification of the ungodly is not about who belongs to the covenant community but about a person's right standing before God. Wright might argue that this is involved when he describes justification as a matter of covenant membership because it is based on the 'representative death and resurrection of Jesus'. He can say in connection with Romans 4:24-25 that the resurrection 'is God's decla-ration that Jesus, and hence his people, are in the right before God.'[54] But that is not what comes across in his neat definitions. We cannot take the important subject of our standing before God for granted. It must be clearly present in any definition of justification. As we have explained in chapter five justification is the declaration of a verdict of not guilty and of being in a right legal position before God. It is significant that no mention is made by Wright of the fact that justifi-cation is the opposite of condemnation. Yet in Romans 5 and 8 this is how we find it described. 'Justify' is used in opposition to 'condemn'. Moreover, righteousness is paralleled with obedience to God's will and standards and unrighteousness with disobedience to God's will. The overwhelming body of scholarly opinion directs us to this conclusion that it refers to a right legal position before God. We concur with Leon Morris in holding that 'justification is in essence a matter of right status or standing in the sight of God, the status which shows that we are accepted with him.'[55]

Membership of God's covenant people then, is not what justification really means. Covenant family membership is, as we shall argue in the final chapter, one of the results of justification along with sonship or adoption which is closely associated with it. Those not condemned and who are in a right position before God through faith in Christ receive the Spirit of sonship, belong to Abraham's descendants, heirs according to the promise and members of the righteous community (Romans 8:14-17; Galatians 3:24, 26-29; 4:4-7).

If then the essence of justification is God's legal pronouncement that those who belong to Christ are righteous in his sight, Wright's dismissal of the doctrine of imputation must be challenged. Justification involves the non-imputation of sin on the one hand, and the imputation of Christ's righteousness on the other. In Romans 4:7-8 Paul quotes Psalm 32:1-2 in which David speaks of the happiness of the person whose sins are forgiven, 'whose sin the Lord will never count against him'. Paul uses this along with the quotation from Genesis 15:6 to argue for a righteousness credited to the believer by God. This righteousness is associated in Romans 5 with the obedience of Christ, an obedience that characterised his whole life and culminated in his death on the cross (5:18-19; Philippians 2:8).

Paul's argument concerns the gift of righteousness by which the believer is justified. The gift is not only the status of being in a right legal position before God but having Christ's moral righteousness credited to the believer. As once we stood in the guilt and sin of Adam so now we stand in the righteousness of Christ. Union with Christ in his life, death, resurrection and ascension is essential for understanding our righteous position before God. It is in Christ that we are forgiven and stand righteous in God's presence.

According to Wright, 2 Corinthians 5:21 has nothing to do with imputed righteousness. Paul's statement that 'in him we might become the righteousness of God' is taken to mean that he has become a new covenant ambassador, a living embodiment of the covenant faithfulness of God. 'He has become, by the Spirit, the incarnation of the covenant faithfulness of God'.[56] As with his interpretation of Galatians 3:13 this is not the most natural and obvious way of understanding the text. Can the verb 'become' bear such a startling meaning as '*becomes* the living embodiment of' or 'incarnation of'? There is no justification for it in the text. In addition, the balance between the two halves of the verse is lost and the full paradoxical nature of the language which Paul is so fond of using, is reduced.

We believe that the Reformers got it right. Here is the great exchange that Luther found so precious. The Lord Jesus who knew no sin became sin for us. Sin was imputed to him. All our transgressions and iniquities were put to his account and he himself received the divine punishment. This was in order that in union with Christ we might not only have a righteous status before God but have placed to our account the moral righteousness of Christ who fulfilled all God's righteous requirements. In 1 Corinthians 1:30 the same thought is presented: Christ Jesus 'has become for us... our righteousness'. Paul again expresses the truth in Philippians 3:9 when he speaks of being found in Christ, 'not having a righteousness of my own that comes from the law, but that which is through faith in Christ - the righteousness that comes from God and is by faith'.[57]

6. Faith

Wright objects to the Reformed position which presents faith as the means or instrument of our justification because, in his view, it merges justification with the atonement and makes faith a luxury.[58] There have been those who have thought in terms of the justification of the elect from eternity, which would have the effect of downplaying the importance of faith, but this is a minority view.[59] One argument often used in support of this notion of eternal justification is to couple it with the justification of Christ in his resurrection (cf. Romans 4:25). But it is misleading to think of the elect being justified in the resurrection of Christ prior to faith and the New Testament does not speak in this way. The elect are not justified until they embrace Christ by faith. This has been the evangelical Protestant position, and thus Wright is criticising not the Reformed position but a distortion of it.

Wright's position moves in the direction of merging justification with regeneration when he speaks of justification on the basis of faith, because God would be justifying on the ground of a change within the sinner. Of course, justification takes place in the context of regeneration: justification is never divorced from regeneration, just as justification is not divorced from sanctification. Nevertheless, as justification must not be confused with sanctification, so justification must not be confused with regeneration. God does not justify sinners on account of the Spirit's work in granting faith.

According to Wright's definition, God would be declaring a person to be in the covenant on the basis of a *fait accompli*. God sees faith which is already an indication of covenant membership and so he pronounces a person justified, i.e. a member of the covenant. This is saying, in effect, that God justifies those who have been justified! There is something nonsensical about such a description of justification. He objects to the idea that justification is about how a person becomes a Christian because as he understands it justification is a declaration that one is already a Christian. In Wright's interpretation, the person has already heard that the crucified and risen Jesus is Lord, has responded by being baptised and has begun to live as a member of Christ's family. Justification becomes a confirmation that one is a Christian. But the apostle goes out of his way to show that God pronounces justified the ungodly and wicked when they look to Christ alone to save them. It is at the point of entry into the Christian life that the pronouncement is made. What is more, justification is never *on the basis of* faith but always *through* or *by* faith. It is important to stress again in the light of what Wright says that God does not justify because he sees evidence of a change in the person. It is through faith, through self-despairing trust in Christ alone that God pronounces us not guilty.

Wright's proposal to use the expression 'justification by belief', which he himself admits will be frowned on by many, is unacceptable and contrary to the biblical evidence. Faith as the badge of new covenant membership is now being defined in terms of assent to a Trinitarian belief. The 'boundary-marker' of the early Christian communities, he argues, is 'the confession which we find in 1 Corinthians 8:6: One God, one Lord'. It is, he suggests, 'a rewriting' of the Jewish confession of faith, the *Shema*, of Deuteronomy 6:4 'Hear, O Israel: The Lord our God, the Lord is one.'[60] The biblical understanding of faith involves not merely an acceptance of a Trinitarian belief but a personal reliance on the person and work of Christ alone. When Paul discusses justification by faith in Romans and Galatians he is at pains to show that it is through faith in the sense of trust that we are justified. God is the one 'who justifies those who have faith in Jesus' (Romans 3:26). 'So we, too, have put our faith in Christ Jesus, that we may be justified by faith in Christ' (Galatians 2:16).

Dangers

There are a number of serious dangers in the approach of Wright, Dunn and other revisionists like them. No doubt they would want to argue that every position has its dangers and to add that they have sought to guard against going down blind alleys. Nevertheless, for the sake of others, especially those who, unlike the scholars we are criticising, have not had the privilege of growing up in an atmosphere where the gospel rediscovered by the Reformers was preached and loved, it is necessary to warn and to pinpoint areas of deep concern.

1. An inadequate view of sin.

There is the danger of not treating sin with the seriousness it deserves. Can Luther's quest for a guilt-free conscience before the good and pure God be dismissed merely as a western preoccupation? Are we not rather in danger of being influenced by an age which dismisses absolute standards of right and wrong and has a very superficial attitude to sin? The emphasis on viewing the law of Moses in the context of the history of salvation, right though that is in itself, is adding to this inadequate view of sin. The law of Moses is also part of the holy Scriptures which are able to make us 'wise for salvation through faith in Christ Jesus' (2 Timothy 3:15). The Old Testament law as preached by Moses, the prophets and the New Testament, and as lived out by our Lord himself, is the means of leading us to Christ by awakening those so-called 'robust' consciences and bringing us to the end of ourselves.

2. Underestimating the human tendency to trust in one's own efforts to gain favour and acceptance with God.

Wright is correct to draw our attention to the issue of 'racialism' and 'nomism'. Paul does attack Jewish dependence on belonging to the race of the Old Testament covenant community (cf. Galatians 4:24-25; Philippians 3:5). The apostle also confronts those who depend on keeping some kind of works for *staying* in after depending on grace for *getting* in ('nomism') as we have seen in Galatians 3:3. Where Wright and others go wrong is in dismissing legalism as an important factor in Judaism of the New Testament period and, as a consequence, failing to show that it was the main issue in Paul's confrontation with the Jews. It must never be forgotten that self-satisfaction and pride in human achievement, using religious devotion to establish a claim on God, is typical of fallen human nature in every generation and in every part of the world despite protestations to the contrary. Reinterpreting the New Testament material to remove the evidence that the Jews thought in this way is, as we have sought to argue, quite inadmissible.

3. Presenting justification more in the context of the church than of salvation.

Instead of the emphasis being placed on the sinner's status before God this newer understanding is making the sinner's acceptance in the church (covenant community) primary. Wright maintains that 'the idea of justification properly belongs not in an individualistic soteriology but in the context of God's affirmation that this or that person is a member of his covenant family.'[61] Indeed, not only justification, but sin and the cross are thought of in terms of the community rather than of the individual. There may be some truth in the allegation that certain branches of evangelicalism have encouraged an individualistic, anti-church mentality. But the pendulum has shifted in the other direction with the stress on the church, and this is again something which Rome finds very acceptable. The individual's standing before God must never be allowed to take second place. Paul was able to write to the Galatians of the Son of God 'who loved me and gave himself for me'.

There is the danger of thinking that the particular group with its badge is the all-important thing. True, Wright would say that his teaching on Christ as our representative guards against such a false view. Nevertheless, it is necessary to give a warning when justification is described in terms of covenant membership and the badge of faith is spoken of as the boundary marker. The whole biblical revelation directs us to understand that the fundamental nature of the human predicament is not a matter of alienation from the group but alienation from God. What is more, sin is rebellion against God and he is right to be angry and to punish sinners. Justification speaks of the divine grace through Christ pronouncing such sinners to be in a right legal position before him. 'The Pauline Gospel has a heavenly horizon in view'.[62]

There needs to be a reassertion of the biblical doctrine of the remnant. The covenant community of the first century represented by the Pharisees and Sadducees despised and rejected Jesus as it had done the true prophets of old. Outcasts like 'the tax collectors and sinners' who repented of their sin and turned to Christ belonged to the true people of God and went home justified. In the sixteenth century 'the covenant community' represented by pope and prelates excommunicated and burned many Protestants, who were, nevertheless, assured that they were right with God. The individual's standing before God is primary and any interpretation which weakens that emphasis must be challenged. This understanding of justification is not individualistic in the way so often associated with modern western secular society. In Mark Seifrid's words, 'Rather than standing in opposition to the corporate dimension of Christianity, the article on justification provides its necessary precondition'.[63]

4. Presenting justification more in relational than judicial terms.
This is probably the most subtle of all the dangers. It arises out of the modern appreciation of justification's covenantal setting. Great stress is placed on viewing the lawcourt language within the context of the Hebrew covenant. This is a helpful insight but it does have its drawbacks in that it can actually underplay the very judicial element it is meant to support. When we think of God's covenant with his people the relational element is uppermost in mind and in that context justification and righteousness are seen primarily as relational words. The legal implications in the word 'justification' are then coloured by the covenantal where the people are collectively described as God's son and

he is their Father, or as God's wife and he is their husband. It is easy therefore to blur the distinction between the Father/son, Husband/wife relationship which God has with his people within the covenant community and the Judge/sinner situation that exists between God and his rebellious creatures. This is something we shall come back to in the final chapter when we consider God our Judge.

At a time when the forensic or judicial dimension is increasingly being dismissed as medieval we need to be on our guard. There is not only a broken relationship, but a *broken law* and a new *legal* position where God is now the Judge and all humanity face him as guilty, condemned sinners. The questions put to Adam and Eve in Eden demanding an account of their disobedience, point to the divine Judge, as do the verdict and sentence that follow. Again, in relation to the impending judgment on Sodom, Abraham pleads, 'Will not the Judge of all the earth do right?' (Genesis 3:9-24; 18:25). God passes judgment on their rebellion and this is followed by punishment.

The biblical truths concerning God's punishment of sinners and the reality of hell emphasise the judicial in a very glaring and awesome way. Justification, therefore, must be viewed against that dark scene. More than a restored relationship is involved. Justification has to do with the removal of God's wrath which hangs over us and our being constituted righteous in his sight. All of which takes place in Christ our representative and substitute who kept the law on our behalf and was punished in our place and thus we are pronounced by the divine Judge to be in a right legal position before him.

5. The new position on justification has no place for the imputed righteousness of Christ's life.

'The righteousness of Christ' is not a Pauline expression according to Wright and so there is no need for a verb such as 'to impute' to describe how one lot of righteousness gets from A to B. This means that such expressions as being clothed in Christ's righteousness about which we sing in our hymns do not, according to these scholars, accurately convey the biblical truth. But the apostle Paul does refer to Christ as 'our righteousness' in 1 Corinthians 1:30 and justification is described in Romans 4:1-13 and 5:17-19 as both the non-imputation of sin and the imputation of righteousness. Though Wright would say it was out of the question, a denial of this truth certainly leaves the door ajar for moralism and legalism to enter with all their accompanying evils.

6. It has the effect of marginalizing the evangelical significance of Christ's death.

The cross and resurrection of Jesus are important in Wright's understanding of justification and he does refer to Christ's substitutionary sacrifice for sinners. However, if justification is defined as covenant membership, the propitiatory nature of Christ's death is no longer seen to be essential. What is more, key verses, such as Galatians 3:13 are being reinterpreted so that they no longer apply as once they did in our understanding of the atonement.

Stephen Travis, Vice-Principal and lecturer in New Testament at St. John's College, Nottingham, has made use of Wright's understanding of Galatians 3:13 in an essay which seeks to prove that Paul did not have a retributive understanding of Christ's death. 'I have argued', says Travis, 'that Paul's understanding of the death of Christ does not include the idea that he bore the retributive punishment for our sins which otherwise would have to be inflicted on us.'[64] This is no isolated case, it is becoming a far too common feature in evangelical scholarly circles to minimize and even to deny Christ's death as a propitiatory sacrifice.[65] All the emphasis lies on expiating sin, none on appeasing the wrath of God. They may believe in substitution but not in propitiation. The modern phraseology often used is 'absorbing sin' and 'outlasting evil'. 'Standing where we stand, he bore the consequences of our alienation from God. In so doing he absorbed and exhausted them, so that they should not fall on us.' Enduring the God-ordained consequences of human sinfulness is 'not the same as to say that he bore our punishment.'[66]

God's justification of sinners is no longer inextricably linked to Christ's death as a propitiatory sacrifice. Yet the only way a righteous God can justify the ungodly without compromising his own righteous character is by the loving act of propitiating his own wrath. He has done this through the sacrifice of His Son who not only represents sinners but stands in their place and takes the full force of God's wrath. Christ as substitute, bearing the punishment that sinners deserve and so propitiating the divine wrath, of foundational importance to a previous generation of evangelical scholars in appreciating God's justifying grace, does not seem to figure strongly, if at all, in this new understanding of the cross.[67] The words of Packer are apposite at this point when he reminds us that 'penal substitutionary atonement and the righteous justification of sinners are the two sides of a single coin, the two elements in the one saving transaction whereby God rescues us from hell.'[68]

7. Justification is no longer 'the article on which the church stands or falls'.

Wright is correct to emphasise what many commentators have failed to notice or stress in the past, that there is a wider dimension to Paul's treatment of the subject in Galatians 3-4 and parts of Romans. He is right to expound justification as part of the historical outworking of God's overall plan of salvation in which Jew and Gentile are united in Christ. According to Wright, however, we must resist the temptation to regard the Pauline doctrine of justification as the article by which the church stands or falls. Other doctrines such as the Trinity would be better placed to merit that distinction, he suggests. He also points out that we are justified by believing in Christ and not by believing in the doctrine of justification. While it is true that our trust is in Christ and not a doctrine, we must not drive a wedge between the person and the truth connected with him. If the doctrine of justification by faith alone is not clearly presented, there will soon arise a distorted message and people will be led to trust a distorted Christ.

The importance of justification in the gospel message and the church's life deserves a separate chapter and it is to this matter that we now turn.

Notes

1. E. P. Sanders, *Paul and Palestinian Judaism,* SCM, 1977. Cf. also *Paul, the Law and the Jewish People,* SCM, 1983.
2. Sanders, *Paul and Palestinian Judaism,* p. 57.
3. *The New Testament and the People of God,* p. 335.
4. Cf. D. A. Carson, *Divine Sovereignty & Human Responsibility,* Marshall, Morgan & Scott, 1981, pp. 87-89. 'Essentially, then, E. P. Sanders is correct in his basic contentions, and Bousset, Billerbeck, Bultmann *et al.* are basically incorrect when they deal with the same areas.'
5. Sanders, *Paul and Palestinian Judaism,* p. 183-198.
6. Carson, *Divine Sovereignty,* p. 91; cf. G. B. Caird, reviewing Sanders' book in *Journal of Theological Studies* 29, 1978, pp. 539-40, who also criticises him for ignoring the legalistic drift in Jewish theology.
7. Cf. R. H. Gundry, 'Grace, Works, and Staying Saved in Paul', *Biblica* 60, 1985, pp. 35-36.
8. Gundry, 'Grace, Works, and Staying Saved in Paul', p. 12.
9. Carson, *Divine Sovereignty,* pp. 69, 106.
10. Cf. S. Schechter, *Aspects of Rabbinic Theology,* Schocken Books, 1961, p. 174.
11. 1QS 3:6-8, 8:6-10, 9:4-5. Cf. F. García Martínez, *The Dead Sea Scrolls Translated: The Qumran Texts in English,* Brill, 1994, pp. 3, 12-13.
12. M. A. Seifrid, 'Justification by Faith: The Origin and Development of a Central Pauline Theme', Supplements to *Novum Testamentum,* vol. LXVIII, Brill, 1992, pp. 89-99; cf. also Carson, *Divine Sovereignty,* pp. 75-83.
13. 1QS 5:20-24. Cf. Martínez, p. 9.
14. Seifrid, 'Justification by Faith', p. 133.
15. M. A. Seifrid, 'Blind Alleys in the Controversy over the Paul of History', *Tyndale Bulletin,* 45.1, 1994, p. 82.
16. *Antiquities,* viii.295.
17. Carson, *Divine Sovereignty,* p. 112.
18. Sanders, *Paul and Palestinian Judaism,* p. 409. Cf. C. L. Quarles, 'The Soteriology of R. Akiba and E. P. Sanders' Paul and Palestinian Judaism', *New Testament Studies* 42, 1966, pp. 185-195. Quarles shows that older rabbis like Gamaliel II clearly held the view that the divine standard of justice required perfection, as expressed by Paul in Galatians 3:10, a point which Sanders seems to have forgotten. Rabbi Akiba revised this extreme view by arguing that 'although judgment was based in divine goodness or

righteousness, judgment based upon the majority of deeds rather than the totality of deeds was somehow possible'. His words 'all is according to the amount of the work' suggest a balancing of good deeds and evil deeds (cf. Mishnah *Aboth* 3.16).

19. J. R. W. Stott, *The Message of Romans*, IVP, 1994, p. 27.

20. Stott, *The Message of Romans*, p. 29.

21. D. J. Moo, '"Law", "Works of the Law" and Legalism in Paul', *Westminster Theological Journal* 45, 1983, p. 80-82.

22. Moo, "Law", pp. 85-90.

23. Moo, "Law", pp. 84-85. For the moral teaching behind the so-called 'ceremonial' law, cf. G. J. Wenham, *The Book of Leviticus,* Eerdmans, 1979, p. 18-25; 274-5.

24. Our Lord recognised primary laws: Matthew 23:23; Mark 12:29-31; cf. also 9:13. This is in line with the Torah itself, cf. Deuteronomy 6:5. Leviticus 19:18 also 'epitomizes and expresses the principles governing all the laws that surround it' (cf. G. J. Wenham, *Leviticus*, p. 274). The Decalogue is also given unique status within the Torah itself: 'the ten commandments' (Exodus 34:28; Deuteronomy 9:17), 'the words of the covenant (Exodus 34:28), 'the tablets of testimony' written with 'the finger of God' (Exodus 31:18), and placed in the Ark (Exodus 40:20). Reference is made to all ten in the New Testament (cf. Mark 10:19; Romans 13:9; etc.).

25. F. F. Bruce, *The Epistle of Paul to the Galatians*, (The New International Greek Testament Commentary), Paternoster, 1982, p. 181.

26. Wenham, *Leviticus*, p. 269-270.

27. Cf. Josephus, *Antiquities*, 20.34-48.

28. M. A. Seifrid, 'The Pauline Gospel in a Postmodern Age', note 16, p. 205 in D. S. Dockery (editor), *The Challenge of Postmodernism: An Evangelical Engagement*, A Bridgepoint book, 1995. Cf. N. T. Wright, *The New Testament and the People of God*, p. 232.

29. J. Calvin, *Institutes*, Bk.3, ch.xi, para.19, p. 749. (Calvin refers to Origen but according to Battles note 36 the reference is to Pelagius).

30. Moo, '"Law", "Works of the Law" and Legalism in Paul', p. 90-100. Cf. also D. J. Moo, *Romans 1-8*, The Wycliffe Exegetical Commentary, Moody, 1991, pp. 210-211.

31. K. R. Snodgrass, 'Justification by Grace - to the Doers: an Analysis of the Place of Romans 2 in the Theology of Paul', *New Testament Studies* 32, 1986, p. 84 and D. P. Fuller, 'Paul and "The Works of the Law"' *Westminster Theological Journal* 38, 1975, pp. 31-33.

32. Qumran reference, 4QFlor 1:7 in F. García Martínez, *The Dead Sea Scrolls*

Translated, p. 136. Cf. also the *Halakhic Letter*, 4QMMT, Martínez pp. 76-85.

33. Moo, *Romans*, pp. 209-210.

34. Cf. C. E. B. Cranfield, *The Epistle to the Romans*, Vol.1, T. & T. Clark, 1975, pp. 197-198.

35. Moo, '"Law", "Works of the Law" and Legalism in Paul', p. 98.

36. Seifrid, *Tyndale Bulletin, 45.1*, pp. 77-79.

37. Seifrid, 'Pauline Gospel in a Postmodern Age', pp. 196-197.

38. *The New Testament and the People of God*, pp. 167-214.

39. Seifrid, 'Justification by Faith', pp. 88f.; *Tyndale Bulletin, 45.1*, pp. 79-81.

40. Moo, *Romans*, p. 210.

41. Stott, *Romans*, p. 104.

42. K. Stendahl's original article *The Apostle Paul and the Introspective Conscience of the West*, is reprinted in *Paul among Jews and Gentiles and Other Essays*, SCM, 1977, pp. 78-96.

43. J. D. G. Dunn, *Theology of Paul's Letter to the Galatians*, Cambridge, 1993, p. 68. In a private communication Dr. Wright agrees with me on this point against Dunn.

44. Cf. Moo, *Romans*, p. 452 note 7 for a full list of those who take this view.

45. While Douglas Moo argues the case for taking the 'I' in Romans 7 to mean 'Paul in solidarity with Israel' he finds that more and more scholars are insisting that 'some reference to Paul himself cannot be excluded', cf. *Romans*, pp. 451-456, 466-467.

46. Cf. Dunn, *Romans* 1-8, p. 405.

47. F. F. Bruce, *The Epistle to the Galatians: A Commentary on the Greek Text*, Paternoster, 1982, pp. 143, 146.

48. J. G. Machen argues for Jews only in *Machen's Notes on Galatians*, ed. J. H. Skilton, Presbyterian and Reformed Publishing Company, 1973, p. 179.

49. A. Caneday, '"Redeemed From the Curse of the Law" The Use of Deut. 21:22-23 in Gal. 3:13', *Trinity Journal*, Vol. 10 No.2, 1989, p. 208.

50. R. Y. K. Fung, *The Epistle to the Galatians*, Eerdmans, 1988, p. 149. Wright believes that he strengthens the position of T. L. Donaldson's study, "The 'curse of the Law' and the Inclusion of the Gentiles: Galatians 3.13-14", *New Testament Studies 32*, 1986. An earlier view to that of Donaldson was held by G. S. Duncan, *The Epistle of Paul to the Galatians*, Hodder and Stoughton, 1934, p. 99.

51. Cf. D. B. Garlington, 'Righteousness' in *The New Dictionary of Christian Ethics and Pastoral Theology*, IVP, 1995.

52. Moo, *Romans*, p. 242; Cranfield, *Romans*, p. 211; D. M. Lloyd-Jones, *Romans*

3:20-4:25, Atonement and Justification, p. 98.

53. Stott, *Romans,* p. 63.

54. Wright, 'Justification', *New Dictionary of Theology,* p. 360.

55. L. Morris, *The Apostolic Preaching of the Cross,* Tyndale Press, 1960, p. 266.

56. Cf. N. T. Wright, 'On becoming the righteousness of God: 2 Corinthians 5:21', in *Pauline Theology Volume II,* ed. D. M. Hay, Fortress Press, 1993, pp. 200-208.

57. In *Justification by Faith: Can we get it right now?* Tyndale Lecture, 1994, Wright admitted that 1 Corinthians 1:30 was a reference to Christ's righteousness. Its relevance to the subject of imputed righteousness was dismissed by reasoning that no one believes in the imputation of Christ's wisdom. But then the language of imputation is never used in the Bible of wisdom or, for that matter, of sanctification and redemption, but it is used of righteousness.

58. Wright, 'Justification: The Biblical Basis & its Relevance for Contemporary Evangelicalism' in *The Great Acquittal,* ed. Gavin Reid, 1980, pp. 26, 30.

59. Cf. L. Berkhof, *Systematic theology,* Banner of Truth, 1958, pp. 517-520; Wright, 'Justification...', p. 110 note 9: 'it is even possible to speak of the atonement itself as the justification of those in Christ, in that in the resurrection God declares that the Messiah, and hence his people, are in the right'. He cites T. F. Torrance and Karl Barth as holding this view. Cf. also G. C. Berkouwer, *Faith and Justification,* ch.VI 'Justification from Eternity', Eerdmans , 1954, pp. 143-168 for a critique of this view.

60. Wright, *Climax of the Covenant,* p. 2. Cf. also pp. 120-137.

61. Wright, *Climax of the Covenant,* p. 203.

62. M. Seifrid, 'Pauline Gospel in a Postmodern Age', p. 194.

63. M. Seifrid, 'Blind Alleys', p. 93.

64. S. H. Travis, 'Christ as Bearer of Divine Judgment in Paul's Thought about the Atonement', in *Jesus of Nazareth Lord and Christ,* eds. J. B. Green and M. Turner, Eerdmans/Paternoster, 1994, p. 344.

65. Cf. J. D. G. Dunn, *Romans 1-8,* p. 171, where he criticises Ridderbos for being 'surprisingly and unjustifiably dogmatic on the issue on the side of Morris'. Also, J. M. Gundry-Volf, 'Expiation, Propitiation, Mercy Seat' in *Dictionary of Paul and his Letters,* eds. G. F. Hawthorne, R. P. Martin, D. G. Reid, IVP, 1993, p. 282, 'In summary, not "propitiatory" but "expiatory" is the more appropriate description of Christ's atoning death'.

66. Travis, p. 345.

67. Cf. J. B. Green, 'Death of Christ' in *Dictionary of Paul and his Letters,* pp. 207-208

and J. D. G. Dunn in 'Paul's Understanding of the Death of Jesus' in *Reconciliation and Hope,* ed. R. Banks, Eerdmans, 1974, pp. 139-141 who prefers to describe Christ's death as representative rather than substitutionary.
68. J. I. Packer, 'Evangelicals and the Way of Salvation: New Challenges to the Gospel - Universalism, and Justification by Faith' in *Evangelical Affirmations,* Academie/Zondervan, 1990, p. 129.

Part 4

Justification Today

11 Getting it Right

The importance of justification for the church and the individual is intimately linked to a right view of the subject. Allow justification to have a broader meaning than the biblical one or reinterpret the biblical evidence to produce a revised definition and this will inevitably result in long-term trouble for the church and the individual. This is what happened early on in the church's history. It led to all the terrible abuses and false teachings that arose during the medieval period. The same thing can happen again.

If the biblical truth concerning justification by faith alone is revised, widened, marginalized or denied, its importance for the life of the church and the individual will be obscured. Roman Catholicism has always played down the significance of the subject and that is to be expected. It will not allow any such biblical teaching to stand over-against it to judge and challenge its traditions, errors and false practices. What is disturbing is to find evangelical leaders and scholars indicating, by what they say or do, that justification is not the major item that Protestants of the past believed it to be.

A Central Doctrine

The whole question of the status of justification in Paul's theology is one that is hotly debated. In 1981 Ronald Fung, who teaches theology at the China Graduate School of Theology, surveyed the scene and detected four broad positions among scholars with regard to the importance of justification: 1) that it is of subsidiary significance; 2) that it is of fundamental significance; 3) that it is one of a number of important metaphors; 4) that it is of central significance but is to be set within the wider context of God's saving activity.[1] The debate continues.

Within evangelical scholarly circles, Mark Seifrid has argued that it is 'a central Pauline theme' set in the context of his mission to the Gentiles.[2] P. T. O'Brien of Moore Theological College, Sydney, prefers the word 'fundamental' or 'foundational'. It is foundational in the sense that it deals with the basic issue of a person's 'entry into the Christian life'.[3] Wright, on the other hand, as we saw at the close of the previous chapter, does not consider justification, as he understands it, to be the principle by which to test what is authentically Christian. McGrath, worried lest the biblical concept of justification might turn out not to be of fundamental significance, argues for a broader meaning that will enable the doctrine to maintain its position as the article by which the church stands or falls.[4]

In this whole argument a lot depends on the meaning given to such words as 'central' or 'fundamental'. If the word 'central' is used, it must not be thought that Paul organized his whole theology around justification. Clearly he did not. Neither is the word 'central' to be thought of in a way that makes other Pauline themes like reconciliation or the work of the Spirit seem trivial. They are all important. Again, the word 'fundamental' can have its drawbacks by creating the false impression that all other themes are logically built upon justification. Having said all this, it is appropriate to view Paul's doctrine of justification by faith alone as of central or fundamental significance when set within the context of God's saving purposes.

It is often suggested that justification for Paul is merely a polemical or controversial doctrine, counteracting heretical views or Jewish attitudes and therefore not as central and as important as Protestants have assumed. Wright, for instance, states that 'we must see justification by faith as a polemical doctrine, whose target is not the usual Lutheran one of "nomism" [i.e. depending on some kind of works for final salvation]... but the Pauline one of Jewish national pride.'[5] Mark Seifrid on the other hand, from his study of Romans, has argued convincingly that Paul's teaching on justification cannot be relegated 'to the status of a mere polemical doctrine'. The purpose of the letter is 'not an attack upon adversaries', but a proclamation of the gospel in which justification by faith alone is an integral part. It assures 'Gentile readers of deliverance from the apocalyptic manifestation of God's wrath' and in the light of Israel's example 'it has become the reason for excluding boasting in any religious pride.' In addition, Paul's argument in Romans 7:14-25 far from being a reference to Israel indicates the relevance of justification 'to the existence of the believer'.[6]

An argument sometimes advanced is that because there is no reference to the 'right' word-group in 1 Thessalonians, which may have been written prior to Galatians, this is evidence for believing that Paul had not yet developed any understanding of justification by faith alone. It is quite clear from the letter, however, that Paul had preached a gospel which gave these Thessalonian believers assurance of future salvation and deliverance from the wrath to come, as Seifrid puts it, 'without any mention of obligation to the Law' (cf. 1:10; 2:12, 16).[7]

To emphasise that justification is integral to Paul's message we can do no better than use the points made by J. I. Packer in his article on justification in the *New Bible Dictionary*:[8]

1. In the Epistle to the Romans Paul expounds the gospel and 'the doctrine of justification is its backbone'. The gospel reveals the righteousness of God in justifying the ungodly (Romans 1:16-3:26).

2. Paul's own personal experience and missionary outlook are expressed in terms of justification (Galatians 2:15-21, 2 Corinthians 5:16-21 and Philippians 3:4-14). In Romans 7:7ff his need is described in terms of the law's condemnation which is relieved by God's justifying grace in Christ (Romans 8:1f.).

3. It is 'God's fundamental act of blessing, for it both saves from the past and secures for the future'. We are given a full pardon and accepted as righteous. The judgment of the last day is brought forward and we are pronounced righteous in Christ, a verdict that is final and irreversible.

4. Justification is the basic reference-point in Paul's doctrine of salvation as Romans and Galatians most clearly reveal. All the hints, prophecies and examples of salvation in the Old Testament are explained in terms of justification. (Cf. Habakkuk 2:4; Genesis 15:6; Psalm 32:1f.; Hosea 2:23; etc.)

5. Justification is the key to unlock Paul's understanding of history. The central over-all purpose in God's dealings with humanity since the fall is to bring sinners to justifying faith.

Without denying the importance of other doctrines, justification does lie at the heart of Paul's gospel. In another place, Packer compares the doctrine of justification to Atlas, for 'it bears a world on its shoulders, the entire evangelical knowledge of saving grace'. He concludes with these sobering words, 'When Atlas falls, everything that rested on his shoulders comes crashing down too'.[9]

It is not a subject confined to the apostle Paul. Though the actual vocabulary may not always be found, the theme runs right through the Bible as we have seen in chapters three and four. It is about how sinful human beings are brought into a right legal status before God. The whole history of the working out of God's plan of salvation recorded in the Bible has this at its core. Paul himself directs us to the one whom God called to be the father of the nation and through whom all nations would find blessing. There, in Genesis 15:6, Abraham is accounted righteous through faith alone in the promises of God, promises which find their ultimate fulfilment in the Lord Jesus Christ. John the Baptist told the Pharisees and Sadducees in no uncertain terms not to trust in their birth and background: 'And do not think that you can say to yourselves, "We have Abraham as our father. I tell you that out of these stones God can raise up children for Abraham"' (Matthew 3:9). He preached a baptism of repentance with a view to the forgiveness of sins and pointed them to Jesus Christ as the Lamb of God who takes away the sin of the world (Mark 1:4; John 1:29).

Jesus himself warned the people of his own village that while judgment came upon unbelievers within Israel in the days of Elijah and Elisha, blessing flowed out to those who humbled themselves and believed regardless of their nationality (Luke 4:25-27). The faith of the centurion is presented both as a warning to the Jews who considered themselves children of Abraham and members of the kingdom by right, and as a foretaste of the many from the Gentile nations who will sit down with Abraham, Isaac and Jacob when the kingdom is consummated (Matthew 8:10-12). It is not the self-righteous who are justified but those who acknowledge their sin and need and look only to the grace of God (Luke 18:9-14). Pious Nicodemus no doubt thought himself a member of the covenant community and hoped to be vindicated on 'the last day'. Nevertheless, he was told by Jesus of the necessity for a radical change that would bring him to the end of himself, and that only through faith in the sacrificial death of the Son of God is there eternal life (John 3:1-15). The last book of the Bible, Revelation, which is an encouragement to all who suffer for the sake of the Lord Jesus, likewise presses home this same theme. John Sweet, in his helpful commentary on Revelation, says of the war against the devil in 12:7-12, 'It is Paul's doctrine of "justification by faith" in pictorial form'.[10]

Justification is one of a number of terms used in the Bible to describe the multi-faceted nature of God's saving work. The good news of the gospel speaks of redemption, reconciliation, deliverance, adoption, sanctification, glorification, etc. as well as justification. In theology all these items come under the umbrella of salvation, and they are all vitally important truths. Even so, following Paul and the rest of Scripture, and despite the modern attempts to make it a subsidiary doctrine, the mainstream evangelical view has been that the doctrine of justification is of foundational or central importance for it alone deals with the crucial matter of a person's standing before God. It must not be confused with any other element of the saving message. Reconciliation is a glorious truth that is associated with justification and so is adoption, but they are not to be equated with justification. The same must be said of 'membership of the covenant family'. It is a privilege that flows from our justified state with God.

The results of revising justification

If justification is redefined as a declaration of covenant membership then its significance is greatly impaired and it can no longer be described as the basic element in the gospel and the principle by which to test whether a church is true to the gospel. According to Tom Wright, as a polemical doctrine justification is not primarily opposed to 'the heirs of the Tractarian movement'. On his understanding of justification one can see why. If it is a declaration of covenant membership it has nothing to say to Anglo-catholicism or to Roman Catholicism.

For Wright 'justification calls us to oppose the present trend away from historical Christianity and to wake up to the treasures of membership in the historical and visible people of God.' He states that the basic doctrines on which justification (i.e. membership of the Christian community) is built are 'the incarnation, cross and resurrection of the one who is Lord of all.'[11] Justification, Wright insists, is about who the people of God are. They are those who confess belief in historic Christianity. Justification therefore stands over-against liberalism and paganism and is important in the area of church membership and ecumenism.

This is in line with the ARCIC II statement (see chapter 8) which considers justification in the context of the church. The church is now the dominant concern and many Anglican evangelicals like Wright are happy with this trend. Justification by faith means that all who believe in the risen Christ belong to the same family and belong to the same table. If Wright's understanding of justification is right then the Reformation was a big mistake. No doubt he himself would want to thank God for the benefits which the Reformation brought. Nevertheless, his interpretation of the Pauline theme has the effect of removing the very heart of the Reformers' dispute with Rome, namely, the matter of justifying righteousness.

According to Wright, the gift of righteousness is the gift of covenant member status. The gift of Christ's righteousness put to the believer's account before God, so precious to the Reformers and to Evangelical Protestants for four centuries, we are now told simply does not exist. There is therefore neither any need to choose between the verbs 'to impart' or 'to impute' righteousness nor to decide in favour of 'to declare' or 'to make' righteous. The verb 'to justify' no longer highlights the truth that God declares the wicked righteous but is, instead, a declaration concerning membership of the Christian community. It is, as far as Wright and others are concerned, in the context of church membership that justification has any real significance, in that it sets the ecumenical agenda and defines who should sit at the communion table. No longer is it the cutting edge of the gospel. The one great stumbling-block between Protestants and Roman Catholics has been removed at a stroke. This revision must be very appealing to Rome at the present time.

Similarly, if justification is understood in terms of group membership then there are those who will see its importance lying more in the world of sociological concerns, politics and economics. James Dunn follows Stendahl in thinking that justification by faith alone had no real significance for Paul's own personal salvation and instead of speaking of his conversion it would be better to speak of his 'call' to preach salvation to the Gentiles.[12] For Paul, his 'conversion' was 'a calling' or 'commissioning'. He was 'converted from ... being a persecutor of the followers of Jesus' and 'converted to the Gentiles. Or, to be more precise, he was converted to the equally burning conviction that the good news of Jesus was indeed, after all, for the Gentiles'. It is in this sense, according to Dunn, Paul was converted to the gospel.

In summing up he informs us that 'justification by faith as Paul formulated it cannot be reduced to the experience of individual salvation as though that was all there is to it. Justification by faith is Paul's fundamental objection to the idea that God has limited his saving goodness to a particular people.'[13] He then goes on to emphasise the social dimensions of the Gospel, believing that Luther's move from the 'justice of God' to 'justification by faith' needs now to be reversed in some measure. 'Should justification by faith be so divorced from social justice?' he asks. 'Does the rather dated Protestant talk of "justification by faith" have more to say to contemporary needs and concerns than has been generally recognised?' In the light of this so-called fuller understanding of justification Dunn believes that the justice of God has national and social outworkings. The views of Dunn are applied by his colleague Alan Suggate in formulating Christian responses to such matters as Hitler's Germany, Japanese imperialism and free market Britain under Margaret Thatcher.[14]

This growing tendency to play down the personal nature of justification in favour of the social dimension is very disturbing. We repeat again that the biblical revelation understands justification by faith alone to be, as Carl Henry succinctly puts it, 'the divinely provided entry to the sinner's redemptive relationship with God in Christ.'[15] It is not primarily about moving from one group to another, neither is it in essence a Pauline protest to the idea that God has limited salvation to one racial group.

Of course, justification has social implications. What is more, there need be no dichotomy between the individual's standing before God and a concern for others. However, if, as Dunn suggests, we go into reverse in the direction of social justice, we are turning our backs on the very article, as Seifrid puts it, 'on which all true justice flows: the wrath and love of God manifest in the justifying work of the cross which call us to account not merely for our outward deeds, but for the secrets of our hearts'.[16]

Justification and Sanctification

Before we proceed any further, we need to be clear concerning what is meant by sanctification. The ARCIC II statement, as we saw earlier in chapter eight, confuses two different understandings of the term. From a biblical perspective, 'sanctification' or 'holiness' refers both to a believer's state or position in Christ and to an activity or process in a believer's life. The dominant use of the 'sanctification' language in the New Testament is, in fact, positional and relational.[17] Paul can describe the Corinthian believers as 'sanctified in Christ Jesus' (1 Corinthians 1:2; cf. also 1:30; 6:11). They have been set apart by God for his use. Christians are not seen as striving to *become* God's holy people, they *are* God's holy people. It is from this privileged position that the New Testament calls Christians to behave as God's holy people and live the sanctified life (1 Thessalonians 4:7). We are called to sanctify only what God has already pronounced holy (cf. 1 Peter 1:2 and 2:9 with 1:15; 3:15). When we come to the Reformation debates and subsequent Protestant theology on the subject, sanctification is primarily understood as the believer's progressive growth in holiness. It is in this secondary sense that sanctification is being used in all that follows.

The connection between justification and sanctification has been, and still is the subject of keen debate and concern. Luther's bold statement that the justified person is at one and the same time righteous and a sinner has always been an obstacle to Roman Catholics. Hans

Küng, in his influential work on justification, tries to divide the Reformers on the nature of justification, suggesting that Calvin accepted a relationship between justification and sanctification that was akin to the medieval tradition defined at Trent, while Luther had twisted the truth. In answering Luther, Küng claims that Trent likewise distorted the doctrine to some degree. He is also of the opinion that Karl Barth is in essential agreement with the Council of Trent's decree on justification.

These are incredible conclusions. Barth, in fact, is very strong in his condemnation of Trent's teaching on justification considering it to be 'another gospel'.[18] Alister McGrath questions whether Küng has done anything more than demonstrate that 'Barth and the Roman Catholic magisterium share a common anti-Pelagian, Christocentric theology of justification.'[19]

As for the attempt to divide Luther and Calvin, his arguments are no more convincing. Both Reformers break with the tradition stretching back to Augustine and defined at Trent. Justification is not for them an all-embracing concept. Calvin is even more explicit than Luther in rejecting any notion of justifying righteousness being located within the person. McGrath shows how Calvin clearly distinguished between 'the event of the divine pronouncement (justification) and the subsequent process of regeneration (sanctification).'[20]

The fact that Calvin opens up the theme of justification under his teaching on the Christian life does not mean he has merged justification and sanctification. What it shows is that for Calvin justification stands at the beginning of a person's saving relationship with God. From the initial declaration by God that guilty sinners are acquitted on account of the righteous life and activity of Jesus Christ, the believer goes on to live that life in the Spirit associated with sanctification. Justification and sanctification are inseparably related but must be kept distinct. This has been the evangelical Protestant position.

Where this distinction is lost, works become linked with justification and the gospel is perverted. The ground of our acceptance now and on the day of judgment does not lie in any human activity or attitude, not even in a small way. It does not depend on sacramental observances like baptism and the Mass, physical pains and persecution, charitable deeds or even a loving disposition. If any of these things in the slightest way become associated with justification then the sufficiency of God's action in Christ is called into question and our assurance of salvation is lost.

Even in the matter of our growth in holiness, Luther was deeply anxious that we should not lose sight of the fact that the justified person is still a sinner, ever dependent not on any personal holiness or good work, but on Christ and his good work. This concern is expressed very forthrightly when he warns, 'Beware of aspiring to such purity that you will not wish to be looked upon as a sinner, or to be one ...Accordingly you will find peace only in him and only when you despair of yourself and your own works. Besides, you will learn from him that just as he has received you, so he has made your sins his own and has made his righteousness yours.'[21]

17th Century Protestants

The importance of getting it right in this area of the relationship between justification and sanctification is not confined to the controversy with Rome. Justification by grace alone, as revealed in the Bible and understood by the Reformers, has been undermined within the Protestant constituency. In many cases well-meaning ministers and theologians have been the cause of distorting the doctrine in the interests of upholding other aspects of truth which they felt were under attack. The fear of sinful presumption and living without regard to God and his law (Antinomianism) have been in the forefront of the debate. Many have also been sensitive to the Roman charge of legal fiction and to the problem of reconciling present justification based on Christ's work and the future judgment according to human works.

Two movements arose in the seventeenth century which had a devastating effect on the doctrine of justification, and in turn, on the health of the Christian Church in Britain in the second half of that century and on into the eighteenth. Their influence still pervades the older denominations and much of the evangelicalism of the twentieth century. The first was Arminianism which came from the continent and owes its origins to the Dutch theologian Jacobus Arminius (1560-1609). The

Arminians objected to Christ's imputed righteousness, denied present assurance of future salvation, unconditional election, particular redemption and the penal substitutionary nature of Christ's death, by which means he was punished for the sins of his people. Faith was seen as essentially a commitment to do something rather than self-despairing trust in Christ and what he has done. Faith, as obedience to the gospel and allegiance to Christ, was seen as God's new law which is counted for righteousness.

Arminianism was embraced by Archbishop Laud in the days of Charles I and later by the Anglicans of the Restoration period. It led to a new legalism at the beginning of the eighteenth century where a form of justification by works was the commonly held view.[22] Packer summarises the situation in these words: 'The meaning of faith as trust in Christ's person and work was forgotten; the experiences of conversion and assurance were dismissed as 'enthusiasm', dangerous to the soul; and present justification ceased to be an issue of importance or interest.'[23]

The other movement was called Neonomianism or Baxterianism, after the famous Puritan minister Richard Baxter (1615-1691), and did much harm amongst the English Nonconformists (Independents and Presbyterians) and the Scottish Presbyterians. Baxter's views were greatly influenced by Hugo Grotius (1583-1645), the Dutch rationalistic theologian and politician and the mediating theology of Amyraldism, named after the celebrated theologian and professor of the French Protestant Academy of Saumour, Moise Amyraut (1596-1664). The position that Baxter took on justification differed substantially from that of the Reformers, the Westminster Confession, and the teaching of his fellow Puritans.

In his work *Aphorismes of Justification* (1655) he states that, 'To affirm therefore that our Evangelical or new Covenant righteousness is in Christ and not in ourselves, or performed by Christ and not by ourselves, is such a piece of Antinomian doctrine that no man who knows the nature and difference of the Covenant can possibly entertain and which every Christian should abhor as insufferable'.[24] In place of the objective righteousness of Christ's obedience and blood Baxter substituted the subjective righteousness of a person's repentance and faith. In other words, he was advocating like the Arminians the belief that it was faith in the sense of allegiance and commitment which justifies because it makes us 'just performers of the conditions of the covenant of grace'.[25] While believing in Christ's death as penal and vicarious, it was not strictly substitutionary because Baxter did not believe in particular redemption, that is, he believed that Christ paid the penalty for the sins of everyone, not just for the sins of the elect. What we see in Baxter is, as Packer rightly judges, an early decline in the doctrine of justification and 'of the Puritan insight into the nature of Christianity as a whole'.[26]

Baxter's revision of the Reformation teaching on justification became very popular, but this and the other rationalistic elements of his theology had disastrous results on the Christian Church and evangelical Christianity. In summary, Packer presents this devastating criticism of Baxter that he 'sowed the seeds of moralism with regard to sin, Arianism with regard to Christ, legalism with regard to faith and salvation, and liberalism with regard to God'.[27] It is a salutary reminder to us today of where one influential and dedicated minister's ideas can lead.

There are some similarities between Baxter's views and the revisions to the doctrine of justification that have been recently presented. Sin tends to be externalized with the result that the indwelling power of personal sin is underestimated. Faith as allegiance to Christ and the ground of justification is not dissimilar to the modern notion of faith as belief and commitment, a badge on the basis of which a person is declared to be justified. The cross becomes of peripheral importance; the wrath of God is no longer viewed as his settled opposition to human rebellion and an expression of his eternal and unchangeable holy nature. Like Baxter's scheme the modern revision rejects the imputation of Christ's righteous life.

Learning from Baxter

Baxter's new understanding of justification aroused the interest of many and this in itself merits attention, for it speaks to our own situation today. Iain Murray draws attention to three reasons why Baxter himself was so attracted to it.[28]

1 The orthodox teaching, Baxter felt, was open to abuse. 'If people believed in a once-for-all justification on the grounds of a divine righteousness imputed to them, then the necessity for continued moral effort was surely lessened'. His experience as a chaplain in Cromwell's Army, where he was shocked by the lax attitude to godly living on the part of those who professed faith, led him to attack the Reformation teaching on justification as Antinomian. Murray comments, 'It was not the doctrine of justification which needed adjustment and revision to meet the threat of "easy-believism"'.

Dr. Martyn Lloyd-Jones in his exposition of Romans 6:1 has drawn attention to the fact that 'the doctrine of justification by faith only is a very dangerous doctrine' in the sense that it can be so easily misunderstood in the direction of antinomianism. He continues, 'If my preaching and presentation of the gospel of salvation does not expose it to that misunderstanding, then it is not the gospel'.[29] The teachings of Rome and legalists never result in people asking the question which Paul tackles in Romans 6, 'What shall we say then? Shall we go on sinning, so that grace may increase?' Paul does not revise his doctrine in the light of the assumption that justification by faith alone encourages people to sin more, but shows how wrong it is and gives further teaching to counteract such false deductions.

We must expect the biblical doctrine of justification as rediscovered and understood by the Reformers to be misunderstood. What we must guard against is the ever-present danger, especially when seeking to overcome such misconceptions, of introducing human works as in some way contributing toward a 'final justification'. In January 1982, Norman Shepherd was dismissed as Associate Professor of Systematic Theology at Westminster Theological Seminary, for his views on justification. This should awaken the staunchest Protestant to 'take heed lest he fall'. In one of his statements concerning justification Shepherd said, 'Works done from true faith ... being the new obedience wrought by the Holy Spirit in the life of the believer united to Christ ... are necessary for salvation from eternal condemnation...' At the same time he repudiated 'the inference that man, by his own good works, contributes to his own salvation'. The system he fashioned was to guard against a belief that forgiveness of sins can be enjoyed without repentance and heaven attained without holiness (cf. Hebrews 12:14, 'without holiness no-one will see the Lord.')[30]

Shepherd and those who supported him had extended justification into the sphere of sanctification and had accepted the notion that the good works of Christians have a necessary part to play in their final justification. Hebrews 12:14 is about sanctification. The good works of believers are to be associated with sanctification and not with justification. Justification must never be thought of as some sort of process fused with sanctification.

Nor is it at all helpful to speak, as Don Garlington does, of justification in past, present and future categories.[31] Justification is not in three stages. Even the expressions 'initial and final justification' or 'first and second justification' are misleading. The only justification of *sinners* the Bible speaks of is the one whereby God justifies the ungodly who put their trust in Christ alone. The righteousness of Christ in terms of his obedience and death is put to their account and that is the sole ground of their acceptability before God. Justification is a divine once-for-all pronouncement in the present which is irrevocable. It is not their 'obedience of faith which will justify in the final judgment', as Garlington suggests,[32] but Christ's obedience which has already been put to their account. Rather, the obedience of believers *will show* them to be the already justified people that they are in Christ.

More recently, R. C. Sproul, a well-respected speaker and author in the United States, has been using wording that is a regrettable lapse from his customary precision. In his admirable concern over the rampant antinomianism present in so much of the modern church, he is giving the impression that justification is on the basis of regeneration as well as of Christ's righteousness. His views are set out in a Symposium entitled *Justification by Faith Alone*. The Reformed position on the forensic nature of justification is spelled out, and Sproul clearly insists that the righteousness of Christ imputed to believers, which includes both his perfect life of obedience and his atoning death, is the ground of their justification. He is also right in stating that though justification and regeneration (or sanctification) are to be distinguished they must not be separated. But when he writes that 'Justification, technically considered, may not *mean* a change of human nature but it certainly *involves* a change in nature' he has overstepped the mark. That this is no mere slip of the pen is evident when he uses such expressions as 'the complex or nexus of justification'. He explains: 'Justification in the narrow sense refers strictly to God's forensic declaration. But the complex of justification in the wider sense involves other elements.' These other elements include a change in the person justified. Later, he introduces quotations from John Gerstner who makes comments which imply that justification is more than a legal declaration.[33]

We have every reason to believe that both Sproul and Gerstner are only concerned to emphasise the close connection between justification and regeneration. To talk, however, of a wider and narrower sense to the term is not the best way of expressing this. Justification itself does not involve or include regeneration or sanctification. God does not justify the godly but the ungodly, not the righteous but the unrighteous. In justification God does not justify sinners on the basis of an inner change which has led them to believe. It is not Christ plus an inner change, but Christ alone. We must get it right and not be tempted to alter the doctrine even under the pressures of antinomianism or some other error.[34]

2 The second reason Murray gives why Baxter found his new ideas on justification so appealing was 'that it seemed to offer a better basis for the preaching of the gospel to all men'. His commendable concern and love for lost sinners made him renounce the widely prevailing belief that Christ's death for sinners, though sufficient for all, is effective for the elect alone. It may well have been, as Murray suggests, that his fellow Puritans, in their opposition to Arminianism in which he himself was involved, 'did not give sufficient emphasis to the universal compassion of God'. In seeking to redress the balance Baxter allowed himself to philosophise and explain what Scripture leaves unexplained. It is something which human beings find difficult to accept but there are matters concerning God and his salvation where we are up against mystery and 'where reason fails there faith prevails and love adores'.

Belief in particular redemption has never inhibited the great evangelical preachers of the church from emphasising God's love for a lost world, offering the gospel to every person and urging them to repent and put their trust in the one and only Saviour of the world. God's sovereignty in the salvation of sinners and the responsibility laid upon human beings both to preach the gospel to all and for them to respond believingly to its message are clearly taught in the Bible (cf. John 6:37-40; 17:2). We dare not surrender the truth or pervert it even with the best of motives. If we do all is lost and the devil will have won.

3 The final reason why Murray thinks Baxter was carried away by his ideas 'was his conviction that it provided a genuine *via media* between Calvinism and Arminianism.' He had a great desire for unity among Christians and for an end to all sectarian interests. In this again he has much to teach us by way of warning. Genuine unity between churches and Christian groups cannot be achieved at the expense of truth. Baxter's errors led, in fact, to even more divisions, to the end of cooperation between the Presbyterians and Independents and to a weakening of orthodox Christianity. The fact that he had a reputation for godliness and evangelism, and had suffered for his faith in the Great Ejection of 1662, gave his false views more influence and credibility.

To reduce, expand or revise the doctrine of justification in the interests of Christian unity, even when leading men, respected in the evangelical world are involved, is to be resisted at all costs. History shows the intended aim is not realised, disaster results, the church falls and Christianity suffers. The Reformers were quite right to insist how fundamentally important the subject of justification is for the believer and the very existence of the Christian church.

Its importance to the Reformers, Puritans and 18th century Evangelicals

The doctrine of justification by faith alone with its trinitarian foundations is described by Luther in the Schmalkald Articles of 1537 as the 'first and chief article' of faith, 'upon which depends all that we teach and practise against the pope, the devil, and all the world. We must, therefore, be entirely certain of this, and not doubt it, otherwise all will be lost, and the pope, and the devil, and our opponents will prevail and obtain the victory'.[35] The following year, in his exposition of Psalm 130:4 he maintained that 'if this article stands, the church stands, if it falls, the church falls.'[36] Later theologians expressed the matter in the well-known dictum that this is 'the article on which the church stands or falls.'

John Calvin stressed the importance of this doctrine. In his *Institutes*, as he comes to open up the subject of justification, he declares that it 'is the main hinge on which religion turns, so that we devote the greater attention and care to it.'[37] He also made clear in a treatise presented to the Emperor Charles V that 'the safety of the church' depended upon this doctrine and 'if the purity of this doctrine is in any degree impaired the Church has received a deadly wound' and 'brought to the very brink of destruction.'[38] In a letter to Cardinal Sadolet Calvin wrote: 'Wherever the knowledge of it is taken away, the glory of Christ is extinguished, religion abolished, the Church destroyed, and the hope of salvation utterly overthrown.'[39]

Archbishop Cranmer, who was burnt alive at the stake in Oxford on 21st March 1556, is very forceful in his famous homily *Of Salvation*. He describes justification as 'the strong rock and foundation of Christian religion: this doctrine all old and ancient authors of Christ's Church do approve: this doctrine advanceth and setteth forth the true glory of Christ, and beateth down the vain glory of man: this whosoever denieth is not to be counted for a true Christian man, nor for a setter forth of Christ's glory, but for an adversary of Christ and his Gospel, and for a setter forth of men's vainglory.'[40] Evangelicals, who are inclined to call those who have turned their back on justification by faith alone for the Roman system 'brothers and sisters in Christ', would do well to think through what Cranmer says.

The Protestant historian John Foxe (1516-1587), in his *Acts and Monuments* (popularly known as *Foxe's Book of Martyrs*) speaks of Luther beating down the Roman errors by the article on justification. 'Luther gave the stroke...by opening one vein, long hid before, wherein lieth the touchstone of all truth and doctrine, as the only principal origin of our salvation, which is, our free justifying by faith alone, in Christ the Son of God.[41] John Knox (c. 1514-1572), the great Scottish Reformer, likened the opposition between the Reformers and Rome to that of Paul and the Galatian heretics. What was at stake, he said in his debate with the Jesuit, James Tyrie, was the gospel of God's grace, 'for it concerneth the chief head of justification'.[42]

The point is that in these quotations from the Reformers this doctrine of justification is not some theoretical matter for university scholars and theologians to debate, it is one which has profound practical implications for the church and the individual. Remember too, that for believing and preaching this gospel truth and for showing people the implications of it, these men lived in danger of their lives and some paid the ultimate price in most cruel circumstances. Justification by faith alone calls into question all the errors, superstitions and abuses that have crept into the church down the centuries.

In his work *A Disputation of Purgatory* (1531), John Frith, the gifted Cambridge scholar clearly saw that the doctrine of justification necessarily put a question-mark over Rome's teaching on purgatory. According to David Daniell in his recent biography on Tyndale, 'Frith's *Purgatory* is one of the finest, answering Rastell, More and Fisher on the subject of purgatory, showing its lack of biblical authority.'[43] Frith was burnt for his views on 4th July 1531 at Smithfield, London. From the opposite side, Cardinal Cervini never said a truer word at the start of session VI of the Council of Trent when he declared that Luther's doctrine of justification was at the root of his 'errors' on the sacraments, the power of the Keys, indulgences and purgatory.[44] When the doctrine of justification by faith was grasped reformation followed. At the Council of Trent Rome closed its mind to justification by faith alone and so there could only be counter-reformation.

If a body calling itself 'church' loses this central message of justification, it will soon have no good news to present. It will become another superstitious, religious institution, falsely bearing the name of Christian. What is more, the people will continue to be in the dark, heading for hell, while at the same time trusting in a Jesus of faulty human thought and heretical church tradition.

John Owen, the Nonconformist leader and theologian of the seventeenth century, wished that Luther 'had not been a true prophet, when he foretold that in the following ages the doctrine hereof would be again obscured.' Owen points out that the doctrine of justification 'gave the first occasion to the whole work of reformation, and was the main hinge whereon it turned'. Even the 'papal church' he declares is 'comparatively at ease' from the abuses that were prevalent before the Reformation. Yet so many wrong traditions remain 'blinding the eyes of men from discerning the *necessity* as well as the truth of the evangelical doctrine of justification.'[45]

Both George Whitefield (1714-1770) and John Wesley (1703-1791), the Methodist leaders of the great Evangelical Revival in England, saw the importance of justification by faith alone and denounced what they saw as the moralism and legalism that prevailed in the Anglican church. Not only at grass roots level but from the Anglican hierarchy the thinking was very much in the direction of a justification that included works as well as faith.

Archbishop John Tillotson, for instance, preached that 'the great condition of our justification and acceptance with God, is the real renovation of our hearts and lives ... and this, whether by justification be meant our first justification ... or our continuance in this state, or our final justification'.[46] No wonder that Wesley and Whitefield accused him of knowing 'no more of true Christianity than Mohamet'! Wesley was as vehement in his opposition to the prevailing Anglican thinking as Whitefield, showing the importance of keeping justification 'wholly distinct from sanctification, and necessarily antecedent to it.'[47]

In his Journal for the year 1735, when he was only twenty, Whitefield wrote of how his eyes had been opened by God's grace to 'the necessity of being justified in His sight by *faith alone*'. He described it as 'the good old doctrine of the Church of England. It is what the holy martyrs in Queen Mary's time sealed with their blood, and which I pray God, if need be, that I and my brethren may seal with ours.'[48]

Summarising the state of evangelicalism within the Church of England after the Great Evangelical Awakening of the eighteenth century, Alister McGrath states that the doctrine of justification was recognised as 'the milk of the gospel, and the salve for troubled consciences. The evangelical love-affair with the doctrine of justification gave rise to a profound spirituality, inspired and nourished by the knowledge that God had freely forgiven the sinner through Christ's death on the cross. It is that profound spirituality which led evangelicals to proclaim the saving love of God at home and abroad.'[49]

The great philosopher and preacher of the Evangelical Revival in New England in the eighteenth century, Jonathan Edwards (1703-1758), has a discourse on justification. In his concluding remarks he shows that the Scriptures treat the doctrine as one of very great importance and that Paul strenuously and zealously defends it by opposing justification by works of the law. The apostle, says Edwards, 'speaks of the contrary doctrine as fatal and ruinous to the souls of men...as subversive of the gospel of Christ, and calls it another gospel' and calls down a curse on those preaching it. 'Certainly we must allow the apostles to be good judges of the importance and tendency of doctrines; at least the Holy Ghost in them. And doubtless we are safe, and in no danger of harshness and censoriousness, if we only follow him, and keep close to his express teachings, in what we believe and say of the hurtful and pernicious tendency of any error.'[50]

We do well to remember these words of Edwards especially at a time when it is not popular to condemn false views. Getting it right is not an optional extra for armchair theologians to debate. We are dealing with matters which affect our eternal destiny and greater will be the judgment on preachers and teachers who have presented an uncertain or false message. No wonder people of old were prepared to die for their belief in justification by faith alone!

When the ARCIC II report on justification appeared in 1987, Clifford Longley of *The Times* commented on 'a certain wetness' among modern churchmen compared with those of the Reformation period. He wrote: 'Evidently there was something about this subject which caused hot tempers...salvation was perhaps more highly valued then, or damnation more feared: it mattered enormously which was the road to one, which to the other.'[51]

Conclusion

The biblical doctrine of justification brings us, as we have seen, to the very heart of the Christian message of salvation, human beings in a right relationship with God. It is often said that we are not called to believe a doctrine in order to be saved, but a Person. Surprisingly, Packer uses this argument in his support for grassroots collaboration with Roman Catholics in ministry. 'What brings salvation, after all, is not any theory about faith in Christ, justification, and the church, but faith itself in Christ himself.'[52]

We thoroughly agree that faith is directed toward Christ himself and not to any statement about him. However, the link must never be severed between the Person and the truth revealed about him in Scripture. We would not know anything about the Lord Jesus were it not for the Bible. The Jesus that we trust is the Jesus revealed in the Bible. To this, Packer would concur and indeed he refers to 'the Christ of Scripture'. Going a step further, we must say that, while it is perfectly possible to be saved through believing in Jesus Christ without having actually heard of the doctrine of justification, nevertheless the Saviour we are called to trust is the One revealed in the Bible whose blood and righteousness alone put us right with God.

The message concerning Christ presented in the Roman Catholic system of belief which the faithful are called to accept for salvation is a false gospel. It is the duty of evangelicals lovingly to challenge their belief and humbly to show them the truth of the gospel. When the biblical doctrine of justification, as rediscovered by the Reformers, is explained to those who say they have faith in Christ, and they do not accept and embrace it, neither we nor they can have any assurance that they are genuine believers. If, on the other hand, they do accept it they will be glad to put their signature to a statement on justification that includes the all-important word 'alone'. Furthermore, those who claim to appreciate something of the wonder of justification by faith alone, will eventually see how utterly repugnant to the gospel are all the unre-formed doctrines and practices of Roman Catholicism, Eastern Orthodoxy and the aberrations that have emerged within the Protestant denominations.

Unless the church clearly understands and proclaims the biblical truth concerning justification by faith alone, individuals may well be lulled into thinking that if they do their best, become members of the church and practise all that is required of them they will be accepted by God. A church made up of people who do not know what it is to be justified by faith alone is a sad sight and one that cannot rightly be called a Christian church.

One of the famous sayings, a truth well-known in the early church, quoted by the apostle Paul, includes this emphasis on justification:

'He saved us, not because of righteous things we had done, but because of his mercy. He saved us through the washing of rebirth and renewal by the Holy Spirit, whom he poured out on us generously through Jesus Christ our Saviour, so that, having been justified by his grace, we might become heirs having the hope of eternal life' (Titus 3:5-7).

In the final chapter we shall consider what this biblical truth means for us today.

Notes

1. R. Y. K. Fung, 'The status of justification by faith in Paul's thought: a brief survey of a modern debate', *Themelios* 6.3., April 1981, pp. 4-11.

2. M. A. Seifrid, 'Justification by Faith. The Origin and Development of a Central Pauline Theme', *Supplement to Novum Testamentum* Vol.68, Brill, 1992, pp. 255-270.

3. P. T. O'Brien, 'Justification in Paul and Some Crucial Issues of the Last Two Decades', in *Right With God: Justification in the Bible and the World*, ed. D. A. Carson, Baker/Paternoster, 1992, pp. 84f.

4. A. E. McGrath, *Justification By Faith: What It Means for Us Today*, Academie Books, Zondervan, 1988, pp. 143f.

5. N. T. Wright, 'The Paul of History and the Apostle of Faith', *Tyndale Bulletin* 29, 1978, p. 71.

6. M. A. Seifrid, 'Justification by Faith', p. 249.

7. Seifrid, 'Justification by Faith', pp. 144-145.

8. J. I. Packer, 'Justification', in *The New Bible Dictionary*, ed. J. D. Douglas, IVF, 1962, p. 684.

9. J. I. Packer, 'Introductory Essay' in *The Doctrine of Justification* by James Buchanan,

Banner of Truth, 1961, pp. 2-3.

10. J. Sweet, *Revelation,* SCM/Trinity Press International, 1990, p. 199.

11. Wright, 'Justification...' in *The Great Acquittal,* pp. 35-36.

12. K. Stendahl, *Paul Among Jews and Gentiles,* SCM, 1976, pp. 78-96.

13. J. D. G. Dunn & A. M. Suggate, *The Justice of God: A fresh look at the old doctrine of justification by faith,* Paternoster Press, 1993, pp. 17, 22, 24, 28.

14. J. D. G. Dunn, 'The Justice of God', *Journal of Theological Studies,* Vol.43, 1992, p. 21; Dunn & Suggate, *The Justice of God,* pp. 45-80.

15. C. F. H. Henry, 'Justification: A Doctrine in Crisis', *Journal of the Evangelical Theological Society* 38/1, March 1995, p. 62.

16. M. A. Seifrid, 'Blind Alleys', *Tyndale Bulletin* 45.1, 1994, p. 94.

17. J. Murray, *The Epistle to the Romans,* Marshall, Morgan & Scott, 1987, Part One p. 234; D. Peterson, *Possessed by God. A New Testament theology of sanctification and holiness,* Apollos (IVP), 1995; Cf. P. Toon, *Justification and Sanctification,* Marshall, Morgan & Scott, 1983, pp. 39-41.

18. K. Barth, *Church Dogmatics* 4.1, p. 626.

19. A. E. McGrath, 'Justification: Barth, Trent, and Küng', *Scottish Journal of Theology* Vol.34, pp. 517-518.

20. McGrath, 'Justification: Barth, Trent, and Küng', pp. 518-520.

21. *Luther's Works* Vol.48, *Letters* 1, Fortress Press, 1963, pp. 12-13.

22. Cf. A. E. McGrath, 'The Emergence of the Anglican Tradition on Justification, 1600-1700', *Churchman* 98, 1983, pp. 28-43.

23. J. I. Packer, 'The Doctrine of Justification in Development and Decline among the Puritans' *By Schisms Rent Asunder,* Puritan and Reformed Studies Conference, 1969, p. 25; reprinted in *Among God's Giants,* Kingsway, 1991, p. 206. For a helpful article on the Anglican view of justification at the time of the Methodist Revival cf. J. S. Chamberlain, 'Moralism, Justification, and the Controversy over Methodism', *Journal of Ecclesiastical History* Vol.44, No.4, October 1993 Cambridge, pp. 652-678.

24. R. Baxter, *Aphorismes of Justification,* Hague (alias Cambridge), 1655, p. 65 quoted by Iain Murray, 'Richard Baxter - "The Reluctant Puritan"?', *Advancing in Adversity,* Westminster Conference, 1991, p. 8.

25. R. Baxter, *An End of Doctrinal Controversies Which have lately Troubled the Churches,* London, 1691, p. 274 quoted by I. Murray, p. 9.

26. Packer, *By Schisms Rent Asunder,* p. 28 or *Among God's Giants,* p. 210.

27. Packer, *By Schisms Rent Asunder,* p. 28 or *Among God's Giants,* p. 210.

28. I. Murray pp. 15-16.

29. D. M. Lloyd-Jones, *Romans*, Exposition of Chapter 6, *The New Man*, Banner of Truth, 1972, pp. 9 and 8.

30. Quotations taken from *Christianity Today*, January 1, 1982, p. 49.

31. D. B. Garlington, in an address on justification at the Carey Ministers' Conference. Cf. 'The Obedience of Faith in the Letter to the Romans', *Westminster Theological Journal* Vol. 52, Fall 1990, pp. 201-224 and Vol. 53, Spring 1991, pp. 47-72.

32. Garlington, 'The Obedience of Faith...', Fall 1990, p. 223.

33. R. C. Sproul, 'The Forensic Nature of Justification' in *Justification by Faith Alone*, Soli Deo Gloria, 1995, pp. 44-46.

34. For further criticism of Sproul see *Chalcedon Report*, November 1995, pp. 26-28. For a good summary of the distinction between justification and sanctification cf. J. C. Ryle, *Holiness*, James Clarke & Co., 1956, pp. 29-33.

35. P. Schaff, *The Creeds of Christendom Vol.I*, Eerdmans, p. 255.

36. *Luther's Works* XL3, 352, Weimar edition.

37. J. Calvin, *Institutes of the Christian Religion*, Bk.3, ch.xi, para.1 (Battles Edition, Vol.1, p. 726).

38. J. Calvin, 'The Necessity of Reforming the Church' in *Tracts and Treaties Vol.I* Eerdmans, 1958, p. 137.

39. Calvin, 'The Necessity of Reforming the Church', p. 42.

40. *Miscellaneous Writings and Letters of Thomas Cranmer,* Parker Society, 1846, p. 131.

41. *The Acts and Monuments of John Foxe*, Vol. 4, Seeley, etc., 1846, p. 259.

42. *The Works of John Knox*, Vol.6, ed. D. Laing, Edinburgh, 1847, p. 499.

43. D. Daniell, *William Tyndale: A Biography,* Yale, 1994, p. 218.

44. J. Waterworth, *The Canons and Decrees of the Council of Trent*, Dolman, 1848, p. ci.

45. *The Works of John Owen*, Vol. 5, Banner of Truth, 1967, pp. 65-66. Cf. A. E. McGrath, 'Justification in Earlier Evangelicalism', *Churchman* 98, No.3, 1984, 218-219, for a treatment of Owen's doctrine of justification.

46. *The Works of the Most Reverend Dr. John Tillotson*, London, 1712, Vol.5, p. 416 quoted by J. S. Chamberlain, in *Journal of Ecclesiastical History* Vol.44, No.4, October 1993, Cambridge, p. 673.

47. *Wesley's Journal* 13 Sept. 1739, Vol. 1, Everyman's Library, Dent & Co., p. 225.

48. *George Whitefield's Journals*, Banner of Truth, 1960, p. 62.

49. A. E. McGrath, 'Justification in Earlier Evangelicalism', *Churchman 98*, No. 3, 1984, pp. 226-227.

50. *The Works of Jonathan Edwards*, Vol. 1, Banner of Truth, 1974, p. 652.

51. C. Longley, 'Lesson of the centurion's faith', *The Times*, 2 February, 1987.

52. J. I. Packer, 'Why I Signed It', *Christianity Today*, December 12, 1994, p. 37.

12 Right with God

In many ways the situation today is similar to that of the late medieval period. Cherished views are being questioned. There is uncertainty over terminology. In the popular mind great ignorance prevails. Added to this, the climate of opinion is against theological precision. People are more interested in feeling than in truth. We are living in what is called the post-modern era. It is an age of relativism, existentialism, mindless enthusiasm and pluralism. How can the gospel truth concerning justification be conveyed in this prevailing situation? Do we compromise the truth, capitulate to the modern trends or cleverly revise it to gain maximum support? Certainly not. There is a better way. We follow the long line of apostles, prophets, martyrs and preachers who have been gripped by the truth of justification by grace alone, through faith alone, in Christ alone, to God's glory alone.

There is something very exciting and wonderful about justification. True, there are aspects of the subject which are mysterious, but that goes for every element of the Christian Faith. Justification is a message unique to Christianity. It needs to be preached with feeling and in a way that shows its relevance now and on into the twenty-first century. Not only must justification be preached from the pulpit it must be expressed in the way life is lived and be a constant theme in prayer and conversation.

In order to appreciate justification by faith alone, it is essential to take into account some very basic, yet important, biblical truths concerning God, humanity and Jesus Christ:

God
Absolute Standard
In this age of relativism, people have been led to believe that there are no moral absolutes. The argument is that behaviour that is acceptable in one period of history or in one particular culture may not be acceptable in another age or another culture. The conclusion is then drawn that what is right for one person need not be right for others. The 'feel good factor' is an example of this way of thinking. Street-level morality often works on the assumption that 'if it feels good' it must be right.

All is not relative, however. There are absolutes. Now and then, even today, belief in absolute standards of right and wrong comes to the surface as, for example, in popular and universal condemnation of apartheid in South Africa.

The Bible does not speak in abstract terms of what is right and just. Any idea of an impersonal and absolute standard of righteousness and justice to which both God and man must comply is foreign to the Scriptures. God is the Absolute One, and he is the ultimate standard for what is right. No-one is good but God. He only is the righteous one. 'The LORD is righteous and my people and I are wicked' confesses Pharaoh in Exodus 9:27. God has made known what is right and good in the Bible. The law, given by God through Moses, is not an arbitrary set of rules; it expresses the character of God who is holy, righteous and good (Romans 7:12). What is more, people without knowledge of God's law show by their behaviour some knowledge of the divine moral standards (Romans 2:12-16). Humanity created by God, and in his image, is not ignorant of God's law. In addition, God's unique Son, Jesus Christ, reveals the divine character (John 14:9). The absolute standard of goodness and righteousness is seen not only in the letter of the law but in the Person of the God-man, the Word made flesh (John 1:14-18).

Attitude to Sin

God's attitude toward all human depravity and sin is one of holy, righteous anger (Romans 1:18). He hates all sin and his wrath remains on all sinners who do not repent and believe the gospel (John 3:36; 1 Thessalonians 2:16). To think of God as wrathful and as an avenging God is not a pagan or archaic idea. Of course, there is no thought of God breaking out in an uncontrollable fit of rage as is often depicted in the Babylonian and Greek myths concerning the gods. To safeguard against any false notions, some scholars have redefined wrath in impersonal terms as no more than 'an inevitable process of cause and effect in a moral universe'.[1] But this is unacceptable, for God's wrath is as personal and as active as his love. It is an aspect of God's holy nature whereby he refuses to condone rebellion against himself and his law.

God's wrath involves his righteous reaction in punishing those guilty of such rebellion (Numbers 11:1; Psalm 90: 7-12; Hebrews 3:11). All present expressions of God's vengeance are merely foretastes and warnings of what will happen on the day of judgment (Romans 9:22; Ephesians 5:6; 2 Thessalonians 1:9-10; Revelation 6:16; 19:15).

Ability to Justify Sinners

God is able to do the seemingly impossible: he justifies the ungodly (Romans 4:5). But how can an unrighteous person be right before God? How can God who is righteous (and that includes being virtuous and fair as well as being true to any covenant obligations into which he has entered), possibly pronounce not guilty those who are guilty of rebellion against his Person and law? 'He who justifies the guilty and he who condemns the innocent are both alike an abomination to the Lord' (Proverbs 17:15 [AV]). It would be inconsistent with his own character and law for God to do such a thing. Yet, in his great love and concern for lost sinners, he has devised a way by which he can and does pronounce such people not guilty without compromising his own nature and standards (Romans 3:26).

Humanity
Accountable to God

Human beings have been created by God and for God. God created man, male and female, in his own image for fellowship with himself and to rule over the earth on God's behalf (Genesis 1:27-28; 5:22,24; Deuteronomy 6:5). It is because we are created in the divine image that there is this built-in sense of God and of right and wrong. Within the limits of our existence as finite creatures, we also have the god-like freedom and power to act according to our own individual wills. Human beings are not robots or machines. It is because we are made in this way that we are responsible for all our actions. This means that ultimately everyone of us must answer to God for our own personal lives. No church, no institution, no human agency can shield us from that final day of reckoning (Romans 2:16; Hebrews 9:27; Revelation 20:12).

Accused by God

All are agreed that there is something wrong with human beings. While many can point to a variety of secondary causes, it is the Bible alone which gets to the root of the matter. Humanity is fallen and the death sentence hangs over us all (Romans 3:23; 6:23a). Sin is rebellion against God (cf. Psalm 51:4). It is acting contrary to God's law (1 John 3:4). We are all rebels. Every human being is a sinner by nature and practice. Already polluted by sin and associated with the guilt of Adam, every person is also guilty of breaking God's law (I Kings 8:46; Romans 3:10-19; 5:12). In this condition we sinners are already in the condemned cell and deserve and can expect nothing but God's wrath to be fully poured out on the day of judgment in final rejection and unending punishment (Mark 3:29; 9:43ff.; John 3:18-19, 36; Ephesians 2:3; Hebrews 10:27-39; 2 Peter 2:9; 3:7). Such is the plight of humanity in sin.

There are three matters, however, that need to be spelled out in more detail and re-emphasised in the light of recent trends in the evangelical world:

1. God our Judge

It must be remembered that humanity in sin is no longer in a parent/child relationship before God but rather in a judge/criminal relationship. The old liberal view, which had a devastating effect on the churches, frowned on the idea of human beings as criminals standing guilty before God the Judge. Though the law-court metaphor is used by Paul, they insisted that it should not be taken too seriously but should be viewed in the light of Jesus' teaching on the lost son needing to find his way back home into the arms of the heavenly Father. They considered the Reformers to have been influenced by the legal concepts which so governed the culture of their day, and that is why justification as a legal term was so popular and important to them. In order to speak to the present situation, legal terminology is out of place. God's dealings with his creatures, so the liberals argued, would be better represented by a more personal and fatherly approach.

Such sentiments have been expressed more recently in evangelical quarters and in a way that makes them sound acceptable. We are being told that we must liberate ourselves from the legal language of the sixteenth century and present justification in a way that meets the needs of twentieth-century Westerners.[2]

Legal terminology, however, is biblical and the sixteenth century Reformers were right to insist that justification refers to a legal pronouncement and not to a transformational activity. To preach justification in legal terms is therefore not a case of being in bondage to the culture and theological expressions of the sixteenth century; it is an instance of being true to the biblical revelation. In addition, the new emphasis on presenting 'righteousness' in covenantal terms, while helpful at many points, can lead to a denial of the biblical insistence that God's relationship to people in their sin is not that of Father/children but of Judge/lawbreakers. Unless we understand rebellious humanity's relationship before God in the legal terms employed by the Bible, we will do great damage to the gospel of justification, 'making it seem simply irrelevant to man's basic need'.[3]

2. Solidarity with Adam

The historicity of Adam is taken for granted by Paul and is essential to his whole argument in Romans 5:12-21. This is an embarrassment to those who jettison the Genesis account of the creation of human beings in favour of an evolutionary theory. According to the biblical record, Adam stands at the head of the human race in two senses. He is, in the first place, the natural head of the race. We are all descended from him. All the races of the world are ultimately of one stock as Paul reminds the Athenians (Acts 17:26). Adam also stands in a representative position as head of humanity. This is the point that Paul stresses in Romans 5:12-21 and 1 Corinthians 15:21-22. The whole of humanity is bound up with the sin of Adam. All sinned 'in Adam'; all stand condemned 'in Adam'; all die 'in Adam'. Adam was appointed by God as our federal or representative head so that his original sin is placed to our account. All of us sinned in and with him, so that when he fell, we fell. We all stand guilty and condemned 'in Adam'.

This solidarity between Adam and the whole human race in sin and death is something which many find unacceptable today. Having a

Western individualistic mentality we have difficulties with the idea of a corporate relationship to a person of the past. Furthermore, to suggest that we today are guilty and condemned for an act at the beginning of history by one man is regarded as grossly unfair, fatalistic and a failure to treat people as morally responsible for their own actions.[4] It is not fatalistic, however, nor does it treat people as morally irresponsible. The fact that we are born with a corrupt and sinful nature does not mean that we are not responsible for our actions (Mark 7:21). We constantly commit sin from our earliest days by not doing what we ought to do and by doing what we ought not to do. For these personal transgressions and failures we are responsible before God. It is because of our present privatistic view of life that our solidarity with Adam is regarded as unfair. To human reason it may be thought offensive, but is such a reaction so surprising, given our natural dislike of the Bible's general estimate of our sinful condition? Have we such a high opinion of ourselves to think that if we were in Adam's position we would have handled the situation differently? Unless we appreciate our position by nature in Adam, we shall not see the significance of the representative nature of Christ and his activity for all those who belong to him. Lose the truth concerning the historical Adam and our solidarity in his sin and condemnation, and a further hole is made in the gospel of justification.

3. God punishes sinners

It is precisely because people are created in God's image that hell awaits all unrepentant sinners. It is as divine image-bearers that we will be judged and punished. That image is defaced on account of sin but it is not eradicated (Genesis 9:6; James 3:9). Just as it is a most heinous crime to take human life unlawfully because it involves killing a divine image-bearer, so human beings in their sinful rebellion are an affront to God and deserve the ultimate penalty, namely, the second death which is everlasting punishment in hell.

There is a growing tendency to play down God's active involvement in the final destiny of the lost. The Church of England Report *The Mystery of Salvation* states that hell is 'the ultimate affirmation of the reality of human freedom'. 'It is the final and irrevocable choosing of that which is opposed to God so completely and so absolutely that the only end is total non-being.'[5] The Bible presents hell, however, not only as the inevitable destiny of human choice but as the ultimate demonstration of the divine wrath, where all who are opposed to God experience divine punishment. It insists that vengeance or retribution belongs to God, he will exact the full penalty. 'It is mine to avenge; I will repay, says the Lord' (Romans 12:19; cf. Deuteronomy 32:35).

In God's mysterious yet amazing action the future judgment was brought forward and experienced by Christ the sinner's substitute in order that all who belong to him might be justified here and now and escape the wrath to come. What happened to our Lord on the cross during those three hours of uncanny darkness and dereliction was absolute hell. 'My God, my God, why have you forsaken me?' (Mark 15:34). He endured the awful judgment of God in body, mind and spirit. That figure on the cross was still a human being. Even though his appearance 'was marred beyond human likeness' (Isaiah 52:14), he was not in a state of 'total non-being'. The eternal punishment and torment which is to come on all those who do not belong to Jesus Christ was experienced by him. 'The punishment that brought us peace was upon him' (Isaiah 53:5). There on that central cross we have a glimpse on earth, in time and space, of what the future torment will be like. But the full horror cannot be depicted; it is veiled behind the three hours of silence and darkness.

God's wrath or punishment of sinners is sometimes described as a cup. In the agony of Gethsemane Jesus prayed to the Father, 'Take this cup from me. Yet not what I will, but what you will' (Mark 14:36). Later, when Jesus had to rebuke Peter he said, 'Shall I not drink the cup the Father has given me' (John 18:11). This cup of the Lord's wrath is spoken of by the prophets, in such passages as Isaiah 51:17-23 and Jeremiah 25:15-29. When Jesus, who knew no sin, became sin for us, there on the cross he tasted the full fury of God's wrath in the place of sinners. The same cup will also be poured out full strength on the day of judgment. 'If anyone worships the beast and his image...he, too, will drink of the wine of God's fury, which has been poured full strength into the cup of his wrath...The smoke of their torment rises for ever and ever. There is no rest day or night' (Revelation 14:9-11).

The Lord Jesus Christ who received the full force of that punishment when he became the sinner's substitute is the very Person who has been appointed Judge on the Day of Judgment and 'He will punish those who do not know God and do not obey the gospel of our Lord Jesus. They will be punished with everlasting destruction and shut out from the presence of the Lord and from the majesty of his power on that day...' (2 Thessalonians 1:8-9; cf. Matthew 10:28; 25:41; Mark 9:43).

Criticism is made of preachers of the past for trying to frighten people too much. When the Church of England Report was published the headlines in *The Times* read: 'No pit, no torment: damnation is not as cruel as it is painted, says Anglican report.'[6] Hell is a disturbing subject but would that more people were frightened into realising what awaits them if they do not repent and believe the gospel! 'It is a dreadful thing to fall into the hands of the living God' for 'our God is a consuming fire' (Hebrews 10:31; 12:29; cf. Deuteronomy 4:24). 'Fear him', say Jesus, 'who, after the killing of the body, has power to throw you into hell. Yes, I tell you, fear him' (Luke 12:5). Those who deny the conscious, everlasting punishment of sinners in hell are chipping away at the foundations of the gospel of justification.[7]

Unable to please God
We always live in hope. Even someone in a condemned cell thinks of the possibility either of escaping or of behaving so well that the authorities may consider amending the sentence. But there is no escape from God's all-seeing eye. In addition, we cannot do anything to change the position in which we find ourselves. The human mind, will, affections, conscience are all contaminated by sin. Though people are capable of many fine and noble achievements, in God's sight, they are all unclean and fallen. The understanding is darkened, the mind depraved and the heart corrupt (Isaiah 64:6; Jeremiah 17:9; Ephesians 2:2-3; 4:17-19). Thus we are totally incapable of doing the good or amending the damage done. 'Those controlled by the sinful nature cannot please God' (Romans 8:8).

This is the tragedy of human beings made in the image of God. We are still human beings: sin has not made us into something else. We bear the divine image in a fallen state. Our whole beings are affected by sin and we are powerless to right the situation. When Paul says that 'all have sinned' he is not speaking merely in general terms of Jews and Gentiles as nations, as some maintain. No, this is the position of every single person conceived in the womb. There are no exceptions. It is into this bleak situation that the Gospel shines in all its glory and at the heart of it is the truth concerning justification by grace alone, through faith alone, in Christ alone, to God's glory alone.

Jesus Christ

The Divine Answer

Christ is God's answer to the human predicament (John 3:16; Galatians 1:4; 4:4; Titus 3:4-7). The gospel of God, which he promised beforehand through the Old Testament prophets, concerns his Son who took human nature in order to live, suffer, die and rise from the dead for our sakes. This promised Person came as Jesus of Nazareth who was fully God and truly human - the God-Man. (Romans 1:1-4). It is through what God has done in Christ that sinners are justified.

The Last Adam

Jesus Christ is the second and final representative figure. As Adam was appointed by God to be the representative head of the old humanity, so now Christ is the divinely appointed head of the new humanity (1 Corinthians 15:45-47). The Puritan, Thomas Goodwin (1600-1680), commenting on Paul's phraseology 'the first man Adam' and 'the second man from heaven', puts it very graphically in these words: 'He speaks of them as if there had never been any more men in the world, nor were ever to be for time to come, except these two. And why? but because these two between them had all the rest of the sons of men hanging at their girdle.'[8] As 'in Adam' all die, so 'in Christ' all will be made alive (1 Corinthians 15:22). As 'in Adam' all sinned so 'in Christ' all are righteous. Christ is the representative of his people so that the righteousness of his obedience is put to their account. We stand guiltless and justified 'in Christ' (Romans 5:15-21).

The Atoning Sacrifice

The substitutionary death of Jesus Christ as a sacrifice to propitiate or appease the wrath of God is another element so essential to the biblical doctrine of justification. By his atoning death Christ has made full, sufficient and final satisfaction for the sins of those he represents. He is the Lamb of God who takes away the sins of the world, who placates God's righteous wrath and who completely satisfies the demands of the law. The liberals of the past rejected Christ's propitiatory sacrifice and many modern evangelicals seem to be embarrassed by it. Without it, however, it would be a sheer impossibility for God to justify sinners. Justification would be a legal fiction and a denial of God's righteous nature and activity.

In order for God to remain true to his character, sin must be justly dealt with. Only through Christ, the sinless one, identifying himself with sinners and receiving what sin deserves can guilty sinners who rely on Christ be immune from punishment. God has presented Jesus Christ as the propitiatory sacrifice in order to 'demonstrate his justice at the present time, so as to be just and the one who justifies those who have faith in Jesus' (Romans 3:25-26). Sinners need not only a representative head who is righteous, but one who will act as their substitute and endure the penalty which their sin deserves.

Propitiation is sometimes presented as though Christ were appeasing God's wrath in order to make God love us. This is completely wrong. It is the love of God in Christ which is at work propitiating his own righteous indignation for the benefit of us sinners. 'Herein is love, not that we loved God, but that he loved us and sent his Son to be the propitiation for our sins' (1 John 4:10; cf. also 2:1-2 [AV]).

What is justification?

A popular evangelical explanation is to take the term justified to mean 'just-as-if-I'd-never-sinned'. As with most clever little definitions it is too simplistic and could be misleading. While it indicates that there is no condemnation, it fails to show that believers will always be aware that they are guilty sinners who have been forgiven and pronounced not guilty on account of Christ's obedience and atoning death.[9]

We may define justification like this:

Justification is a legal pronouncement made by God in the present, prior to the day of judgment, declaring sinners to be not guilty and therefore to be acquitted, by pardoning all their sins and reckoning them to be righteous in his sight, on the basis of Christ, their representative and substitute, whose righteousness in life and death is put to their account when in self-despairing trust they look to him alone for salvation.

Justification is a legal declaration. It has to do with the judge's sentence or pronouncement. There is no question of people justifying themselves. Justification is not sinners trying to make excuses for themselves. It is 'an instantaneous legal act of God'.[10] The biblical doctrine of justification concerns the Judge of all the earth uttering a legal pronouncement in the offender's favour, in advance of the day of judgment, which takes immediate effect and which cannot be changed. It means the offender can walk free. 'If the Son sets you free, you will be free indeed' (John 8:36). The person is in a right legal standing before the heavenly court. It is the opposite of condemnation (Romans 5:16,18; 8:33-34). 'To condemn' means to declare a person guilty and to pronounce sentence. 'To justify' is to declare a person not guilty, and acquitted of all charges. 'He will not be condemned; he has crossed over from death to life' (John 5:24; cf. 3:18).

This legal declaration includes two items:
1. Sinners are given a full pardon.
When dealing with justification, Paul quotes Psalm 32:1-2 in Romans 4:6-8 showing that it involves the forgiveness of sins. 'David ...speaks of the blessedness of the man to whom God credits righteousness apart from works: "Blessed are they whose transgressions are forgiven, whose sins are covered. Blessed is the man whose sin the Lord will never

count against him."' Sin is covered. It is blotted out. The slate is wiped clean. The sinner will never be charged with it as a crime needing to be punished. Past, present and future sins have all been paid for. 'Who is a God like you', declares Micah, 'who pardons sin and forgives the transgression of the remnant of his inheritance?' (Micah 7:18) 'As far as the east is from the west, so far has he removed our transgressions from us' (Psalm 103:12).

Some scholars have been content to leave it at that - full and free forgiveness. But this is only one aspect of the truth, wonderful though that is. Forgiveness is the negative aspect of justification. It has to do with our sins and involves the cancelling of the debt we owe. Though we have sinned God does not impute sin to us. Sin is no longer reckoned to our account. But there is more to it than that.

2. Sinners are declared righteous in God's sight.
At the heart of justification is the truth that God declares the sinner to be righteous. It is the positive aspect of justification. Not only are our sins not reckoned to us but beyond that we have righteousness credited to us. God puts righteousness to our account. Some stop short of this. They hold that all that is meant is a new righteous status: justification is the statement of a person's right legal status before the heavenly court. In line with the Reformers and Puritans, however, we would want to add that it includes 'the merits of perfect righteousness before him'.[11] Abraham was in a right legal status before God because he had righteousness, or 'God-like behaviour' credited to him (Genesis 15:6). Isaiah rejoiced greatly in God who 'arrayed me in a robe of righteousness' (Isaiah 61:10). In Romans 5:19 Paul argues that just as through the disobedience of the one man Adam the many were constituted sinners, so through the obedience of the one man Jesus Christ the many are constituted righteous. Ethical righteousness, the perfect undefiled righteousness of Christ is credited to the account of sinners and so they are declared righteous.[12] It is in union with Christ that the pronouncement is made.

This legal verdict is therefore, not about *making* sinners righteous but *declaring* them righteous. Justification itself does not mean that

God changes people within making them morally upright. That is something connected with regeneration and sanctification. If justification were about a change within people then they would have some righteous act of their own on which to depend. Justification is about the righteous activity of someone else which is put to the account of those who have absolutely nothing in themselves to plead. It is about a change of *status* not a change of *nature*. It concerns the righteousness of another put to the sinner's account. When Paul states in Romans 5:19 that 'the many will be made righteous', he does not mean that they are made morally upright. The verb 'to make' there means 'to appoint', 'to constitute'. He is referring to God's judicial act in regarding them as righteous: they are set in the category of the righteous. In their legal status before God they are really and truly righteous because of the righteous character and work of Christ. Dr. Lloyd-Jones explains the meaning in this way: 'Look at yourself in Adam; though you had done nothing you were declared a sinner. Look at yourself in Christ; and see that, though you have done nothing, you are declared to be righteous. That is the parallel.'[13]

It must be added that this legal pronouncement is not merely a declaring in the present of what people will one day become on the day of judgment. We object to those who, with the best of intentions, take away from the radical nature of God's declaration. For instance, in reply to the claim that justification is a legal fiction, one respected author has written, 'God does not treat us as if we were righteous; he declares that we will be righteous...The sinner, who one day will be righteous, can rejoice in that hope'.[14] Of course sinners in Christ will be morally upright one day, and that will be because of God's sanctifying work in us. But justification is a declaration of what sinners in Christ are now. God treats them as morally upright now. He declares not only that we *will be* righteous but that we *are* righteous in his sight. The grounds on which he does so, without there being any legal fiction, are Christ's obedience and atoning death and are set out in more detail below. In the light of the context, the future tense in Romans 5:19 is used not of the final declaration on the judgment day but of any time in the present before the end whenever people believe the gospel.[15]

Whenever people trust Christ for salvation there and then they are declared righteous.

We drew attention in chapter eight to a common idea in ecumenical circles of thinking that when God justifies he not only pronounces the sinner righteous (declaring righteous) but his powerful word effects what is declared (making righteous).[16] This is supported, so it is claimed, by Paul's words in Romans 1:16 that the gospel is 'the power of God unto salvation'. But we are not dealing with the wider topic of God's salvation in general but the specific matter concerning justification. Dr. David Samuel, former Director of Church Society, pointed out in an article in *The Times* that when God condemns, he does not make someone a sinner. Why should we then think that God makes someone righteous when he justifies them?[17]

The origin of justification

Justification is due entirely to the sovereign, gracious activity of God towards undeserving people. It lies in God's free, unmerited love towards sinners ('it is by grace you have been saved', Ephesians 2:5). Such sinners are 'justified freely by his grace through the redemption that came by Christ Jesus' (Romans 3:24). Justification is not on account of any human achievement or initiative. We do not add any merit of our own. 'No-one will be declared righteous in his sight by observing the law' (Romans 3:20). 'He saved us, not because of righteous things we had done, but because of his mercy...having been justified by his grace' (Titus 3:5-7).

The recipients of justification

The people who receive this gracious blessing from God are those who have no merits or works of their own to plead. In fact, we are taught that God 'justifies the wicked' (Romans 4:5). The ones whom God justifies are those who are sinners and enemies of God, who are already condemned, with the wrath of God already hanging over them (Romans 5:8, 10; 3:23; John 3:36). It is not those confident of their own righteousness who are justified but sinners like the despised tax collector (Luke 18:9-14; cf. 15:1-2). Gentiles 'who did not pursue righteousness, have obtained it' while Israel, 'who pursued a law of righteousness, has not attained it' (Romans 9:30-31). Nevertheless, God 'will justify the circumcised by faith and the uncircumcised through that same faith' (Romans 3:30).

The basis of justification

It is based entirely on the representative, substitutionary work of Jesus Christ. Isaiah 53:11-12 shows that justification comes through the Servant's propitiatory sacrifice. Paul indicates this even more clearly in Romans 3:24-26. Peter also writes of Christ, the righteous one, suffering what our sins deserve, in order to bring us to God (1 Peter 3:18). Christ is also the representative head of his people. He is the righteous one and his people are righteous in him.

Christ alone is the ground and basis of justification. God's gift of a righteous status is due to Christ's work on behalf of sinners and this provides the only adequate answer to the charge of legal fiction. It stands on solid foundations. God is able to justify the ungodly on the grounds that:

1 The sinner's guilt has been put to Christ's account and he has paid the penalty. 'God made him who had no sin to be sin for us' (2 Corinthians 5:21). God considered our sin as belonging to his Son, Jesus Christ, who was sinless, and he experienced the awful consequences. In so doing he has made full satisfaction for the believer's sins. There is no more to pay. The punishment fell on Jesus Christ as he bore our sins in his own body on the tree (1 Peter 2:24).

2 Christ's obedience or righteousness is reckoned to the sinner. 'God credits righteousness' to us (Romans 4:1-11). Not only do we need our sins cancelled but, as Wayne Grudem in his excellent presentation of the doctrine of justification puts it, 'We must rather move from a point of moral neutrality to a point of having positive righteousness before God, the righteousness of a life of perfect obedience to him ... God must declare us not to be merely *neutral* in his sight but actually to be *righteous* in his sight.'[18] Of course, Grudem is not suggesting that it is

possible for any sinner actually to be in a neutral state. He is not describing the steps of a process - he is simply analysing the elements of justification. We are given the gift of Christ's righteousness, the righteousness of his perfect life which culminated in his obedience even to the death of the cross (Philippians 2:7-8). Paul speaks of being found in Christ, 'not having a righteousness of my own that comes from the law, but that which is through faith in Christ - the righteousness that comes from God...' (Philippians 3:9; 2 Corinthians 5:21).

As we were constituted sinners in Adam, so in Christ we are constituted righteous. When Adam sinned his guilt was imputed to us all. Christ pleased his Father in every way and his righteousness is credited to all who belong to him. God sees the believing sinner in Christ 'who has become for us...our righteousness' (1 Corinthians 1:30). We stand in the perfect righteousness of Christ. Or to put it another way, we are clothed in his righteousness. It covers all those who belong to him. The clothing illustration picks up themes running throughout Scripture from the tunics which God gave Adam and Eve, the robe of righteousness of which Isaiah speaks, the wedding clothes of Jesus' parable, to the white robes of the innumerable company of those from every nation standing before God's throne (Genesis 3:21; Isaiah 61:10; Matthew 22:11-14; Revelation 7:9).

God does not justify on the ground of the Spirit's work of regeneration and renewal. The Spirit's work enabling the sinner to believe is not a basis of justification. God does not take into account any initial movement on our part and on that basis decides to justify us. When the Bible says that Abraham believed and it was accounted to him for righteousness, it was not his faith as an obedient act of personal righteousness that was the basis of God's verdict. God credited righteousness 'without works'. Abraham believed the gospel promise, he embraced the Christ who is the only ground (Hebrews 11:13; Romans 4:5, 24-25).

The way to justification

It is through faith in Jesus Christ that the sinner is justified. God justifies the one 'who believes in Jesus' (Romans 3:26; 5:1; Galatians 2:16). It is *not* through faith *and* human works that we are justified but through faith *alone*. Not that faith justifies. Faith is only a channel. It is simply the instrument, the empty hand, through which we receive justification from God. Faith is not a work which God regards as meritorious. God does not even justify sinners because he sees faith as a sign of change in the sinner's attitude. It is faith's object that is the basis of justification, namely, Jesus Christ. Justification is never *on the basis of* faith but always *through* or *by* faith. Faith is personal reliance on the Person and work of Christ alone. 'Faith is the absence of self-justification, or at least the recognition that self-justification will not avail with Almighty God'.[19] It is self-despairing trust in the Lord Jesus Christ our only Saviour.

The results of justification

There are many consequences which flow from justification. They include the following:

1. Peace with God

This is the first item that Paul mentions in Romans 5:1, 'Therefore, since we have been justified through faith, we have peace with God through our Lord Jesus Christ.' It is not some personal problem or trouble that is highlighted. Not even the blessing of inner tranquillity is mentioned. The first and fundamental blessing is God-centred rather than centred in any individual need. Right with God means the end of hostilities between God and human beings. Justification brings about reconciliation. The theme of reconciliation is picked up again further on in Romans 5:10-11. All the barriers and obstacles are now removed. The way is open into the very presence of God. We are welcomed home. The relationship which was broken by sin is re-established.

2. A state of grace

In Romans 5:2 Paul writes that through Jesus Christ 'we have gained access by faith into this grace in which we now stand.' It is a 'blessed', highly privileged position in which to be (cf. Matthew 5:3). It is to be no longer in the realm of sin, Satan, law and death (cf. Romans 6). This state is continuing and secure and enables us to come freely and confidently into God's presence (Ephesians 3:12).

3. A glorious hope
Again in Romans 5:2 Paul adds, 'And we rejoice in the hope of the glory of God'. In 3:23 Paul speaks of all humanity having fallen short of the glory of God because of sin. Now, all those who are in this justified position through Christ can boast, exult, rejoice with confidence in the sure hope of sharing in and being part of that stunning greatness and splendour of God.

4. Adopted into God's family
In both Romans and Galatians Paul is eager to show that one of the blessings of being justified is 'that we might receive the full rights of sons' (Galatians 4:5). Both justification and adoption are associated with the promise of the Spirit. In Galatians 3:1-5 and 3:14 Paul refers to the promise of the Spirit in connection with justification. Then in the next chapter this promise is associated with adoption. 'Because you are sons, God sent the Spirit of his Son into our hearts, the Spirit who calls out, "*Abba*, Father." So you are no longer a slave, but a son; and since you are a son, God has made you also an heir' (4:6-7). In Romans 8 where Paul is dealing with the security of the believer as a result of being justified by faith alone ('Therefore, there is now no condemnation for those who are in Christ Jesus') he presents teaching concerning the Spirit. The Spirit is the Spirit of life who applies the benefits which Christ won at Calvary. Those who are led by the Spirit are the sons of God. What is more, the indwelling Spirit also 'makes us deeply aware that we now belong to God'[20] as his own very dear children, using similar language as in the letter to the Galatians. 'You received the Spirit of sonship. And by him we cry, "*Abba*, Father"' (Romans 8:15).

5. Membership of the covenant community
In chapter ten we criticised those who argued that justification means God's declaration that those who believe in Christ are members of the covenant family. Such a definition gives pride of place to the horizontal

state (a right status in the group) rather than the vertical (a right status with God). We all stand naked and exposed in our rebellious condition before God. What we need, if we are to be saved, is for God to clear us of guilt and to declare us right with himself.

Having emphasised that point, we can say that membership of the covenant family is one of the consequences of justification. In his treatment of justification in Galatians 3 and 4, Paul deals with the question of who belongs to the covenant community. There is only one people of God to which both Jewish and Gentile believers belong. Those who believe in Christ are members of the same covenant family as Abraham. 'If you belong to Christ, then you are Abraham's seed, and heirs according to the promise' (Galatians 3:29). Gentiles do not need to become Jews and carry out all the old covenant rituals in order to properly belong. It is not Christ plus any legal requirements that put us right with God and fit us to be members of his covenant community, but Christ alone. In Christ we are among the righteous people of God.

The implications of justification
1. For unbelievers and those trusting false hopes
There are both negative as well as positive points to consider. On the negative side it means that people can never by their religious obser-vances and good works attract God's attention and win for themselves places in heaven. It also means the end of thinking that our good points will finally balance out our bad points and God will be kind enough to overlook the bad and, with a nod and wink, get us into heaven. In addition, there is no hope for those who put their trust in the church and its sacraments to see them right in the end.

On the other hand, the message of justification by faith alone in Christ alone means good news for those who have tried to do their best and yet have failed even to live up to their own standards. There is also real hope for spiritual down-and-outs, people who are painfully aware that they will never make it. Indeed, all those who feel unworthy and weighed down with guilt need no longer despair. Jesus said: 'Come to me, all you who are weary and burdened, and I will give you rest' (Matthew 11:28).

2. For believers in the Lord Jesus

The implications of this glorious truth for believers are enormous.

Contentment

To appreciate the truth concerning justification is immensely liberating and is a source of true joy and contentment of spirit for the Christian. It is a great blessing to wake up each morning and realise that there is no need to strive for recognition, status and acceptance before God. 'Therefore, since we have been justified through faith, we have peace with God through our Lord Jesus Christ' (Romans 5:1).

When doubts and fears arise we are to remember that Christ died and rose from the dead to bring about our justification (Romans 4:25). Our feelings may get the better of us and we may wonder whether we are Christians. Satan, the accuser of God's people, will seek to point the finger at us and accuse us. At that time we can remember, 'It is God who justifies us. Who is he that condemns?' (Romans 8:33-34). God the Father sees us in Christ.

> *When Satan tempts me to despair,*
> *And tells me of the guilt within,*
> *Upward I look, and see him there*
> *Who made an end of all my sin.*[21]

Assurance

Despite what Rome claims, such assurance of our justified state is not sinful presumption, because it does not rest on human ability but on the grace of God. What is more, there are no degrees of justification. We are either declared righteous like the tax-collector or we are not justified like the proud Pharisee. Neither can we be justified one day and not justified the next. The verdict of the final judgment is brought forward and is a once and for all declaration. Those whom God calls and justifies, he glorifies (Romans 8:30).

This also means we can face death confidently as we lean upon the once for all work of the Lord Jesus Christ. There is no such place or state as purgatory. Jesus Christ has made full satisfaction for our sins. 'Just as man is destined to die once, and after that to face judgment, so

Christ was sacrificed once to take away the sins of many people' (Hebrews 9:27-28). The dying thief who trusted Christ was assured by Jesus that he would be, that very day, in paradise with the Lord (Luke 23:43). There is no need to pray for the dead or light candles for them, no need to hold requiem masses or to obtain indulgences. Those who die in Jesus die safely and are with Christ which is far better than anything in this present earthly life (Philippians 1:21-23). There is no sadder occasion than to be present at a funeral service where the doctrine of justification by faith alone is not known. On the other hand, there is something very uplifting and deeply moving to be present at the funeral of one who died believing and to see the family, through tears of loss and sorrow, having that inner joy and assurance in the Lord that comes to those who know the truth of justification.

> My hope is built on nothing less
> Than Jesus' blood and righteousness...
> Clothed in His righteousness alone,
> Faultless to stand before the throne.[22]

The righteous life

From this new justified position in Christ we are called to live the righteous life. Regeneration and sanctification must not be confused with justification as they are in Roman Catholic and ecumenical theology. Nevertheless, they are firmly linked to justification. Justification takes place in the context of regeneration and renewal by the Holy Spirit. The faith which rests on Christ is a living faith. It is a sign of new life, of a repentant, obedient spirit, and of a desire to please God (Titus 3:5-7; Ephesians 2:8-10).

At this point, what James says is important. He is concerned that faith is not a mere acceptance of facts. Such a faith demons have. 'Faith without deeds is dead' (2:14-20, 26). The faith that embraces Christ for justification is a faith that issues in a righteous life. This leads James to speak of the works which a Christian does as an indication of this saving faith (2:21-24). In doing so he uses the word 'justify' to mean 'to show to be righteous', a meaning not uncommon in other parts of the

Bible (cf. Jeremiah 3:11; Ezekiel 16: 51-52; Matthew 11:19; Luke 16:15; Romans 3:4; etc.). Abraham and Rahab were 'justified by works' in that they demonstrated their righteous status by their good actions.[23] Our works arising out of our faith should indicate that our lives have been changed and that we are living the righteous life. We do not do good works to earn salvation but we are saved to do good works (Ephesians 2:8-10; Titus 2:11-14).

Those who are righteous by God's grace 'hunger and thirst for righteousness' (Matthew 5:6; cf. Zephaniah 2:3). They have a deep longing which is expressed in prayer and action to see God's will done on earth as it is in heaven. This means we shall not be satisfied with ourselves but we shall daily desire to be more like the Lord Jesus Christ. There will also be an ache in our hearts to see justice done in the world. The cry of the Psalmist will be our cry, 'How long, O Lord, how long?' We shall long to see lives changed as a result of the gospel. There will be a desperate calling out to God for spiritual awakening in the church that will spill over into society. In eager expectation we shall also pray, 'Come, Lord Jesus'. We hunger for the ultimate satisfaction: for the day when sin will be forever removed, when we shall stand faultless and blameless before God's throne, when all opposition to God will have gone, and when the Lord alone will be exalted. 'But in keeping with his promise we are looking forward to a new heaven and a new earth, the home of righteousness' (2 Peter 3:13). This is 'the hope of righteousness' and it is the Spirit's ministry to assure us of this hope (Galatians 5:5; 2 Corinthians 5:5; Ephesians 1:13-14).[24]

Discipline, not punishment

In all our troubles and difficulties we know that God is for us, not against us. 'And we know that in all things God works for the good of those who love him, who have been called according to his purpose' (Romans 8:28). He disciplines his children in order to conform them to the image of his Son (Hebrews 12: 4-11). Such trials do have a purifying effect, but they must not be thought of as punishments, as though God were making us pay for our sins in some way. Christ alone has paid the full punishment which our sins deserve. We are not to live, then, in a spirit of fear and torment. 'Therefore, there is now no condemnation for those who are in Christ Jesus' (Romans 8:1). Being justified we live neither in fear of purgatory nor of hell. In no way does God bring calamity on us to make us pay for past or present sins. The results of past and present sins we may well have to live with for the rest of our lives. In the same way, we all have to live with ailments, pain and death which are the results of Adam's original sin. But thank God, we do not have to live with them for ever! We do not have to live with them after we pass from this life. After death, those who love the Lord are immediately in his presence and are at peace. 'Blessed are the dead who die in the Lord from now on. Yes, says the Spirit, they will rest from their labour, for their deeds will follow them' (Revelation 14:13). But there is more. The Bible speaks of glorification, of the resurrection of the body, the curse finally removed, no more pain or death, and of a new creation (Philippians 3:21; Revelation 21:1-4).

Our present justified state anticipates the verdict on the day of judgment and this present state is complete and final in Christ, because it is his perfect righteousness that is imputed to us. It is our personal sanctification that is incomplete in this life and it is our work as believers that will be judged on the final day.

Church life

Being declared right with God through faith in Jesus Christ means that we are now counted among the righteous and fit to be members of the covenant community. This does have implications for the church as the people of God. The visible family of God that meets as a local church should receive into membership all who look to Christ alone for salvation whatever their class, colour, sex or race. Jews do not have to become Gentiles in order to belong, neither do Gentiles need to become Jews (Galatians 3:26-29).

For there to be fellowship between churches, a clear statement of belief in the doctrine of justification by faith alone, in Christ alone, is essential. There can be no fellowship between churches where this doctrine is ignored, weakened or compromised. Merely to have a form of words that is agreeable to everyone is meaningless. How can there be cooperation in evangelism when the heart of the gospel, the message of justification, is left imprecise? How can people grow in grace when justification by faith alone is not preached and known? Happy the community of God's people where all are one in spirit and mind in confessing this wonderful gospel truth!

O for a thousand tongues to sing
My great Redeemer's praise,
The glories of my God and king,
The triumphs of His grace!

Look unto him, ye nations, own
your God, ye fallen race;
Look, and be saved through faith alone,
Be justified by grace.[25]

Notes

1. C. H. Dodd, *The Epistle of Paul to the Romans*, The Moffatt New Testament *Commentary*, Hodder & Stoughton, 1947, p. 23.

2. McGrath, *Justification by Faith*, pp. 10-15, 97-114.

3. J. I. Packer, 'Introductory Essay' to J. Buchanan, *The Doctrine of Justification*, Banner of Truth, 1961, p. 6.

4. *New Dictionary of Christian Ethics and Pastoral Theology*, Eds. D. J. Atkinson & D. H. Field, 1995, pp. 641-642.

5. *The Mystery of Salvation*, p. 199. N. T. Wright holds a similar view: 'Part of the horror of hell ... is that those who consciously and continually choose sin instead of God become less and less human, until all that ennobles them as creatures made in God's image has, by their own choice, been altogether obliterated, beyond hope or pity.' (*Colossians and Philemon*, Tyndale NT Commentaries, IVP, 1986, pp. 135-136). In a sermon entitled 'hell', he advances the idea that the final individual human destiny of the lost is a condition 'where some, perhaps many, of God's human creatures do choose, and will choose, to dehumanize themselves completely' (*Following Jesus*, SPCK, 1994, p. 80). He does not say so, but the logic would lead us to believe that such dehumanized creatures, 'beings who were once human but are not now', become no more than animals that cease to be.

Melvin Tinker, vicar of St. John's Newland, Hull in his review of *The Mystery of Salvation*, comments that 'there is a reluctance to say clearly that God punishes sinners because by nature he is opposed to sin...It is not so much that God is to act justly in relation to our rebellion that is key to the writers' thinking, but that he must respect our human freedom' ('Salvation: is it such a mystery?', *Evangelicals Now*, March 1996, p. 11).

6. *The Times* January 11, 1996 p. 3. Cf. also S. H. Travis *I believe in the Second Coming of Jesus*, Hodder and Stoughton, 1982, p. 184-208. He shudders 'not with fear but with embarrassment' at Augustine's description of hell as a fire kept burning 'by the miraculous power of God' and of passages in Jonathan Edwards' famous sermon 'Sinners in the hands of an Angry God'. He rejects hell as eternal punishment. It is not unexpected to find him arguing that 'in Paul's understanding of divine judgment ideas of "punishment" or "retribution" lie on the periphery of his thought...He understands both salvation and condemnation primarily in relational terms: people's destinies will be a confirmation and intensification of the relationship with God or alienation from him which has been their experience in this life'. Cf. 'Christ as Bearer of Divine Judgment in Paul's Thought about the Atonement', in *Jesus of Nazareth Lord and Christ*, eds. J. B. Green and M. Turner, Eerdmans/Paternoster, 1994, pp. 332-345.

7. For an excellent treatment of current discussion on annihilation and hell cf. D. A. Carson, *The Gagging of God, Christianity Confronts Pluralism*, Apollos (IVP), 1996, chapter 13, 'On Banishing the Lake of Fire', pp. 515-536.

8. *Works of Thomas Goodwin*, J. Nichol, 1862, Vol.4, p. 31.

9. Cf. W. Grudem, *Systematic Theology*, IVP/Zondervan, 1994, p. 727, note 4 for a criticism of this definition.

10. Grudem, p. 723.

11. Grudem, p. 725.

12. Cf. J. Murray, *Redemption Accomplished and Applied*, Banner of Truth, 1961, pp. 117-131, especially pp. 122-128 on the righteousness of Christ imputed to us.

13. D. M. Lloyd-Jones, *Romans, An Exposition of Chapter 5, Assurance*, Banner of Truth, 1971, p. 274.

14. McGrath, *Making Sense of the the Cross*, IVP, 1992, pp. 66-67.

15. Cf. Cranfield, *Romans* Vol.1, T. & T. Clark, 1977, p. 291: 'As to the future ... while it could refer to the final judgment, it is probably better understood, in agreement with 5.1 and 9, as referring to the present life of believers'; Moo, *Romans*, p. 359.

16. Cf. ARCIC II *Salvation and the Church*, p. 17: 'God's grace effects what he declares:

his creative word imparts what it imputes'; H. Küng, *Justification*, Burns & Oats, 1981, p. 212-213: 'Unlike the word of man, the word of God *does* what it signifies. God said, "Let there be light" and there was light. He said, "Be clean" and it was clean... The sinner's justification is exactly like this. God pronounces the verdict, "You are just." And the sinner *is* just, really and truly, outwardly and inwardly, wholly and completely ... God's *declaration* of justice is, as God's Declaration of justice, at the same time and in the same act, a *making* just'.

17. D. N. Samuel, 'The Unjustified Case for Church Unity', *The Times*, March 7, 1987, quoted by H. R. Jones in *Gospel & Church*, Evangelical Press of Wales, 1989, p. 100.

18. W. Grudem, *Systematic Theology*, p. 725.

19. P. Toon, *Justification and Sanctification*, Marshall, Morgan & Scott, 1983, p. 143.

20. Moo, *Romans*, p. 533.

21. C. L. De Chenez, *Before the throne of God above*.

22. E. Mote.

23. For a different understanding of James 2: 14-26 cf. D. J. Moo, *James,* Tyndale New Testament Commentaries, 1985, pp. 109-110. He thinks that James is using 'to justify ' in a declarative rather than a demonstrative sense and that it refers to God's ultimate declaration of righteousness, the 'final justification'. The context, however, does not suggest that the last judgment is in mind. James is concerned about the nature of faith. Works show that faith is genuine. Objections to Moo's view are presented by R. Y. K. Fung, '"Justification" in the Epistle of James', in *Right With God: Justification in the Bible and the World*, ed. D. A. Carson, Baker/Paternoster, 1992, pp. 153-154.

24. On Galatians 5:5 see G. Vos, *Pauline Eschatology*, Eerdmans, 1930, p. 30: 'In Gal. 5:5 Christians "through the Spirit by faith wait for the hope of righteousness" (that is for the realization of the hoped for things pertaining to the state of righteousness conferred in justification).' Our justification points us forward to glorification. It is not the hope of final acceptance, for we are already finally accepted, but it is 'the hope of glory' and of final salvation (Romans 5:2ff. and 1 Thessalonians 5:8). See further, R. Y. K. Fung, *The Epistle to the Galatians*, Eerdmans, 1988, pp. 224-228.

25. Charles Wesley.

General Index

Edwards, Jonathan 177, 182, 207
Eichrodt, W. 59
Elihu 57
Elijah 161
Elisha 161
Enoch 39
Evangelical 9, 10, 60-77, 82, 89-96, 126, 138, 148, 151-152, 158, 162-163, 174, 176-178, 186, 192
Eveson, P. H. 87
Exchange, see also Imputation 17, 44, 67, 71, 73, 145
Exile 115-117, 121, 139-141
Existential 104, 106, 183

Faith 15, 17, 18, 21-23, 28, 30, 33-34, 41-44, 64, 78, 83-84, 90, 92-93, 122, 131-132, 145-147, 168-169, 176, 178, 198-199, 203-204, 208
Faith of Christ 17-18, 25, 120
Faithfulness 16, 18, 24, 31-32, 51, 54, 112, 117-118
Florence, Council of 63
Forgiveness 32, 42, 193-194
Forty-Two Articles 61
Fourth Lateran Council 63
Foxe, John 174, 181
French Confession 61, 75
Frith, John 175
Fuller, D. P. 154
Fung, R. Y. K. 24, 141, 155, 158, 179, 208

Garlington, D. 123, 125, 138, 155, 171, 181
Gerstner, J. H. 107, 172
Glory of God 18-19, 200
Goodwin, Thomas 191, 207
Gospel 14, 16, 33, 92, 94, 147, 160, 162-164, 166, 170, 172-175, 178-179, 191, 196, 206
Grace 19, 37-39, 67, 74, 78, 80, 92, 120, 126-130, 196, 199-200
Graham, Billy 91
Green, J. B. 156
Grotius, H. 168
Grudem, Wayne 197, 207-208
Guinness, Os 89
Gundry, R. H. 128, 153
Gundry-Volf, J. M. 156

Hagner, D. A. 36
Haldane, Robert 25
Hall, Edward 65
Hays, R. B. 25
Heidelberg Catechism 61
Hell 188-190, 205, 206-207
Hendriksen, William 36
Henry, Carl F. H. 164, 180
Herveus 68
Hill, David 58
Holy Spirit 23, 31, 82-83, 94, 120-122, 140, 159, 170, 198, 200, 203-204
Homily of Salvation 61, 69, 84, 88, 174
Hughes, Philip E. 36, 76-77

Scripture Index

Old Testament

Genesis

1:26-28	37, 185
2:4	40
2:17	37
2:25	38
3:9-24	150
3:15	38, 46
3:21	38, 198
5:1	40
5:1-2	37
5:22, 24	185
5:29	39
6:8	39
6:9	39-40
9:6	188
10:1	40
11:10	40
11:27	40
15:6	41, 43, 53, 116, 144, 160, 161, 194
15:17	42
18:25	150
22:18	40
49:29-32	40
50:20	40
50:24-25	40

Exodus

9:27	184
23:7	57
32:13	128
32:32	44
34:7	32, 54

Leviticus

18:5	43
19:15	52
19:36	52

Numbers

11:1	185
25:6-13	45

Deuteronomy

4:24	190
6:4	146
6:5	185
7:7-8	127
9:4-6	138
25:1	56, 57
25:15	52
27	139
27-29	115
30	115
30:6	27
30:19-20	43
32:4	32
32:35	189

New Testament

Matthew

1:19	56
3:9	161
3:15	28
5:3	29, 199
5:6	29, 204
5:20	29, 55
6:33	16, 28
7:11	28
8:10-12	161
10:28	190
11:19	57, 204
11:25-30	28
11:28	201
12:37	22, 57
13:17	56
13:38	29
13:43	29
20:28	28
21:32	29
22:1-14	46
22:11-14	198
23:15	132
23:28	29
25:31-46	22
25:37-40	29
25:41	190
26:28	28

Mark

1:2	26
1:4	161
2:17	26
3:29	186
7:21	188
9:43ff	186, 190
10:21-22	137
10:45	26
14:36	189
15:34	189

Luke

1:6	56
1:17	26
1:76	26
3:4	26
3:8	27
3:18	26
3:38	37
4:25-27	161
5:8	136
10:29	57
12:5	190
15:1-2	196
16:15	27, 204
16:19-31	27
18:9-14	27-28, 162, 196
22:37	26
23:43	203

John

1:13	30
1:14-18	184
1:29	161

2 Peter

1:1	16
2:9	186
3:7	186
3:13	29, 204

1 John

1:5-7	31
1:8-10	31
1:9	31-32, 46
2:1-2	31-32, 192
2:29	32, 55
3:1-2	33
3:4	186
3:4-9	31
3:5	32
3:7	32
4:10	32, 192

Jude

24	47

Revelation

3:4-5	35
3:18	35
4:4	35
6:11	35
6:16	185
7:9	198
7:9-14	35
7:13-15	35
12:1-12	46
12:7-12	35-36, 162
13:3	46
14:9-11	190

Revelation *Continued*

14:13	47
15:3	56
19:2	56
19:15	185
20:11-15	22
20:12	185
20:14-15	47
21:1-4	205

Also from Day One

The Lord's Prelude for Today

The Lord's Prayer for Today

Derek Prime

Large format paperback
163 pages   **£5.95**

The Lord's Prayer is the only pattern prayer the Lord Jesus provided and is timeless in purpose and function. It indicates how we are to pray throughout our life in this present world. Its truths do not change. The necessity for us to be reminded of them is essential.
The Lords Prayer reminds us, at its very beginning, that true worship of God arises from a living relationship with Him as our Father through our Lord Jesus Christ.

Derek Prime was for many years the pastor of Charlotte Baptist Chapel, Edinburgh. He is now a well-known convention speaker and author of many books including *Let's Say The Grace Together* and *Gofors and Grumps.*

ISBN 0 902548 68 9

The Beatitudes for Today

John Blanchard

Large format paperback
263 pages   **£7.95**

In his foreword, Eric J. Alexander writes, "this book fills a significant gap in contemporary Christian writing. Although the past thirty years have seen the publication of several excellent volumes on the Sermon on the Mount, we have lacked a full-length treatment of the Beatitudes. The Christian world has been deeply indebted to John Blanchard for his preaching and writing ministry over many years. Both are characterised by an absolute faithfulness to the text of Scripture, a deep concern to apply God's Word to today's world, and a God-given insight into the implications of biblical truth."

John Blanchard is an internationally known British Evangelist and Bible teacher, who has written a number of best-selling books including *Ultimate Questions, Right with God, Pop Goes the Gospel* and *Whatever Happened to Hell?*

ISBN 0 902548 67 0

For further information about other Day One titles, call or write to us:

0181 313 0456

IN THE UK

In Europe: ++ 44 181 313 0456
In North America: 011 44 181 313 0456

Day One Publications 6 Sherman Road, Bromley Kent BR1 3JH England

Other books in this series

Only One Way

Hywel R. Jones

Paperback   £7.99

Is Christ the only Saviour?
Do you have to believe in him in order to be saved?
Evangelicals have always held that the Lord Jesus Christ is the only way to God, and that to be saved, people need to hear the good news about him and to respond personally to him.
Recently, however, some evangelical writers on both sides of the Atlantic, have suggested that it is possible to be saved by Christ without knowing him or even having heard of him.
Dr. Hywel R. Jones, principal of the London Theological Seminary, examines the arguments in support of this new 'evangelical optimism'. He raises again the question, 'What about the unevangelised?'
This is a significant book for all in leadership in the churches and for those involved in mission, since it deals with vital issues concerning the gospel of salvation.

ISBN 0 902548 70 0

Men, Women and Authority
–serving together in the church

Andrew Anderson, General Editor

Paperback   £7.99

The twentieth century has seen a dramatic revolution in attitudes to the place and role of women in society. Whether it be in the board-room or even the Prime Minister's office, people both accept and expect that women will be there. The norms of society in this area, as well as many others, have been rewritten. Additionally, the struggle for women's rights in the secular realm throughout this century has been paralleled by its counterpart in the Church.
This comprehensive book has been written by nine leading evangelical writers who have set out to analyse fully the issues as they are being faced by Christians today, in order to attempt to see how they have been shaped and influenced by the wider sphere of thought.

ISBN 0 902548 71 9

For further information about other Day One titles, call or write to us:

0181 313 0456
IN THE UK

In Europe: ++ 44 181 313 0456
In North America: 011 44 181 313 0456

Day One Publications 6 Sherman Road, Bromley Kent BR1 3JH England